The Other

Her past-life won't let go

by Réal Laplaine

Books by Réal Laplaine

Intrusion: A Keeno Crime Thriller
Quantum Assault: A Keeno Crime Thriller
The One: A Keeno Crime Thriller
The Buffalo Kid
Twilight Visitor
Dead but not Gone
See Me Not
Earth Escape
Deception People
Woman EX
Finding Agnetha

www.reallaplaine.com

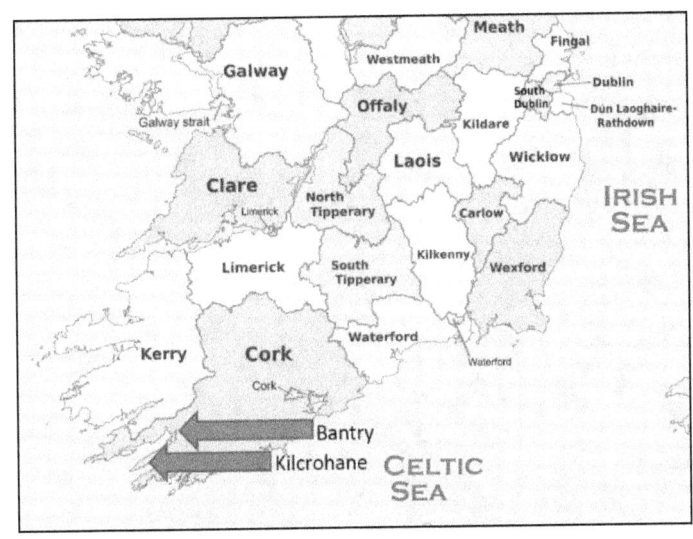

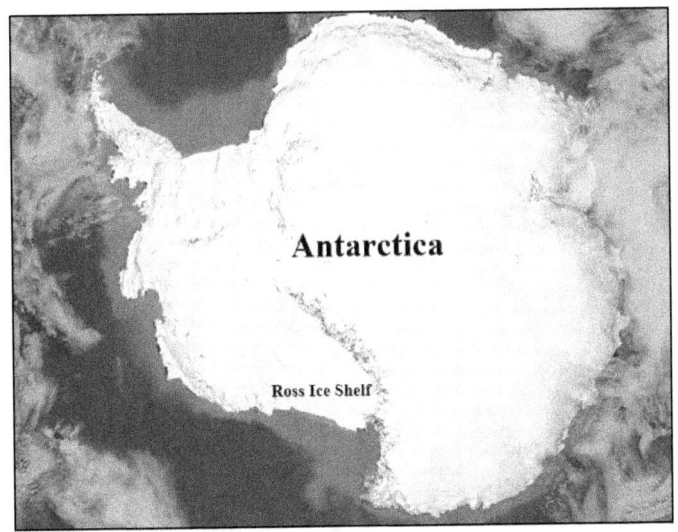

Book One

1

For Kaetlyn O'Sullivan, school was more of a prison of the mind than a place of learning.

The eighteen-year-old was counting the days until her final term ended in June when she could walk away with her *Leaving Certificate* in hand, the official accreditation and ticket to the education she really wanted to pursue as a bio-astrophysicist; all in the hopes that by the time she was in her mid-twenties, she could apply to be one of the few Irish scientists to ever rocket off to **ISS**, the *International Space Station,* and eventually, to Mars.

Ever since she could remember, the stars had called to her – like a gentle voice that whispered to her soul, taunting her to come out and play amongst them.

For reasons she could not entirely explain, and from the first days she could pick up a crayon and draw, her canvass was filled with images of other worlds, planets and aliens. Her foster parents thought it was cute that their young daughter was so engaged, but for Kaetlyn, the expression of her inner thoughts was a way of channeling some deep-seated passion, that out there, beyond the rim of Earth, was a Universe that was hers to explore; a place that seemed as real to her as the one she stood on.

At a very young age she had already done the math; there were billions of suns, countless billions of planets – it was ridiculous, she thought, to assume that human beings were alone in the Universe, and in her life time, she intended to prove it, she intended to meet ET.

But now, she had to make do with the mundane, the droning and tireless monotony of sitting in classes, learning mostly dribble, much of which she had already studied on her own and could recite back to the teachers, or, for reasons she could not explain, she already knew about.

Although the October air had a bite to it, she preferred sitting alone outside the school, nibbling on her sandwich.

She was in the minority, being one of the few black girls in the predominantly white Roman Catholic town of Bantry, located in the far southwestern reaches of Ireland, where the folk were friendly enough, but who also eyed "different" with a constitutionally discerning aspect, all of which made her feel like the black sheep in the flock – literally.

Kaetlyn was different, and she knew it. Not only because of her skin color, but because she simply didn't try to fit in with others, and this gave her an aloofness and apparent arrogance, which in fact, was not there.

She didn't consider herself better than anyone. She didn't think she was smarter. She simply did not want to try and be like anyone else, and she resisted any attempts, through peer pressure, cultural dynamics, trends and other memes, to fit into anyone's box.

What she wanted was to know herself, to explore the depths of what she thought was her limitless soul, and to that end, she refused to imposed accept limitations, false paradigms or conventional views about how she should be in order to better fit in.

Moreover, she had questions. So, many questions.

And then of course, there was the dream – the haunting that visited itself upon her so many nights of every week and had been doing so for several years now.

School had been easy for her, far too easy in the eyes of others, and so, the faculty and other students, tended to regard her with an unstated, but tacit suspicion – as if being too intelligent was a sign of a dysfunctional personality – an oddball.

Her biological parents had immigrated from Nigeria to Ireland in the hopes of finding a new, and better life – a story of hope that had turned to tragedy when her mother died while giving birth to her.

In the wake of that calamity, her father became a broken and depressed human being, left to raise a new-born in a land he knew nothing of, and eventually resorted to alcohol to numb his pain.

When she was old enough to understand why her skin was so black and why her parents, the O'Sullivan's, were as white as milk, she learned that Child Protective Services had intervened and taken her from her father.

Sitting alone at a picnic table in the school yard, idly picking away at her lunch, her mind wandered back to the episode in her last class – just thirty minutes before.

The teacher, speaking about political ideology, had made the mistake of declaring that democracy was the purest form of governance, and that had set Kaetlyn's alarm bells ringing. For reasons she could not yet fathom, her hand speared into the air.

"Mr. Peterson?"

"Yes, Kaetlyn," he said with a reticent tone.

"If democracy is the purest form of ideological governance, why isn't it the predominant form of governance today?"

The teacher tipped a questioning eye at her. "What do you mean – it's all around us?"

"I don't think so." She shook her head. "Clearly, democracy has been hijacked in most every nation in our world."

Murmurs and giggles emitted from the other students.

The teacher raised a brow. "Care to enlighten us on how you came to that conclusion?" he said with a creeping smile.

"Can you tell us about a single government on Earth today which adheres to the purest form of democracy of which you speak?"

"I'm speaking about political ideology, Kaetlyn."

"I understand that," she said with a wave of her hand, "but what's the point of learning ideology if it isn't practiced?"

"It is practiced, Kaetlyn." He answered. "Is there a point here?"

"There is," she continued, "wouldn't it be more useful to us if you demonstrated how the system of democracy has been compromised by nearly every government in the world and how it really works today so we can understand how to avoid the shortcomings and corruption of our predecessors?"

The teacher's slight distemper seeped through as his jaw clenched, but Kaetlyn carried on, her arms crossed, and her eyes forcibly fixed on his.

"Let's take America, a nation which you yourself said was a leader of the free world and democracy. Today, America is nothing more than an oligarchical empire – its wealth and power controlled by a minority of corporate empires, the banking institution and private entities, a hegemony and not a democratic system that governs on behalf of the people. Presidents and parties are elected by the financial support of corporate and banking institutions who buy them out, and once in office, they answer to their benefactors, the rich who run the country, the 1% who own most of its wealth, while the rest of the population is forced to concede to their mandates. That isn't democracy, it's corporate tyranny – just another form of legalized piracy."

"Kaetlyn, this lesson was not meant to be about the relative pros and cons of governances."

She pressed forward with a more belligerent attitude. "That's my point, sir, it should be. Shouldn't you be preparing us for the real world, and not a fake one?

"It isn't a false picture, it is …"

She cut him off. "Shouldn't you be teaching us to think for ourselves, not just to learn and parrot off paradigms that are not working?"

"Kaetlyn, that's quite enough, you've made your point."

Kaetlyn sat, her half-eaten sandwich pinched between her fingers, recalling the moment as she realized that she would soon be called to the Headmaster's office for yet another berating about her lack of discipline and respect.

"Hey weirdo," a voice broke her mental maundering.

She turned to see two boys, both members of her class, standing nearby with a leer on their faces.

11

"What'ch'ya gonna do next, weirdo, tell us that we all came from aliens? You fook'n blackie."

Lurching to her feet, she tossed her sandwich to the ground and marched up to him.

"You know what your problem is, Tommy?" she glared at him. "You're too stupid to know that you're stupid."

He pressed his hand into her chest and pushed her back. She stumbled to the ground. As she did, she saw someone step between her and Tommy, and a second later, Tommy was face down in the dirt, twisted up in pain, while his partner ran.

"Apologize to her," said the intruder.

Tommy's face, flushed red with anguish, conceded. "Sorry – I'm sorry," he said.

When he was gone, the other turned to her. "I'm Shamus Maguire," he said, extending a hand, helping her to her feet.

"I'm …"

"Kaetlyn O'Sullivan, I know," his smile widened.

"Thanks for the help."

Shamus glanced at Tommy as he walked away. "Sometimes, the only way to stop a bully is to show 'em they're vulnerable too. Makes 'em think twice about mess'n with others."

He turned back to Kaetlyn. "Maybe we can talk sometime," he said with an expectant look, one which betrayed something else, some other unspoken message.

2

Harry O'Sullivan plucked the newspaper from a small puddle of water, where the delivery boy had conveniently tossed it.

Obscenities escaped his lips as he entered the house. "Fook'n punk! Can't deliver a paper the right way," he snarled.

His wife looked at him as he dropped into his chair with an audible grumble. She smiled, thinking to herself that her husband would complain until the day he died, but unfortunately, she knew, as did he, that he was part of a dying breed. Most of their neighbors had long stopped reading print-papers, resorting to using smart-phones or tablets, a more sustainable and efficient medium.

She placed a hot cup of coffee, a side-dish of toast, and a jar of her homemade jam in front of him. His bellyaching abated as the pleasing scent reached his nose.

With a bite of toast, followed by a slurp of coffee, he dove back into the paper. "Shite!" he lightly exclaimed. "What's the bloody world com'n to?" He tipped the paper to one side to steal a look at his daughter, Kaetlyn, who was scrolling through her mobile phone across from him.

"Says 'er the Arabs bombed an Israeli settlement – killed a shite load of 'em."

Claire O'Sullivan sat down next to her daughter and fixed an eye on her husband. "Well, I guess god does have a sense of justice after all."

Harry scrunched his nose at her. "God?! What the shite does god have to do with this, Claire?"

Kaetlyn turned an eye to her mom, interested to see how their dialogue would play out.

Humble as always, Claire answered. "Well, I don't mean anything against the Israelis, and certainly noth'n blasphemous against God, but they brought this on themselves with all the kill'n and violence they been doing against those poor Palestinian folk."

Kaetlyn lowered her mobile phone, suddenly compelled to enter the debate. "You think god is punishing the Jews?"

"Well," Claire began with a subtle twist of her head, "you can't go 'round hurt'n folk and stealing their land and call it God's will. There's a reckon'n waiting for those who do that sort of thing," she said with a shudder. "And besides, no decent god is gonna sanction such violence and mistreatment."

Kaetlyn grinned. "Interesting concept, mum."

Harry trained an eye on his daughter. "Won't be so interest'n if the Jews invade Palestine for real – which they're threaten'n to do. Then we'll be see'n all-out war."

It was Kaetlyn's turn to shrug. "They've been killing one another for decades, dad. Until they end their religious intolerance and treat one other as equals, nothing is going to change, and no brokered peace deal will ever last."

Harry flicked a dismissive brow and returned to reading the paper. "Says 're that a team of scientists reckon a chunk of the Antarctic is gonna split off some day soon."

Kaetlyn shook her head. "That's not good news."

Harry lowered the paper once again, fixing his gaze on her. "Let me get this straight," he began, "the Arabs and Jews are killing each other by the droves, and that, you shrug off, but some block of ice split'n in half – that gets yur hackles in a bunch?" He tipped his head at her with a look of mild rebuke.

"I'm not suggesting that anyone killing anyone is good, dad – but the fact remains that the conflicts in the Middle East are manufactured by vested interests and the inflated egos of people on both sides. They hide behind a façade of religious and ideological beliefs, pretending that they are better than the other and acting at the behest of their god which they consider the only true god, but their real agenda is always the same – money, power and real estate. The Ross Ice Shelf is far more critical to our future and survival as a race than all the shite stirred up in the Middle East."

Harry smiled. He enjoyed debates with his daughter, who, as far as he was concerned, was probably one of the brightest minds he had ever known, certainly shining brighter than his.

"Okay, smarty-pants, tell me why I should lose any sleep over this chunk of ice."

Kaetlyn picked up a pen and drew on a napkin. "The Ross Ice Shelf is actually the size of a continent, dad. You could fit ten entire Irelands into that one geographical area. It is nearly a mile deep and rises half a mile above water level at its apex. The fact that it is weak enough to crack apart, means that an entire continental zone of our planet is going to disappear someday. It would be like Europe breaking in half and falling into the ocean. It means that global warming has hit a critical-mass stage."

"So what, it's just ice down there. It'll fill up the oceans – no big deal?"

"You're missing the point, dad. The real issue is that it would critically affect the weather patterns globally. We just had our hottest summer in what ..." she looked to her mum.

"189 years, dear," answered Claire with a concerned look in her eyes. "Read it in *The Local* the other day, five more dairy farms in Cork went bankrupt – too dry to raise feed for cattle – and too expensive to buy it from elsewhere."

Harry lowered the paper to the table and sipped his coffee. "Maybe it's time to stop reading these damn papers," he grumbled once again as he sank his teeth into a slice of buttery toast.

A knock came to the door. Mrs. O'Sullivan answered and returned with Duncan Flowery, the Dean of Saint Michael's School, a man who rarely visited their home.

He nodded respectfully at Harry. Both men had grown up in Bantry, in fact, they had gone to the same school and had attended one another's wedding.

"Sit down, Duncan, take a load off your feet. Claire just cracked open a jar of her homemade jam."

Flowery offered a reserved smile while stealing a transient peek at Kaetlyn. It was a moment, a tacit moment, where the look on his face was enough to alert her that something was wrong, otherwise, why was the Dean of her school showing up at their house just before she was about to leave for her first class that day.

"I'm afraid this isn't a social call," began Duncan, while hovering by the back of a chair – his hands clasping it so tightly that the whites of his knuckles showed. "I'm sorry to impose on you this early in the morning but the matter concerns Kaetlyn."

16

All eyes shifted to her.

"Did I do something wrong?" asked Kaetlyn."

The Dean's face screwed up with evident discomfort.

"The School Council has deemed that you should be temporarily suspended."

The shock struck Kaetlyn like a blow to her head.

Harry O'Sullivan dropped his cup to the table with a definitive crash. "What the fook fer?!" He demanded.

Duncan raised a brow. "I'm afraid that Kaetlyn's behavior has been determined as inappropriate and unsuitable to permit her to continue her curriculum without first addressing the matter."

"What are you talking about?" asked Claire. "How can you simply suspend her from school – she's a top-student?"

The Dean bowed his head marginally, his eyes falling to the floor tentatively as he took a deep breath. "Her grades are not in question, Claire. Nor is her intelligence – she is most certainly above average in that regard. It is her behavior."

"What's wrong with my behavior?" asked Kaetlyn.

Duncan raised his eyes to meet hers. "You are creating a constant stir in the classrooms, Kaetlyn – showing a repeated pattern of rebelliousness and disrespect against the teachers and challenging the curriculum they are teaching. Parents are regularly calling my office complaining that you are upsetting the other students with crazy ideas and disturbing classes." His eyes drifted back to Mrs. O'Sullivan. "Every one of Kaetlyn's teachers has filed reports about her odd behavior of recent and the disturbance she is causing in their classes."

17

Mrs. O'Sullivan pinched her lips as her angst funneled upward, like hot lava about to spew-out.

"You're telling me that my daughter, an A-plus student, does not fit the mold for acceptable behavior and for that reason she cannot stay in school."

A small pad emerged from the man's pocket. He flipped it open and read from it. "Let me provide more details. Kaetlyn recently announced, in the middle of Catechism no less, that religion was a farce, that God did not exist, and that Jesus was a marketing caper dreamed up by the Catholic Church to keep people in the fold."

Harry raised a brow and looked to Kaetlyn. "Did you say that?"

Kaetlyn shrugged.

The Dean continued. "Two weeks ago, she openly challenged the history teacher, saying that learning about a pedophile like Julius Caesar had no value and served no purpose in their lives and that it would be more valuable to learn about recent historical events, people who are changing or have changed the culture."

Kaetlyn shrugged again. "That's true. How does learning about a pedophiliac nut-job give me a leg up in my career? Why not teach us about Martin Luther King, or Nelson Mandela, or even Elon Musk – people who made a difference and who inspired us to be better."

The Dean sighed, clearly irritated by her recalcitrance and flipped to another page of his pad. "In her social studies class, just last week, Kaetlyn challenged the teacher and announced that mental health practitioners were just drug peddlers for the big pharmaceuticals." He paused to look at them. "I could go on if you wish."

"So, what! It's all true," asserted Kaetlyn with a retaliatory look in her eyes.

The Dean turned to her. "Whether these opinions or views are true or not, Kaetlyn, you are a student, the teachers teach, and the curriculum is the curriculum." He turned to Mrs. O'Sullivan. "Bantry is a God-loving town, you know that, Claire. Saint Michaels School is one of its oldest and most respected institutions, and for Kaetlyn to continuously assault the material, claiming, quite discourteously I might add, that what we are teaching is wrong, is in itself a very poor show of character on her part – particularly this close to graduating her final year. It presents the School Council with a problem. Academically speaking, Kaetlyn is far above average, but her behavior is far too radical to permit the matter to go unnoticed, and certainly before the school could ratify her final year. In the interests of seeing that Kaetlyn does graduate and go on to lead a successful life, it was considered best that she be temporarily suspended while undergoing therapy."

Harry was completely slack-jawed as he listened.

The Dean continued. "I know it seems harsh, but I assure you, we have taken every known approach to temper the situation. Unfortunately," he shook his head, "we must insist that you get her professional help to temper her outbursts before we can permit her to finish her curriculum."

"Professional help?" retorted the mother, her wounded look accompanied her words.

The Dean handed her a paper. "We are recommending that she see a therapist to discuss her behavior. This particular one comes well-recommended, and all expenses for her sessions will be covered by her tuition."

He glanced once more at Kaetlyn.

"I'm sorry, Kaetlyn. I really am. You are a very bright girl, and I suspect that one day I will be reading about your accomplishments in the newspaper. But right now, your attitude presents a problem to our school. Maybe we should be more progressive in our ways of seeing things, but this is Bantry. We're a small community and people still hold to Catholic conventions, so when you repeatedly assert your views without regard for the perspectives of others, it offends them and us."

Harry stood. His face black with repressed anger.

"And how long is she expected to see this shrink?"

"Until the therapist's recommendation shows that Kaetlyn can function within the realm of the school parameters. Then she will be reinstated to her classes." He paused. "I highly doubt that her temporary absence will adversely affect her grades anyhow – but her behavior could certainly influence the results of her *Leaving Certificate*."

3

"Hello, Kaetlyn, my name is Serena Bohannon."

Kaetlyn lowered herself into the armchair with a cautious aspect.

Her first impression was that Serena didn't fit her expectancy of a shrink, that is, the image she had of the stereotyped psychologist.

She was quite pretty, with bright blue eyes, milky skin peppered with freckles and long sienna-colored hair, a package that would certainly bewitch any man, she thought.

A framed certificate on the wall announced that she was a graduate of *UCD's - School of Psychology*.

It had taken her mum several hours to convince her, after the news of her temporary suspension from school, that the only road back to admittance was with a clean bill of health from the therapist, and now, reluctantly, she sat there watching the woman, who politely smiled back at her, no doubt, trying to disarm her growing anxiety.

"Can we get to know one other just a little?" asked Serena.

Kaetlyn shrugged. "Sure."

"Tell me about yourself."

"I just turned eighteen last month."

"Well, I'm twenty-nine. Do you feel comfortable talking to someone older?"

"You're not that much older than me."

Serena grinned. "I'll take that as a compliment," she answered with another disarming smile. "I'm told you don't think very highly of my profession."

Kaetlyn raised a brow. "Told by who?"

"I spoke with your school psychologist. He said you called him a drug pusher when he recommended Ritalin for you, and that later, you openly referred to him as just another cultist."

Kaetlyn's head bobbed. "He is part of the cult of pharmaceutical drug pushers. You call yourselves authorities on the mind, but when you can't figure out what's really wrong with folk, you subscribe psychotropics – right?"

Serena fixed her eyes on Kaetlyn. "Harsh words."

"Hard truth?"

"You seem angry, Kaetlyn."

"At least we agree on something."

"What are you angry about?"

"For starters, I just got kicked out of school based on someone's false idea of acceptable behavior."

Serena raised a brow. "How do you know it's false?"

Kaetlyn tipped her head at the other. "Seriously?!"

Serena raised a brow. "I'm not challenging you, I'm just curious why you think it is false?"

"How about this. A society that advocates war, that is destroying the planet we live on, that engages in racial profiling, that objectifies an entire religion as being terrorists, where the one-percenters own most of the wealth while the rest of us struggle to make a living - how does that society set the bar for acceptable behavior?" Kaetlyn's jaw crimped tight as she shook her head. "You sit there and judge me based on some benchmark of normality that someone taught you – but who defines that normality? The people starting the wars? The ones destroying our planet? The one-percenters who have a vested interest in protecting their hoards?"

Serena offered up a smile. "May I offer a suggestion?"

Kaetlyn shrugged.

"Choose your battles, Kaet. Despite your passion and sensitivities, you simply cannot fight everyone on every front. That isn't a good strategy for winning a war," she paused. "Clearly, you have strong views about things, and you assert those, and I wouldn't for a second suggest that you stop speaking up – but there is wisdom in being prudent about where and when to swing your sword."

Kaetlyn was silent for a time, her eyes fixed on Serena. "I'll take that on advisement."

Serena leaned back in her chair, satisfied that they had reached the first rung of the ladder they must climb together. "So, tell me, why do you think you are here?"

"Apparently, I offend people's sense of propriety. Too much truth bruises their minds."

"Do you?"

Kaetlyn rolled her eyes. "If freedom of expression is a sign of a rebel, then I am guilty of that."

"From what I understand, you have opposing views to the school curriculum."

"That's an understatement."

"Tell me more."

"Where do I start?" she shrugged. "For me it's the difference between teaching us *Fifty Shades of Grey* or a *Brief History of Time* by Stephen Hawking. One is soft porn and does nothing to increase our ability to think for ourselves, the other actually expands our minds and teaches us to think and to question the world around us."

"So, you're saying the curriculum is poor?"

Kaetlyn nods. "Why do you think I'm sitting in front of you?" She raised a brow. "I don't want to learn about the same old box, I want to know how to stretch the edges of it, or better yet, how to build a better one. Why must we be stifled by an education system that only tests our ability to parrot back what teachers and text books say? How is that supposed to lead me to a successful life that really taps all my potential?"

"Do you consider yourself different from others?"

Kaetlyn flicked a brow. "I've always felt out of place."

"Why?"

Kaetlyn pointed to her skin. "For one, I'm black, and most of you are white as fook'n cream."

Serena nodded. "How long have you felt this way?"

"As long as I can remember."

"And how far back would that be?"

Kaetlyn grinned. "Pretty much the day I popped out of my mother's vagina."

Serena grinned. She was beginning to like this girl. Her candid approach was both refreshing and feisty, moreover, something about Kaetlyn intrigued her. She had read the brief by the Dean of the school, as well as the one provided by the school psychologist; but it was one thing to read words on a page based on the interpretations of others, and quite another to hear it from the person.

"Are you saying you can remember having conscious thoughts that far back?"

"I can tell you the details of the hospital room where I was delivered, even how the doctor looked and his dialect."

"Impressive."

"Why is that impressive?"

"Most people I've dealt with don't remember their early childhood, let alone birth."

"Well, I do. I remember everything. I can tell you that the chairs in your waiting room outside are made of black leather, that you graduated UCD two years ago in April, you're left-handed and that you are slightly myopic."

"How do you know I have myopia?"

Kaetlyn nodded at the pad balanced on her knee. "By the way you squint when you glance at your notes."

Serena leaned forward in her chair, her eyes probing the other. "Do you remember what your first thought was after you were born?"

Kaetlyn's eyes drifted for a moment. "I remember thinking that the room felt cold. The womb was so warm and cozy – but a tad bit constrictive for my liking."

Serena grinned. "Anything else?"

Kaetlyn was silent for a time as her mind probed its vaults. She drew in a breath and exhaled before answering. "I remember thinking, *why am I here?*"

Serena's face screwed up. "I don't understand."

"Neither did I," she said, clearly exasperated. "And, I still don't."

Serena leaned closer. "What do you mean by that?

Kaetlyn appeared sincerely confused as she stared at the floor before answering. She looked up at Serena. "I've never felt comfortable in my skin, like I don't belong on this planet."

4

The old man had trekked over the same craggy slopes, navigating a narrow, barely visible footpath, for nigh on eighty years now.

His hand-carved walking stick had accompanied him the entire time, its age reflected in the dings and worn grip.

On every outing, he donned his favorite raincoat, a Henry White forest-green tweed and matching cap, both of which his late wife had given him for their 50th anniversary.

Carefully stepping over stones and avoiding the spiked brambles and their thorny bite, conjured up the memory once again, that of the first day his father had taken him along this very trail.

It was the morning of his 5th birthday. His father woke him before the sun had risen. They performed their usual chores in silence, fed the cattle, sheep and chickens, collected up some eggs for mum to cook-up for breakfast, and then, his father handed him the walking stick – the very one he still used to this day.

"Carved it m'self," he proclaimed with a proud smile. "You'll be need'n this where we're goin', lad" said the man, and without further ado, he turned on his heel and headed off with his son in tow.

The trip took well over an hour, he well recalled, because his legs were tired and his stomach screamed for something to fill it.

As they emerged from the thinning tree line, a brisk gust cuffed him in the face with the taste of sea salt. It was the first time he had seen the Old Man, as they called the Celtic Sea.

He remembered the sense of awe, the feeling of being mesmerized by the sight as he stood there on the cliff overlooking what seemed to be an endless expanse of grey, where the sea and the sky melted together on the distant horizon.

The voice of his father broke the enchantment.

Turning, he saw him disappearing through a cluster of tall firs. He found his father sitting atop a moss-covered rock, pointing his walking stick to the precipice a stone's throw away.

"This here's called Witches' Tit, son."

"Why's it called that, father?"

"If'n ya look over that edge," he pointed, "you'll see two bulges in the escarpment to the right, looks like someone carved a woman's breasts in the rock." He chuckled at the confused look on his son's face.

"You'll appreciate it when you get older, son" he said as his hand emerged from his coat pocket with a small package wrapped in butcher's paper. The boy lowered himself tiredly to the ground as the father handed him a pork sandwich.

He promptly devoured the sandwich as his eyes searched the small enclosure.

"Father, what is this place?"

"Old ruins, I imagine - found it a few years back."

"Is it a magical place?" asked the boy, now noticing the arrangement of large stones forming a circle around them, most of them canted and worn by age."

"Could be, don't reckon I know for sure."

"Why'd you bring me here, father?"

The man tilted his head toward the sea, his eyes fixed on a dim spherical glow where the sun hung, obscured by thick clouds. "Ireland's a magical place, boy, with plenty of hidden secrets and treasures just wait'n to be found," he turned and looked at him. "This here's a special place, and someday, if you keep look'n, you'll find your own treasure."

His father's words echoed in his mind, even now, eight decades later. He had planted the seed for a young boy who started to romanticize the prospects of making his own discovery someday and he never lost that passion – as if his father had set him on a mission so many years before.

From the age of five, until now, on the cusp of his 85th birthday, he had searched these cliffs, but his age had caught up with him, demanding precedence over his dream, and all the while his special treasure had not revealed itself.

Today, his legs were not what they were as a young boy. Back then his walking stick was something to poke and bang against trees and rocks, whereas today, he could barely climb small rises or descend rocky slopes without the stick to support his creaky frame.

Standing there on the cusp of the steep precipice, one he had visited more times than he could remember, and yet, one which never failed to dazzle him, he gazed out at the churn of the Celtic as whitecaps pounded into the pebbled-beach far below with a distant crash that thundered upward. He braced himself against the cold and shrieking October wind – its call reminding him that soon enough he would have to cash in his ticket.

Trouble, his Irish Setter, just as old in dog-years, settled at his feet. Trouble's fur was looking mangier these days – and his slow gait betrayed the pain of time-worn joints.

His eyes wandered over the face of the escarpment below – a sheer wall of rock that opposed its adversary, a sea that relentlessly carved away at it, wearing it down, eroding its exterior, increment by increment, in a battle for dominance.

As he pulled his gaze to the right, the odd displacement stopped him dead.

"What the shite is that, Trouble?" he squinted and pointed with his stick, wondering if the light was playing tricks on his old eyes.

5

Serena paused their talk, offering Kaetlyn a drink to keep her occupied.

Leaving her in the interview room, she went to her office and pulled up the notes she had received from the school psychologist and refreshed herself on the details of her case.

There was no doubt about it, Kaetlyn O'Sullivan was an interesting person, but was she delusional, hyperactive, or passive-aggressive, various labels the school counsellor referred to in his brief – that was not clear.

Moments later, they were back at it.

"Do you remember your last Catechism – what you said to the teacher?" she asked, glancing at her notes.

Kaetlyn shrugged with a slight smirk on her lips. "Oh, you mean when I told her that Jesus could not possibly have walked on water."

Serena nodded. "What happened?"

"She got very offended, told me I wasn't supposed to question the Bible, that I was supposed to believe it."

"And what did you say?"

"I told her I didn't believe things just because I was supposed to," she paused to gather her thoughts, "In fact, I remember saying that the whole story about Jesus was an elaborate fiction filled with hyperbole designed to deify him as the son of God, just to give the narrative more power over the minds of people."

Serena restrained from smiling. Not being particularly religious herself, she found the perspective refreshing to hear in a land where many of her Irish brothers and sisters still retained an unswerving faith for the Biblical stories taught to them from the very earliest ages.

"What happened after that?"

"She asked me to leave the class. Later, I was informed by the Head Master that unless I was willing to learn the Catechism, there was no point in my returning to that class."

Serena nodded. "Did that upset you?"

Kaetlyn shook her head. "Fook, no! I was relieved. Besides, I'd wager anything on the fact that there isn't an organization in the world, looking to hire me in the future, that would give a shite as to whether I got credits for attending Catechism, unless of course it was the Church itself."

Serena flicked a brow. "Why did you agree to be here today?"

"It wasn't my choice – I assure you."

"So, you don't think there's anything to be fixed?"

Kaetlyn's head rocked back and forth. "I'm not mentally ill, if that's what you mean?"

"Did someone say you were?"

"Is that a trick question, because the last time I checked, that's exactly what the school administration and psychologist alluded to."

"Just to be clear, Kaetlyn, I make up my own mind about my patients."

Kaetlyn eyed her for a moment before continuing. "Just because my views don't fit mediocrity doesn't make me a freak or mentally dysfunctional."

"These views, as you say, are they random – coming on the spur of the moment?"

"Yes and no."

"Is it like voices in your head?" asked Serena.

Kaetlyn rolled her eyes at the other. "Seriously, you're playing that card already? No, there are no voices in my head, and I don't hear things. It's more like a cognizance, like I suddenly know something without having studied about it..." she paused, "... as if some part of me is woke up and is trying to say something meaningful." She sighed. "And, frankly, I don't a do very good job of relating what I think. My mouth gets away from me sometimes."

"Do you care what others think?"

"It's means shite to me what others think about me. What bothers me is that my situation is affecting my parents."

"In what way?"

"Mum worries a lot about me, a lot more than she lets on. I see it in her face. My suspension was a blow to her and I know she cried her heart out over it that day." She paused. "My dad, on the other hand, he just locks it all up inside, but I know he's pissed."

"You think he's angry at you?"

"No. I think he's mad at the community for rejecting me."

Serena leaned forward. "Do you think any of these ideas you have are delusional?" she asked, testing the waters to see her reaction.

"Absolutely not. I don't understand where they come from, or why I have such a conviction about them, but they're not delusional."

Serena offered a consoling smile as she shifted tactic. "Not everything we know is taught to us, Kaetlyn. There is such a thing as cognitive intuition, as well as cognitive dissonance."

Kaetlyn offered a crooked grin. "Really? That sounds a bit hypocritical coming from you."

"Why?"

"Your entire profession is predicated on the whole gray-goop theory – that our brains are the source of everything and that we're nothing more than the net sum of the interchange of chemicals and synapses in our heads?"

"That's an over-simplification."

Kaetlyn shook her head. "Maybe, or maybe that's your delusion," she said with an impish smile.

"Tell me more about these ideas you get."

Kaetlyn paused before answering – reticent to expose herself to more criticism – because it seemed that anytime she opened her mouth, people felt entitled to pass more judgement her – as if it was a national pastime.

Serena saw her hesitation. "You're not on trial, Kaetlyn, if that's what you're worried about. I just want to understand what is going on."

Kaetlyn exhaled, "Since the day I can remember, I have seen the world around me more like a glass-bowl, as if I was standing on the outside, looking in – like I don't belong."

"Belong where?"

Kaetlyn looked at her, her brown eyes almost pleading with the other. "I told you already – I don't feel as if I belong here and I don't understand why."

6

Not much happened in Kilcrohane, a small hamlet located on the remote southwesterly tip of Ireland – a place where tourists sometimes outnumbered the local population.

Old man O'Brien, or *geezer* as most called him, sat in his small kitchenette, romancing a cup of hot tea while trying to shake off the pervasive cold which afflicted him more than he cared to admit. The old house, which his great grandfather had built, hewed of stone and timber from this very land, creaked to the pressing hand of a brisk wind that swirled and besieged it, like Indians circling a wagon train.

Across from him sat Finn, his grandson and only living heir on this Earth. Death had come far too easy to his family, losing his daughter and son to disease, his wife to old age, leaving Finn alone in this world.

"How was yur walk, grandad?"

O'Brien shrugged. "Blustery as fook'n hell out there, but a fine autumn day nonetheless." He sipped on his tea as he patted Trouble. The old dog seemed more interested in sleeping than anything these days. "Saw sometin' out by Witches' Tit."

Finn raised a brow, his interest suddenly piqued. "Like what?"

The old man's eyes narrowed. "Don't know, to be sure. Somethin' was stick'n out from the escarpment. Didn't look right to me."

Finn pushed his phone aside and looked at his grandad. "You seen it before?"

"Nope!" the old man's head shook. "I been to that lookout since Jesus was a born, never saw it once. I think the recent rains must'a exposed it." He fixed a look at Finn. "I was plan'n to go back there, but I'm feel'n a bit out of sorts today. Maybe you can take a gander."

Finn nodded.

"Take my binoculars," he pointed to a nearby shelf, "and take Trouble with you. The old shite needs the walk."

Finn stood, plucked up the binoculars and blew off a layer of thick dust. Trouble creaked to a standing position and rubbed up against his leg.

Old man O'Brien tipped his head at his grandson. "You know, I been look'n for sometin' out there most of my life, so ..." he teased him with a wink, "you be sure an' let me know if it's a treasure, sometin' special, sometin I can say is mine before I let go of this carcass I'm drag'n about."

Finn was pretty sure it would turn out to be nothing at all, but he humored his grandad whose days were numbered, smiled at him and then stepped into the arms of frigid wind.

7

Kaetlyn sat leaning against the headstone.

The inscription carved into it read: Norbert Finnigan. April 12th 1861 to 28th July 1914.

Her mind never stopped working the details of things, even now. It was either a gift or a demon, she wasn't sure which one.

Nonetheless, puzzles were meant to be solved, mysteries delved into, and impossibilities made possible – that was how she saw the world.

She questioned everything, challenged the mediocrity and never accepted conventions, driven by some sonorous desire to know the bottom line, the truth, and not "sanctioned" versions based on collective thought.

While others her age were engaged in socializing and developing relationships, she was usually found with her nose buried in a book, or researching the internet, or simply sitting alone, here, with Mr. Finnigan, listening to the wind or watching the stars materialize in the night sky.

Why did she feel so different, she wondered?

Why couldn't she just be happy with finding normality in life, like others seemed to be able to do?

Why was it that every time she sat alone, something inside taunted her, poked her, scratched at her soul, like a ghost from her past?

She had read countless books about the mind and the soul, in the hopes of connecting the dots about who she was; but nothing answered the questions, nor the mystery about the haunting that came calling to her most every night in the form of a dream, a nightmare, a specter from somewhere.

Was it just dreaming? she thought.

Or, was it something else?

Was it a sign, a voice from somewhere, some awakening deep inside her – something trying to escape?

She sighed as the answers eluded her for the umpteenth time.

Her recurring dream wasn't something she could talk to others about, except her one and only real friend, Alana, who seemed to have the fortitude to listen to her rants when others would probably have called time out and left her far behind.

"D-TEKT?" she said as she turned an eye to her mobile phone – tapping the icon of the latest and most advanced search-app available on the web.

"Yes, Kaetlyn, how can I help you?" answered the avatar, its alien-like-face with its bulbous eyes and exaggerated lips, as if aliens used Botox too.

She turned an eye to the inscription on the gravestone and noted the date of Mr. Finnigan's birth. "What happened in 1861?"

"Any special search-parameters?"

"No, just tell me about the first significant event you can find, anywhere."

Seconds later, D-TEKT responded, its rubbery lips moving with animated precision. "1861, is the year the American Civil War began, when the Confederates, under General Pierre Beauregard's command, opened fire with 50 cannons on Fort Sumter in Charleston, South Carolina."

She grinned. "Interesting. And what about 1914."

"World War I began that year," responded the app without delay.

"Wow," she said, turning to wink at the dead man's gravestone. "Born and died the same years as to two major wars started. You're a real shite-stirrer, Mr. Finnigan."

The Bantry Church graveyard was quiet, rarely visited by people, usually just a handful of locals who came by to pay their respects to the long gone. There was a certain solace about it; moreover, the dead didn't talk, and they certainly didn't pass judgement on her either.

If there was a virtue in death, she thought, *it was silence.*

She listened as the cold October wind rustled through the trees around her, feeling the warmth of a waning sun on her face, and the touch of a good book in her hands.

"It's a beautiful day, isn't it?" she announced.

The avatar's eyes flickered as it tried to process the statement as a subjective question. "The forecast for today is partially sunny until mid-afternoon, with possible rain by dinner time."

"Thanks."

"You're welcome."

She enjoyed dialogues with the app, but even it had limitations.

Her mind drifted back to her last interview with the psychologist, Serena Bohannon. She was nice enough, seemed sincerely interested in her, but ... there was that stigma, she was a mind doctor and Kaetlyn had no trust in a profession that claimed to be authorities, and yet, who could not provide sensible answers about the human condition, beyond assigning it labels and feeding people drugs.

"D-TEKT, look up Serena Bohannon, in Cork County, please."

"Serena Bohannon, PhD. Twenty-nine years of age. Born in Dublin. Completed University of Psychology – majoring in trauma therapy. Currently employed as a trauma psychologist by the Cork County Health Care Services."

"That's all?"

The avatar blinked. "I can summarize her Facebook and Instagram accounts if you wish

"No, thanks."

Her gaze returned to the graveyard – looking at the small plots of colorful flowers not yet deadened by the cold touch of autumn.

A movement caught her eye, a subtle shift in the shadow of a cluster of trees ahead.

Someone was watching her.

8

While she had other clients, none of them intrigued her like the eighteen-year-old, Kaetlyn O'Sullivan.

It wasn't that delusion, hyper-imagination, or any other of a dozen labels her profession assigned such maladies, was anything new to her. It was the fact that Kaetlyn didn't fit any mold, that was the oddity. She spoke with both clarity and conviction, which made her utterances sound more creditable than just pure fantasy.

And while the school psychologist was convinced that Kaetlyn suffered from something, Serena wasn't so sure – although it was too early in the therapy to draw any lines in the sand.

She wondered about the veracity of the Council's decision to suspend her from school.

Was she being fairly judged in the matter of her outspokenness, or was she simply being thrown under the bus to protect mediocrity from something, or someone, they could not control?

The problem, which she knew all-too-well from her years at UCD's School of Psychology, was that delusion-cases were the most difficult ones to break through. Their grip on their illusions, their resistance to letting anyone

38

penetrate their protective armor, was to a degree, a survival mechanism against a world that no longer accepted them as normal. And clearly, Kaetlyn, as shown by her emotional defensiveness during their first two sessions, felt the need to suit-up each time she was challenged about her state of mind.

What struck her as particularly odd, and that which cast the dice in yet another direction, was the fact that Kaetlyn was aware that sometimes she did not know why or how she came to the conclusions she did, or the source of her utterances – and that very self-awareness was not an attribute of the classic delusion case – in fact, it suggested that Kaetlyn was not living in a world of self-imposed illusion at all.

So, what was she dealing with, she wondered?

Was she a child prodigy – a born genius? History was certainly replete with the inexplicable phenomena of children, who, at very young ages, could sit down at a piano and play an entire concerto by Mozart or Beethoven – start to finish, without having studied their music or taken a single piano lesson. "Experts", even in her field of mental health, had no explanation for the fact that phenomenon. And yet – it happened repeatedly. So, like most, they simply categorized it as paranormal - a convenient way of tucking the inexplicable mystery under the rug in order to protect the status quo.

There was always the possibility of autism, of which Serena seemed to manifest the slightest signs. High intelligence compounded by an absence of empathy – and an introvert, but a brilliant one.

The subtle knock shook her from her thoughts.

"Come in."

Kaetlyn entered, with a reserved smile on her lips.

"How are you today, Kaetlyn?"

She shrugged. "I'm okay."

Everything aside, Kaetlyn was a very beautiful young lady, with intensely dark skin and equally long black hair and bright eyes.

"Take a seat. What have you been doing since our last talk?"

"Helping mum around the house. Reading – the usual shite."

"No friends?"

"My best friend …" she paused, "actually, my only real one, is off in London visiting relatives."

Serena smiled. "Ready to get started?"

"One thing before we do."

"Yes?"

"What benchmark do you use to judge if someone is sane or not?"

"There is no absolute measuring stick for sanity, Kaetlyn."

"Then how do you measure abnormality if there is no absolute standard for normality, and how can I be judged by you and given a clean bill of health if there are no clear lines of delineation?"

"We look for certain markers that help to identify the extremes – but they're only guideposts."

"Such as?" asked Kaetlyn.

"That's hard to summarize in one brief statement – considering I spent years studying the subject."

Kaetlyn grinned. "Humor me."

"Well, extremes are the clue. Extreme behavior, abnormal obsessions, recurring delusions, constant paranoia, these are classic markers, but there are also less obvious ones, like those that define sociopathic behavior."

"Do you see any of those in my behavior?"

Serena paused, offering a disarming smile. "It's a bit early in the therapy for me to make any conclusions."

"Hmm. And what if I disagree with your findings? Do I have any say in the matter or is your word final?"

"No, Kaetlyn, my word isn't final. Like any doctor, if you disagree with my diagnosis, you can go to another one." She tipped her head at her. "I promise, I will remain objective. Shall we get started?"

Kaetlyn nodded.

"In our first session, you said that you could remember things from birth."

"Yes."

"Do you remember the name of the doctor who delivered you?"

"No, but I remember that he was about forty-five, wore glasses and was not Irish."

Serena jotted down notes. "Do you remember any other details of your birth?

"When I popped out, the first person I saw was the doctor who delivered me. The second person I saw, who I didn't know at the time, was my father, and he fainted on the spot."

"Fainted?"

"Apparently, the sight of blood was not his strong point."

"And your mother?"

41

"She died several minutes after delivering me."

Serena's face sobered. "I'm sorry to hear that."

Kaetlyn shook her head. "It's okay." She paused. "I didn't understand what was happening when the nurse took me away from her, but I could hear the voices of medical personnel as they tried to save her."

"Do you know what happened to your dad?"

Kaetlyn's head wagged slightly. "You know the story, I'm sure. He became an alcoholic, reneged on his fatherly duties, so social services swooped in and I was adopted by the O'Sullivans."

"What happened to him – do you know?"

"He drank himself into a stupor and drowned in his own vomit. Not a very respectable man."

Serena was silent for a time. Kaetlyn broke the taciturnity.

"You want to ask me how I feel about all of this, right?"

Serena offered an amiable smile. "The thought did occur to me."

"My father was a disappointment at best."

"And your mum?"

Kaetlyn's eyes glazed-over as she sighed. "I think I would have liked her a lot."

9

It was late in the afternoon, with a dimming sun filtering through a cloud-scudded sky, when Finn set out to Witches' Tit to inspect what his grandad had spoken of.

An hour later, following a good pounding by a strong headwind, he eased up to the cliffside overlooking the spot, pulled the binoculars to his eyes and located the two infamous breast-shaped protrusions extruding from the escarpment to his right. From there, he worked his way down the escarpment.

"Good lord!" he exclaimed, although the piercing wind was quick to squelch the expletive.

He looked long and hard at the oddity, which, from his perspective, appeared like a cylindrical object, maybe a meter or two in length, protruding from the cliffside. It was smooth and clearly not made of the rock in which it sat.

He estimated that it was two hundred feet down from where he stood, or midway from the top to the rocky shores below, and there was certainly no way for him to get any closer.

He pulled out his mobile, snapped off some shots and headed back.

When he got home, his first thought was to get a second opinion, so he looked up the *Irish Military War Museum*, just outside Drogheda, north of Dublin, a place he had visited once before.

"This is Mr. Chandry, proprietor of the IMWM, how can I help you," answered the man.

"My name is Finn O'Brien, I live in Cork County, near Kilcrohane."

"How can I help you, Mr. O'Brien?"

"I found something today which I think might be a war artifact of some kind."

"I see," said the man. "Why do you say that?"

"It was my first thought when I saw it, which is why I decided to contact you."

"That region was a popular shipping-route for warships and U-boats during World War II. In fact, several battles happened not far from where you live."

"Yes, I've heard that from my grandad. If I were to email you several pictures of this object could you look at them and tell me if it resembles anything from your historical records?"

"Certainly. Happy to do so."

Within minutes, Finn had uploaded and sent the images to the man.

Some hours and several cups of coffee later, he received an email.

> *"Mr. O'Brien, I have checked with my colleagues and compared the images to our digital-data base, and there was nary a match to anything in our records. In fact, as you described in your email, having no apparent signs of weathering or damage, despite its rather odd location protruding from the face of this cliff, I can only surmise that it isn't a wartime artifact. I wish you the best of luck in your search."*

10

Serena Bohannon contacted Kaetlyn's mother and arranged to meet both her and her husband the next morning.

"Thank you for coming on such short notice."

Claire O'Sullivan's face betrayed her anxiety, a face that seemed to have worn such anxiety for many years judging by the deeply trenched lines in her brow and the harried look that exuded from her eyes.

"As you know, I've had several sessions with Kaetlyn and some questions have been raised which I am hoping you can assist in answering."

"Anything, of course," responded the mother, while Harry nodded somberly.

"Kaetlyn is a unique case, at least from my experience. She shows an amazing degree of mental clarity, and yet, as already noted by others, her views about certain things are intensely strong."

"We noticed," uttered the father with an annoyed tone.

Serena smiled disarmingly at the man, who, clearly, was sitting on a mountain of upset.

"Kaetlyn mentioned something which I found profoundly unusual." She paused. "She claims to be able to remember details from her birth."

The mother's face remained unchanged, as if this was nothing new to her. "Kaetlyn has always shown a remarkable ability to remember things which…" she paused to look at her husband… "we could not explain."

"She says that when she was born, the first person she saw was a doctor," she glanced at a notepad in her lap, "possibly around forty-five years of age, and she distinctly remembers that he was not Irish."

A light chuckle emitted from Claire's throat. "Actually, he was an American, a Texan, who was interning at the hospital at the time."

"How do you know this?" inquired Serena, her interest piqued.

"When we picked up Kaetlyn at the office of adoption services, this very doctor stepped from that office and congratulated us. Apparently, he was called in to confirm the baby's certification and identity as part of their due process."

"Impressive," said Serena. "She also said that the second person she saw was her biological father, and that upon seeing her coming out of the womb, he promptly fainted."

"I've heard Kaetlyn mention it once or twice when she was young."

"Is there any way that Kaetlyn could have known about the details of these incidents?"

Harry O'Sullivan leaned forward as he leveled a defiant stare at the psychologist. "Not unless she got on the phone to that doctor who delivered her, or her mother and father suddenly came back from their fook'n graves." He glared at her. "Look, Ms. Bohannon, my daughter isn't crazy. She's not weird or strange or anything – she's just smarter than the lot of them."

Serena leaned back in her chair, assuming a more casual pose. "The school psychologist is of the opinion that Kaetlyn might be delusional, or possibly even autistic."

"That's just bull crap," retorted the father, his anger suddenly unleashed. "The only delusional people are the fooks who can't see her for what she is."

46

"That may be true, Mr. O'Sullivan, which is why I asked you to come here so that I could confirm for myself whether or not Kaetlyn's story was creditable."

The mother sighed with frustration clearly etched on her face.

"Of course, we've had our doubts at times, believe me," she cast a transient look to Harry. "We've tried to temper the storm with her school and friends, but it's been a difficult road these past few months because Kaetlyn has become more outspoken, as if she's trying to make a stand – and she comes across strong, assertive, even insensitive at times, but she doesn't mean it – she just says what's on her mind." She paused and then looked up at Serena. "We know our daughter, Ms. Bohannon, and like my husband said, she's not crazy, and she's not delusional, we know that much to be true."

"But there is something, isn't there?" probed Serena, seeing the concern painted on Claire's face.

The father broke his silence once again, his tone more tempered and hushed. "What I'm gonna tell you, lass, I haven't told anyone."

"Our talk is protected by the codes of my profession, Mr. O'Sullivan."

He grimaced, as if it pained him to open this door. "When Kaetlyn was five, I walked into her room one day and found her sitting on the floor with a large sheet of butcher paper spread out. She had her back to me, so I just stood there to see what she was doin', think'n that maybe she was making a drawing of sorts, like most kids." He sighed. "Anyhow, when I looked at it, she had drawn a complex chart."

"What kind of chart?"

His face still held an element of incredulity as he answered. "T'was nothing that a five-year-old child would draw."

"What was it?"

"The *Periodic Table of Elements.*"

"What do you mean?"

"Just what I said, lass. She drew the bloody Table of Elements and then some."

Serena's face betrayed her manifest confusion. "... and some"?

The father's eyes fixed on Serena's. "There were names of elements on that chart that don't exist in our world."

"And you're sure she never memorized it from a book?"

The father grinned. "Seriously, do you know of any five-year-old who reads the periodic table?"

Serena shook her head. "No, of course not."

Claire stepped in. "As Kaet got older, we saw other things, many things, small and large, which suggested that she was a very special child."

"Such as?"

The mother fished a small tattered book from her purse and handed it to Serena who promptly opened it and flipped through the pages."

"What is it?" she asked as she looked up at the two?

The father's shoulders heaved. "You tell us, you're the mind doctor."

11

Finn had combed the internet for anything that might suggest what the object could be.

Nothing made sense. In some ways it looked like a bomb, or a missile, and yet, its shape was not quite right. The very idea of trying to dislodge the object from the face of the cliff, short of having an entire excavation crew at his beck and call, was ridiculous; and, the option of calling in a specialist to analyze it, was also outside his league and certainly his budget. His frustration mounted by the hour.

His grandad shuffled into the small kitchenette with Trouble at his heels. He prepared a tea and then eased himself into a chair, pain exuding from his eyes as his failing joints announced their antiquity. He looked up at Finn.

"You didn't tell me what you saw at Witches' Tit."

Finn drew in a deep breath. "It's somethin' alright."

The old man waved a hand to the air. "Course it's sometin, but what?"

"Don't know, grandad, been wondering 'bout it myself."

O'Brien sipped on his tea, his wrinkled visage and bright blue eyes still fixed on Finn.

"Why not call your friend at the Naval Base, what's his name, Dookey..."

Finn grinned. "Deek, his name is Deek."

"Right. Ask him to check their military files. As I recall, those Navy boys keep perfect records," he chuckled, "since they got no wars to fight, they just sit 'round recording shite for posterity. Gotta be some record of a crash, maybe a plane, maybe the fook'n Yanks lost a nuke..." he smiled, revealing his nicotine-stained teeth.

Finn took his grandpa's advice and rang his friend who worked at the *Irish Defense Forces Naval Base* on Spike Island, just south of Cork.

"Damn, Finn, it's nearly ten o'clock at night. What's so fook'n important?"

Finn went on to describe the object.

"Why you call'n me 'bout it?"

"Figured you might be able to ask around or check military records, I don't know. I need some help here, mate."

Deek sighed. "Okay. Shoot me the pics and where you found it and I'll get back to you if anything comes up."

Finn promptly did so and then called it a night.

Little did he know that he had just lit the fuse to a global event that would change the world.

12

Kaetlyn stared at the small leather-bound book sitting on the coffee table between her and Serena.

"My parents gave you this?"

Serena nodded.

She shook her head – clearly annoyed. "Whatever happened to privacy?"

"You may not agree with me on this, Kaetlyn, but I think it's time that you came to terms with something."

"Which is?" she responded as her eyes shot up from the book.

"If you want my help you have to be completely transparent with me."

"I'm answering your questions, what more do you want?"

"We can tip-toe around your issue. Me asking questions, hit or miss, or you can just start telling me the depth of your..." she paused.

"Delusion?"

"I wasn't going to say that."

"But you were thinking it."

Serena drew in a breath with slight exasperation. "Cut me a little slack here. I'm a psychologist. It's my job. That said, I'm not judging you. I can't – because to be honest, I simply don't understand what the hell I am dealing with here."

"Neither do I," Kaetlyn's voice pitched high with anger.

"Then let's work together. If I can help you, it's a win-win scenario. If I don't then I promise you one thing, that I will recommend your reinstatement to school."

"Why would you do that?"

Serena shrugged lightly. "Frankly, you haven't convinced me, yet, that you are mentally dysfunctional."

Kaetlyn was silent.

"Are you afraid of finding out the truth?"

"No," responded Kaetlyn defiantly. "I'm afraid that you will try to impose your shite on me."

"I would never do that."

Kaetlyn's head wagged as she pinched her lips. "That's what the school psychologist said before insisting I take his fook'n pills."

"I'm not him." Serena leaned forward, looking the other in the face. "This ..." she pointed to Kaetlyn and then

51

to herself, "… only works if there is some level of trust between us. Otherwise, you're better off going to someone else."

"Or I just quit school, forget about getting my final grades and try to move on with my life?"

"It's not that grim."

"Sure, it is. If the last thing in my curriculum is that I am a delusional and disruptive student, who the hell is going to accept me at a higher institution of learning – particularly where I want to go?"

"Then let's work together to solve it. There is only way out and that is through the shite of it all, Kaet."

Kaetlyn tempered the storm brewing inside. Finally, she picked up the book from the coffee table and slowly leafed through its pages of handwritten notations.

A sigh escaped her throat. "One day, I think it was two years ago, I woke up from a dream, thinking this stuff," she nodded at the book. "It was like a stream of consciousness. Inside my head it sounded like it should mean something and that I should understand it, but when I put the thoughts to paper, this is what came of it."

13

As he stepped into the house the next morning, Finn's mobile buzzed.

"Hi Deek."

"Finn," the man's voice sounded with shrouded anxiety, "I gave those pics and the information to one of our analysts and asked him to see if he could find anything 'bout them, and ..." he paused, as if speaking in secret, "there's a shite storm com'n your way, mate."

"What are you talk'n about?"

"I'm putting my arse out on a limb by call'n you back, but someone took a big fook'n interest in this thing."

"What d'ya mean?"

"I just got interrogated about how I got them and about you."

"But, why?" asked Finn – feeling the bile rising in the base of his throat.

"I don't know, mate, but whatever it is, it's important to someone. Just giv'n you a heads-up."

14

Kaetlyn sat alone in the waiting area.

It was nearly time for her next session with Serena.

Staring at the austere walls and the empty chairs, her mind meandered along the byways of her early life. She had always known that this day would come – the point where the pressure inside her head would build until it simply had to be released. For years, she had successfully capped it off, never truly revealing her sense of disenfranchisement or vocalizing her state of mind as she had done over the past months.

She knew she was burning bridges faster than she could build them, but she didn't understand why.

There were so many mysteries for which she had no answers.

The specter that haunted her nearly every night.

The fact that since a young girl she knew things without having studied or learned about them – things that came to her mind from a place she could not yet even fathom.

And then there was the strange language that swirled in her head, whispering in her ear as if she should understand it – sounds and words which she had written in the very book her parents had found and handed over to Serena.

But the most disturbing thing of all was the pervasive sense of guilt that shackled and ghosted her – making her feel as if she was accountable for something terrible – but what? What had she done to prompt such an intensity of guilt?

"Kaetlyn?"

She looked up to see Serena standing there with a friendly smile on her lips. As they settled into the room, Serena spoke. "I hope you don't mind," she began, more reserved than usual, "but since our last session I contacted a friend of mine at the University in Dublin. He's a language specialist. I showed him a page from your notes and asked if he could check it out for us."

"And?"

"I received this email from him this morning," she handed Kaetlyn a paper.

"So, he couldn't make sense of it."

"No."

"So, what, does that make me, delusional?"

Serena grinned. "If we labelled people delusional just because they heard things in their head, we'd pretty much have a planet full of sick people. Hearing things, or voices, whatever you want to call it, particularly in dreams, isn't a mental disorder, Kaet."

"Okay, good to hear that."

"So, are you ready to start the session?

Kaetlyn settled comfortably into the sofa and nodded.

"What is your worst fear, Kaetlyn?"

Her face morphed, almost instantly, as if a storm had suddenly blown in. Silence reigned for a time, time during which she debated whether she should open-up to Serena. But then she remembered the pact she had made – *transparency*.

"Feeling guilty for the rest of my life."

Serena's brows rose. "What do you mean by that?"

Kaetlyn drew in a breath. "I don't know why, or how, but ever since I can recall, I've had this heavy sense of culpability hanging over me."

"Is it associated with anything?"

Her head wagged.

"When did you first notice it?"

"Like I said, I've felt it most of my life."

"I see. And this scares you?"

Kaetlyn's eyes surged back to meet hers. "It terrifies the shite out of me to think that I might feel this way for the rest of my life."

"Why?"

"I don't know where it comes from? It haunts me and follows me, like a shadow, day and night, and I can't get rid of it." She pressed her lips together, repressing the small tremor inside, as tears pooled in her eyes and slowly skidded down her cheeks.

Wiping her cheek she continued. "When I look at the world, it's like I'm seeing it with two different pairs of eyes, or even two different mindsets. One sees opportunity, the other feels guilt. The two seem to work against each other, like a raging battle inside of me, both fighting for relevancy." She paused to wipe the - tears from her eyes. "One of them I know and understand, the other one, I just don't get – it's like another personality altogether." She paused to look at Serena. "It's making me feel crazy, Serena."

"And you've never talked about it to anyone?"

Kaetlyn tipped her head with a look of subtle surprise. "Would you?"

"Why, because people will think you're…"

"Crazy … yeah. I'm already the black sheep, ousted from the pack, and they don't have a clue what's going on inside my head."

"Let's take a time out for some coffee."

During the break, Serena called her colleague in Dublin, her mentor for most of her studies at the university. She explained the latest development and he came back to her with some advice.

Returning to the session, Serena dove right in. "I just consulted with my colleague at the University and he suggested that we try regressive therapy to see if we can find the source of this guilt that you feel?"

"How does that work?"

"Simply put, we try to find the first time you felt that way, or a sequence of memories, or markers as they are sometimes called, which might lead back to an anchor, an incident that is the root of the feeling."

"Like a hidden trauma?"

"Yes."

Kaetlyn considered it a moment. "But I have no traumas in my life."

Serena tipped her head with an inquisitive look in her face. "How would you know? Traumas are, by their very nature, often buried so deep in the subconscious mind, out of sight and forgotten about, or encysted by pain, that one often has no idea they are there."

"Well, unless something happened to me that I don't know about, it seems like a stretch."

"It could be. However, studies have shown some interesting results. For instance, women who have been subjected to abuse often develop unnatural fears and mental disorders, even physical obsessions or disabilities, and when they finally show up for help, they are desperate to deal with the symptoms, having forgotten that the source of it all started with the abuse. We tend to bury our pain and live with the side-effects. Regressive therapy can be a very powerful tool to help dig up the real causes."

Kaetlyn thought about it for a time. "Okay. I'm game."

15

Finn couldn't sleep a wink the whole night as the warning from Deek frothed inside him like a boiling kettle.

What the hell could it mean? He wondered.

Why would those pics cause a stir with the military?

Was it a secret weapon of some kind? A crashed satellite? Or maybe even part of a terrorist plot?

His imagination had taken over and was waging war on him, and all he could do was pace the kitchen, imbibing a string of coffees.

When the first rays of the morning sun crept over the horizon a black Hummer pulled in front of his home. Two men exited as Finn, underscored by panic, stood at the window watching them approach.

A minute later he was facing them.

"Finn O'Brien?" a man, fiftyish in age, and outfitted with naval colors and a respectable amount of braid on his shoulders, asked.

"Yes."

"I'm Colonel Desmond – head of Military Intelligence at the Irish Defense Forces Naval Base. This is my associate," he tipped his head at the other uniformed man, "Special Operations Officer, Raymond Statler."

Finn's eyes met theirs, a distinctly stoic-like ambience surrounded them, despite the polite smiles on their lips.

"May we come in," asked Desmond.

They sat across from Finn.

"It's come to our attention that you've found something of interest to the military."

Finn nervously nodded.

The man tipped his head. "Have you told anyone else about this discovery?"

"My grandad was the one who first saw it. He asked me to check it out."

"Good, good," said the man, followed by an uncomfortable pause as his eyes rolled around the inside of the small farmhouse. "Does your grandfather live here?"

"Aye."

"Anyone else?" he asked with a raised brow.

"I talked to someone at the war museum, you know, the one north of Dublin, but they had nothin' to offer."

Desmond stole a glance at Statler. "I'm not at liberty to provide you with any details at this point, and given that we haven't yet inspected the object, it would be pointless to do so, but ..." he fished a paper from a small portfolio ... "We are going to ask you to sign this non-disclosure bond, and we will do the same with your grandfather."

"Why?"

Colonel Desmond straightened his back, assuming a distinctly authoritative pose. "The photos you provided, and in particular, that exact location, suggests that this object might bear some relevance to something we lost track of many years ago."

"What was it?"

The man smiled, but it was cryptic smile. "Again, at this time, I cannot provide further details." His eyes dropped to the paper in front of Finn. "Please sign the bond Mr. O'Brien, and then I must ask that you and your grandad not visit that site again until we have had time to thoroughly investigate the matter. When we have answers, we will let you know."

16

Kaetlyn arrived at her favorite spot in the Garryvurcha Church graveyard, anxious to see her best friend, Alana Gallagher, who had just returned from London.

In contrast to Kaetlyn, Alana was white as chalk, with rust-colored hair and a small lacing of red freckles – as if someone had lightly sprinkled them over her face. A year older than Kaetlyn, she still had the air of a young girl about her.

"How was London?" she asked as they hugged.

"Oh, you know, fook'n cabbie's everywhere, tons of people, the traffic was mental as always – but it felt great to be in civilization and not stuck here in the middle of bum-fook nowhere."

"I gotta go there one day. I need to get out of this place," said Kaetlyn with a wave of her hand.

"Yeah, Bantry will mess you up but good if you stay too long. Too small for the brain. Personally, I plan to head to the Continent when I finish school – maybe do Uni in Paris, hitch my wagon to a career there and find some good-look'n Frenchie to hang a leg over." Her eyes leveled on Kaetlyn. "What's going on with you, girl? I heard they suspended you."

Kaetlyn shrugged. Her silence was her answer.

"Oh, I get it, that mouth finally pissed 'em off, uh?"

Kaetlyn twitched a brow. "Guess so."

"Don't fret over it. You're smarter than the lot of 'em, students and faculty combined. You'll be fine."

"I'm seen a shrink."

Alana's faced displayed her surprise. "Why?"

"I have to get a clean bill of health, otherwise, they won't let me back in."

"Nasty shite. And just before the finals too. You need your credits."

"If I want to go to Uni, I have no choice."

"How is she?"

"She's okay."

"Have you told her about the dream?"

Kaetlyn's head wagged.

"Are you going to?"

"Yeah, maybe … I don't know yet."

"Maybe this nightmare is what's got your nipples in a twist, Kaet. Maybe it's why you're kick'n up so much dust and act'n out. Have you considered that?"

Kaetlyn nodded. "I have – but..."

Alana poked her in the arm. "Listen to me, girl. You're my best friend and we've known each other since fifth grade. Most of those other punks don't get you, but I do. I understand you and what makes you so different is what I like so much about you. But trust me on this one, since this nightmare has been bash'n at your head these past months, you've become impulsive and lash'n out at folk, and it's getting you in a shite-load of trouble."

She lowered her eyes to meet Kaetlyn's. "I think you should tell her about it. What have you got to lose?"

17

"Make yourself comfortable," said Serena.

Kaetlyn stretched out on the sofa.

"This is pretty stereotyped."

Serena chuckled. "I know. But believe it or not, a comfortable lying position accommodates the process."

Kaetlyn settled in and took a deep breath. "Whenever you're ready, doc."

"Any questions before we start the regressive therapy?" asked Serena with a tipped head.

"No. I studied up on it, last night."

Serena smiled. "Of course you did. First, I will try to locate a marker, a time which we can associate with this feeling of guilt."

"Okay."

"Do you experience any noteworthy dreams?"

Kaetlyn stiffened. "What classifies as noteworthy?"

"Well, dreams that are recurring would be the most important ones – particularly nightmares."

Kaetlyn drew in a deep breath and exhaled, recalling her talk with Alana the night before. "There is one," she answered hesitantly, not having revealed the nature of the nightmare to anyone, not even her mum.

"Tell me about it."

"It's just a bad dream," added Kaetlyn, defensively trying to downplay it.

"You don't have to worry, Kaetlyn. Dreams are dreams. They can be bizarre. They can be anything. They do not reflect the state of mind of the person – but they are sometimes useful in helping to narrow the target in therapy."

After a long pause, Kaetlyn started speaking. "I have nightmare that comes back over and over – usually several times a week. It started a few years ago, but back then I'd get it every once in a while. In the past few months, it's been getting worse, sometimes visiting me every night."

"Tell me about."

"I'm in space, and it feels like I'm flying inside something, or maybe nothing, it's difficult to say. It seems so clear to me when the dream is happening, and yet, every time I wake up and try to get a grip on it, it's like clutching at smoke."

"You said that you are inside something?"

"It feels that way because I have this sense of movement." She was silent for a time before continuing. "Anyhow, we're flying, maybe inside a ship of some kind … and then there's an explosion, at least it feels like one, and everything goes black. Usually I wake up in a panic, gasping for breath. It freaks the shite out of me every time and I feel this pain in my chest."

Kaetlyn turned to face Serena. "I've read a lot about dreams, trying to figure mine out, and one thing that people often comment on is that they never see themselves dying in their dreams. If they're falling, they wake up just before hitting the ground. In my case, I get a clear sense that I die, and that's when I wake up in a panic."

"Does the guilt feeling come then?"

"I don't know if it starts there, but I do feel that somehow the guilt and the dream are connected."

Serena raised a brow as she jotted a note. "Here's the thing, Kaet, the subconscious mind is like a protective mechanism that serves us. On one hand, it's the mind that records our routines, the regimens that we train ourselves to do, over and over, without having to think about them; like driving a car, or walking, so that subconsciously we perform those mechanical acts without even having to think about them. On the other hand, the subconscious is where we bury our pain. Like a buffer, it protects us from the negative things we have experienced, but at the same time, it has a backlash effect, because, by its very nature, and the fact that we lose our cognitive awareness of what is buried there, that pain can also be used to control us for our own *good* – at least, that's how the subconscious mind sees it."

"Like fears and phobias?"

"Exactly. Your experience, this nightmare, could be the ambassador, a sort of message from your subconscious, trying to reveal something to you."

"But that's the thing, how can it reveal something that never happened to me? I've never been in that circumstance and I certainly haven't died."

Serena grinned. "I never said that the subconscious mind is the purveyor of absolute truth."

Kaetlyn nodded. "Oh, I see, so that's where the delusions come in."

"It happens, yes. It's all part of the protective armor we use to shield ourselves from our past. Let's try the regressive therapy and see where it goes, okay?"

Kaetlyn nodded, settled back into the sofa and closed her eyes.

"Try to locate the first image of that incident or dream."

A moment passed before she answered. "It's clearer now. I'm definitely standing by a rail or a window of some kind, looking out into space."

"And then?"

"There's noise in the background, like voices, or something."

"What do you feel?"

"Anxiety."

"What happens next?"

"There's an explosion, like something hitting us, and then we're falling into blackness. It feels as if I die."

"You refer to "we" – are you aware of others in your dream?"

Kaetlyn paused, her head shaking side to side as her face tensed with frustration. "I don't know why I said that, maybe."

"Okay, I'm going to ask you to relax, and then empty your mind. Let me know when you've done that."

After a moment she answered. "Okay."

"Go back to the last time you can remember having had that dream."

"Okay."

"Go to the first moment of that dream sequence, the very first instant it appears."

"Yeah."

"Now, describe to me what you see or hear."

Minutes passed as Kaetlyn's eye lids fluttered as if in deep sleep. She finally spoke in a hushed voice, as if she was a very long way away. "It's just space, everywhere around us is empty, dark space, except ..." she paused. "There is something there ..."

"What?"

Her eyes suddenly opened with a look of bewilderment. "I saw it this time, something was coming at us, it was right in front of us, and then ..." she paused, "... it disappeared in the explosion."

18

Special Operations Officer, Raymond Statler, watched as his men rappelled down the cliffside hundreds of feet above, dangling from ropes as they approached the anomaly – the official term now being used to refer to the object and the target of their mission dubbed *Fish Hook*.

The initial inspections, using military drones which photographed the object close-up, had provided enough evidence to warrant a full-scale deployment.

The first phase of the mission was to cordon-off the entire perimeter above and below the rocky precipice, which the locals adoringly called, Witches' Tit, so that no civilians or other prying eyes could interfere with the operation.

Two teams worked twelve-hour shifts patrolling the area.

His airborne team, dangling high above, finally arrived just above the anomaly and began to drill into the cliffside. They had to establish a working platform from which the excavation team could do their jobs and that required securing anchors into the escarpment. Then they would hoist up platforms and begin to carve into the cliff around the object, eventually freeing it from the clutches of its stony tomb.

Of course, there was no way to know how large it was. The assumption was that it could not be more than a meter or two in length, certainly no longer than that, considering that it was embedded in solid rock.

Statler braced himself against the Celtic gust that whipped in from the sea. It was late autumn, and the Irish coastline was anything but inviting.

Several hours passed before the platform was finally hoisted into place and the crew began to cut into the rockface with handheld hydraulic drills. He watched as chunks of rock splashed downward, crashing to the ground as the drills bored into the rock.

Every member of his team had been bonded to complete secrecy. Their families could know nothing of their whereabouts, and for the duration of their stay here, they were expressly restricted to this small piece of rocky coast. Supplies and equipment would be ferried in by naval ship – with two smaller ships standing off at sea – like sentries. It seemed that no expense was being spared for this operation. And his only contact was directly to Colonel Desmond himself, the head of Military Intelligence at the Irish Defense Forces Naval Base.

He lifted the binoculars to his eyes and peered upward at the strange object protruding from the escarpment.

"What the fook are you?" he muttered into the maws of a wailing wind.

19

After a short break, Serena and Kaetlyn were back in the small room, one containing a sofa, a chair, a lamp and a singular framed picture on the wall – a generic print of a lone cow standing in a pasture.

Kaetlyn looked about. "I didn't notice before just how creepy this room is."

"Creepy, why?"

Kaetlyn flashed a disparaging eye at the picture on the wall. "For starters, a painting of a cow, hello?!"

Serena smiled. "Art is a matter of perspective isn't it?"

Kaetlyn shook her head. "I think art should at least stimulate the imagination, and a cow in a field may be pastoral, but it's boring as shite."

"Well… on that positive note, should we dive back in?"

Kaetlyn nodded as she stretched out on the sofa, letting her eyes casually roam the ceiling before closing them.

"Let's go back to the beginning of the dream sequence, what do you see?"

"Empty space – just space everywhere."

"What do you feel?"

Her eyelids fluttered momentarily. "To be honest, I feel kind of stunned by it."

"How so?"

"There's so much of it. It seems endless."

"Okay, do you hear anything?"

Kaetlyn's brow furrowed as she focused her attention deeper into the vision.

"There is a noise of some kind."

"Describe it to me?"

"Very high-pitched – like nothing I've heard before."

More silence ensued as Kaetlyn delved deeper into the confines of her mind. "I feel nervous. Something is about to happen?"

"Tell me."

Her breathing suddenly hastened as her chest began to pump up and down, and her hands formed into fists as her entire body tensed like a board.

Kaetlyn's jaw tightened, as if gripped by something. "I see it now. It's coming closer. I can't breathe ..."

Her eyes burst open as she gasped with desperation.

Serena gently gripped her by the arm. "Are you okay?"

A film of sweat layered her skin as she sat there, reconciling what she had seen.

"Something hit us. I felt it this time. It was stronger than before ..." she paused, her eyes and face now consumed with confusion. "Whatever it was, it definitely killed us."

"It's okay, Kaet, it's just a dream."

Kaetlyn's head rocked back and forth. "No, it's not."

Serena tipped her head at the other. "What makes you think that?"

Kaetlyn drew a deep breath. "Because, each time we go back, every detail I remember seems to remind me that I was actually there."

20

As dawn broke the cloud-scudded sky and a rugged northerly gusted, driving whitecaps into the rock-strewn beach with a crash, Statler had his crew up, fed and positioned on the gantry high above, by the time the first rays of the sun had managed to squeeze through the gray mantle.

Twelve men and women formed four teams. Two teams armed the hydraulic drills designed to pulverize rock, while the other two teams managed the fallout, clearing away rubble and debris from the platform, and then, after a time, switching out with the other team.

Back and forth they went until the call for lunch, and then back up to the gantry, again. Endless drilling, it seemed, but in truth, the stone was giving way, and the cavity on each side of the anomaly had widened and deepened until his men had disappeared inside the orifice to each side, pushing steadily into the cliffside.

He hadn't anticipated that it would be this much work, or take this long, but whatever it was they were excavating, it was big – bigger than anticipated.

During a break for tea and sandwiches his crew huddled inside a portable hut which provided some protection against the whipping hand of the wind that incessantly harassed them.

Statler looked at their dirt-covered faces. He could see by the looks in their eyes that they had the same question going through their minds – a question that no one asked because of the stringent security protocols imposed upon them. They all knew that it was better to shut up than to face a military tribunal for serious security breach.

"Look, lads…" he paused to smile at the women present, "and lasses, "I realize that the secrecy on this project is probably killing you – and I wish I could share something revealing, but I have nothing. I know what you know." He flicked an eye to the cliff above. "Whatever that thing is, it's got everyone's balls in a fook'n knot."

He stood. "Finish up," he smiled at them. "Let's get that thing out of there so we can all go back to warm beds and warm mates."

21

Making herself a sandwich, Kaetlyn announced to her mum that she'd be out for a few hours and then hopped on her moped.

Her mother stood at the window, watching her daughter disappear down the road, her long black hair swirling in the wind behind.

Claire O'Sullivan didn't understand the world anymore.

What had seemed right to her, now appeared wrong, and the morality of a community she had lived in her entire life, no longer made any sense.

After years of trying to have children, she had been distraught that she would never get her chance at motherhood, something she had dreamed of doing since a little girl. Harry had suggested adoption, and the lights of a dimming opportunity had brightened once again when Kaetlyn came into their lives shortly thereafter. She became the brightest star in their sky.

But now, that star seemed to fade under the mantle of deep dark clouds as the world around her daughter tried to shackle her, that which made her so special and so beautiful.

She watched Kaetlyn turn the corner, and instead of happiness, she felt a pang, a deep pain that accosted her motherly sense.

How could she protect her daughter from this abuse, when an entire community had turned on her just because she was different?

All the secrets both she and Harry had kept locked up about Kaetlyn, her special talents, her intelligence, her ability to know things which were inexplicable, all of it, had been carefully packed away to shield her from a world that could be brutally indifferent towards anyone or anything "different".

She sighed. She wanted to talk to Harry – but he was off in his own world. An angry man, and Irish at that.

22

Kaetlyn arrived at the Bantry Library just moments later. It wasn't as if Bantry was a large town – so getting around on her moped was easy.

Soon, she was sitting in a corner with several books piled in front of her. The first book she delved into was entitled *Souls on Earth*, by Dr. Linda Backman. Two hours later she dropped it to the table, fished her sandwich from her backpack and nibbled away at it while considering what she had just read.

She wondered to herself if it was possible? *If her "dream" was actually a past life remembrance, how could she prove it – how could she really know her mind wasn't just playing tricks on her?*

She knew that Serena, by the nature of her profession, would lean in another direction. She didn't blame her, psychology was, after all, predicated on another premise entirely and past lives was certainly not one of them. She signed-out one of the other books and then took off to her favorite spot next to the tombstone of Mr. Norbert Finnigan – in the Bantry Church graveyard.

Despite a cold gust, she felt sheltered there, amidst the tombstones, and enclosed by a bank of trees.

The additional inscription on his tombstone, barely visible after a century, read:

HERE LAYS NORBERT FINNIGAN:
DEVOTED HUSBAND AND FATHER

Offering a tilted smile at the slab of stone that symbolized a life once lived, she added, *"It's okay, I'm sure you were a good bloke and all."*

She settled next to his headstone, cracked open the book entitled: *Regressive-Therapy: Techniques for Uncovering Forgotten Lives*. Three hours later she was done reading it.

As she watched the choreography of clouds dancing across the heavens, she played back the scenario of her dream, comparing it to the material she had just studied.

Something had been sparked in her last talk with Serena, some cognitive awakening deep inside. And if it was her past life speaking to her, it presupposed so much more to be discovered – maybe even the very answers she had been seeking for most of her life.

Gathering up her backpack she turned to leave the graveyard when she saw the vague shadow once again, just the transient glimpse of a figure in the distant trees.

Jumping on her moped she nervously glanced back at the stand of trees but the figure was gone.

23

The man unhitched his repelling rope just as his feet touched the ground, and made a beeline for the officer in charge, Raymond Statler.

"What is it?" asked Statler, seeing the look in his eye.

"Sir, we've reached a portal on the side of that thing."

Statler's face lit up with genuine surprise. "You mean it's a ship?"

"Aye."

"What kind of ship could be lodged in solid rock?"

"Can'a say that I know ... certainly noth'n like I've ever seen before." The man stole a glance up at the hole in the cliff above. "To be honest, I'll be need'n a few ales before I'd venture a educated guess."

Statler fixed a firm gaze on the man. "Speak freely, Sergeant."

The man turned to him and drew a breath and exhaled. "If you ask me, I'd say it's not from this world."

24

Ever since his daughter had been suspended from school and ostracized by the community he had lived in his whole life, Harry O'Sullivan felt like someone had unlocked Pandora's Box inside his head.

All the encysted doubts, feelings, worries and secrets associated with Kaetlyn, a daughter he loved more than life itself, but who presented a bizarre and disturbing package, had been unleashed.

He didn't have anyone to talk to about it – not now.

Claire was already walking her own tenuous path, having had her maternal sense of propriety violated to such a degree that she was like a ship lost at sea. It was best to leave her alone to deal with her internal meltdown.

Meanwhile, he tried his best to numb the emotional tide inside him with enough ales to forget that his community had just ostracized his daughter.

He didn't blame Kaetlyn, not in the least. She was maturing, becoming her own woman, and he knew this day would eventually come, the day when the truth about her would be unveiled.

If anything, he felt the burden of responsibility, because he had seen, early-on, that she was special, and in those formative years, he had tried to protect her from the outside world – a world he knew would treat her as different, something to poke and prod, like a circus freak. He knew people could be harsh, even cruel at times, because what they did not understand they generally attacked or shunned – and he didn't want his beautiful daughter to experience that abuse.

Sitting at the pub, he quietly imbibed another ale. He needed time and distance away from it all and the pub afforded him that solace.

"Harry O'Sullivan!" the familiar, but unlikeable voice cut the air like a shrill violin.

Stan Murphy, a local loud-mouth, amongst other things, edged up next to him at the bar. The scent of alcohol was thick on his breath.

"Heard your girl got kicked out of school."

Harry stared at his half-empty glass – his fingers tightening around it as his anger grew.

Stan continued, even louder, his blithering voice now echoed around the small pub.

"Yup, heard she's a bit of a witch. Don't like god and thinks aliens made us all – some shite like that."

Harry turned to face him. "Murphy, you best shut that trap before I shut it for ya."

The other smiled, revealing tobacco-stained teeth.

"You been hiding her all this time, Harry? Keeping the little bitch safe so we don't find out the truth 'bout her? Meanwhile, all our kids been infected with her shite ..."

Harry's fist speared out before the man could finish the sentence, landing squarely on Murphy's jaw, knocking him to the floor.

Harry stood, his fists balled up and white knuckled as he looked around the bar at the faces of the others who watched on with a mix of shock and judgement in their eyes.

"Anyone else got somethin' to say 'bout my daughter, best say it now, otherwise, keep your fook'n mouths shut."

He stepped over Stan Murphy and stormed from the pub.

25

Claire O'Sullivan placed a hot cup of coffee in front of Kaetlyn, along with a dish of her sumptuous scones.

The steaming scent of fresh-baked pastry was enough to make Kaetlyn forget about the world for a time. It was also a signal.

Whenever her mum wanted to talk about something important, something awkward or uncomfortable, she would throw up the white flag and lure her to the kitchen with the promise of a freshly baked incantation, and then, once shackled to the delights, launch into her platform.

"How's it goin' hon?" she asked, her eyes filled with worry.

Kaetlyn shrugged. "You mean, with the mind doctor?"

She smiled.

"It's okay, mum. We're making some progress."

Claire's face continued its transformation from her usual maternal facade, that calm, always placating visage, to a deeper, darker one.

"What's worrying you, mum?"

Her mother sighed. "It's your dad. He got himself into a brawl at the pub today."

"Seriously? With who?"

"That dimwit, Stan Murphy, insulted you in front of the others, so your dad punched him to the floor."

Kaetlyn lowered her cup to the table. "Dad nailed Murphy?"

"You sound happy about it."

"Murphy had it coming. He's always shooting his mouth off with his hypocrtical puritan Christian bias about the holy and the unholy. Kind of glad that dad stood up to 'em," she grinned.

"The point is…" her mum fiddled with her tea cup as her eyes grazed the table and then rested back on Kaetlyn, "people are talking shite 'bout you."

"People do that, mum. Who cares."

"I care that you are being rejected by this community."

Kaetlyn fixed a calming eye to her. "Come on, mum, you must have expected this would happen someday. Besides, I haven't exactly been the poster girl of perfection at school – I've pissed some people off, I know that. This was my responsibility."

Her mother paused, trying not to show the pain that roiled within, her eyes deflecting momentarily. "You're being punished for speaking up, something that shouldn't be treated as a crime." She shook her head as her eyes revealed the depth of her dread. "But, you're right, I did expect this day to come," she said in a hushed voice. "I just didn't expect it to happen like this."

Claire looked to the window as she spoke – her voice stifled and nostalgic. "Mrs. Gantry died last month," she pointed to a white house on the far corner, one with a wilting white picket fence to match. "I used to visit them when I was a kid. She made the best scones in Ireland, at least, that's what she said, and I tended to agree." She sighed as she turned to her daughter. "Your dad and I bought this house when we got married, with the dream of raising a family. After three miscarriages and all hope lost, God led us to you.

She smiled with teary eyes. "You were the best thing that ever happened to us, Kaetlyn. I just want you to have a happy life – that's all," the tears skidded down her cheek as she pinched her lips.

Kaetlyn reached a hand across the table and squeezed her mum's hand.

"You've both done a fab job raising me, I couldn't have asked for better parents." Her eyes drifted momentarily before continuing. "This isn't your fight anymore, mum. You and dad did your part. I'm 18 now, it's time for me to face the dragons on my own."

26

Enveloped by a darkness so black, so thick and so imperceptibly fathomless, it felt like a murky veil pressing in on her, smothering the life from her and with it came the same sense of desperation of struggling for a breath of air while being pulled into a watery grave.

A distant spot suddenly blazed in the morose gloom – growing like a specter of death, like a dragon belching fire as it streaked toward her.

The explosion that followed rocked her world.

Kaetlyn's eyes shot open as she heaved from the bed clutching at her throat, gasping for air.

A brutal terror cut through her like a knife.

Trembling, she groped in the darkness, clutching for something to hold onto, something to stop herself from reeling and falling – but she wasn't falling, she was sitting upright in her bed.

A gentle touch to her shoulder startled her. Turning, she saw her mum standing there. "You were having a nightmare, honey."

Beads of sweat trickled down her face, her chest rising and falling as the adrenaline pumping through her veins began to abate.

Drawing in a deep breath to calm herself, she spoke. "Thanks, mum – it was a bad one."

"They're all bad."

Leaning over she kissed her daughter on the cheek. "Should I make some tea?"

"No, I'm fine. I'll just sit here for a while."

Her nighttime specter had struck yet again, she thought, as her mum left the room.

This time, it felt different. It was more intense, more real, more subjective in ways she could not yet even grasp.

One thing was absolutely clear, her demon was not going to relent until she opened up the door to her past.

27

Statler checked his safety harness one more time before extending his right foot out onto the rocky ledge, straddling the narrow gape between the gantry and the cliff and some 200 feet to the rocky shore below.

Blistering gusts screeched up the escarpment, causing the platform to rock and sway, its metal edge scraping along the stone face, reminding him of the immense power which the Celtic could muster.

He slipped into the narrow space that had been carved-out by his team, roughly a meter in width, and extending deep into the rock.

A string of lights illuminated the way.

Behind him, the wind howled – as if beckoning him to leave this place. He turned to face the sleek creature and then cautiously ran his hand along its surface. It was smooth and cool to the touch – with not even the slightest nick or defect to be felt.

Taking a nearby spotlight, he pointed it at the anomaly, his eyes carefully working the surface.

"How is this even possible?" he muttered to his senior engineer.

The man shrugged.

"Not a scratch, not even a dent – and yet, here it is, embedded in solid rock," said Statler with a look of complete bewilderment.

"Aye, sir," answered the other, "but that's not what I wanted to really show ya, Cap," he pointed toward the top of the cavity.

"Take a look up there," he pointed to a nearby ladder.

Statler climbed the rungs and aimed the light into the darkness.

His exclamation echoed off the walls of the small cavern.

28

"Was this the worst one you've had?"

Kaetlyn nodded. "Certainly the worst version of it, yeah," she answered as the specter of her nighttime haunting paraded itself through her mind. "It's never been this strong before."

"That could be a good sign that we're getting closer."

Kaetlyn flicked a brow. "I hope so, because sleep isn't coming easy these past few days," she answered as she handed Serena the book, one she had read the previous day. "I've book-marked the pages I want you to read."

Serena looked at the cover. "I'm familiar with this author's work on regressive therapy."

"I also read another book about past-lives, called *Souls on Earth*, by Dr. Linda Backman."

"Past lives?" responded Serena with a hitched brow.

Kaetlyn's head subtly tipped to one side.

"So, you think the dream is an actual experience from a former life?"

Kaetlyn offered up a dismissive shrug. "How else do you explain it?"

"I can't explain it."

"So, what, you don't buy the whole "past-life" thing, is that it?" asked Kaetlyn with a challenge.

"It's not my field of specialty, Kaet. The question is, do you believe in past lives?"

Kaetlyn paused a moment before answering. "Honestly, I never thought about it until we started poking around with the regressive therapy. But now, yeah, I do think it is possibly the only logical answer."

Serena leaned back in her chair, studying Kaetlyn for a moment.

"I have never used therapy to explore that domain, or inexplicable phenomena."

"What do you mean, inexplicable?"

"Well, your parents told me some things."

"Oh, besides giving you my little secret book of notes?"

Serena smiled. "Like knowing the Table of Elements at the age of five."

Kaetlyn flicked a hand to the air. "That's nothing. When I was six, I was working out advanced algebraic equations for fun – and I hadn't even studied algebra yet. By the time I was eight I could point to the sky and tell you the names of nearly every constellation up there, again, without having studied a single book on the subject." She turned to Serena. "How could I know this stuff? unless I had learned it earlier than this life?"

29

Within an hour of reporting the lastest details on the anomaly, a military chopper swooped in, its massive blades hammering the ground and churning up a storm of sand and water as it touched down.

Moments later, Special Operations Officer, Raymond Statler, was being couriered back to the Irish Defense Forces Naval Base outside Cork. Two armed men met him at the Helipad and escorted him to a room where Desmond himself, as well as two other men, sat waiting.

"Have a seat, Raymond," said Desmond with a definitive wave of his hand. "These two gentlemen are from the G2, the Directorate of Military Intelligence. Their names are not important at this time."

Statler nodded at each – realizing that discretion was clearly senior to social conventions at this time.

"I want you to relate the details of what you told me on the phone," he said, clasping his hands behind his back, with an expectant look on his face.

"As I said in my brief, we found what appears to be an entry or portal to the anomaly, but as yet, we have not been able to figure out how to get in without attempting a forceful incursion."

Desmond nodded, letting his silence encourage Statler to continue.

"Of course, the most shocking discovery is that the object appears to be a craft of some kind."

"What led you to that conclusion," uttered one of the G2 men.

"Well, although there are no signs of propulsion, not in a conventional sense, its shape is aerodynamically structured, and ..." he paused, "there is a pilots window made of what appears to be tinted glass or some other material."

Colonel Desmond's eyes narrowed as he waited for the punchline. "Go on."

"We could barely see what looked like a bridge or cockpit, only much larger. There were several chairs visible, a console of sorts, but it was difficult to make out much detail through the window."

"And ...?" asked Desmond, inviting him to continue with a tip of his head.

"There were skeletal remains visible on the floor."

Colonel Desmond cast a furtive look at the other two.

"Skeletons," one of them chimed.

"Yes, sir. But they were different."

"How so?" asked the G2.

"They didn't appear to be human."

30

It was a cloudless morning in Suitland, Maryland.

Rear Admiral, Norman Patterson, head of *The National Maritime Intelligence Center*, or *NMIC*, and one of the military's most trusted people, was enjoying his first coffee for the day before addressing the prodigious pile of papers carefully stacked in the center of his blotter.

He cast a dreaded eye to the stack, and then turned to the window, looking wistfully toward the Atlantic Ocean, some twenty clicks due-east.

"I'm just not cut out to be a landlubber," he thought, feeling the tug of the sea and a longing for its touch.

For years he had headed up the North Atlantic Fleet, the nation's defensive arm for the entire northeastern seaboard.

His love affair with the sea had been stolen from him when the new Presidential Administration had seen fit to promote him to head of Naval Intelligence. It was an honorable promotion, and to decline such would have been a career mistake, but that notwithstanding, Norman Patterson was first and foremost a seaman. He had started working on his dad's fishing trawler at the age of seven, earned his first skipper's license at seventeen, and by the time he was twenty-four, was commanding a naval ship. The sea was his true love-affair in life, and all else was relevant to it.

The light rap on his door, followed by the smiling face of his secretary, forced him back from his daydreaming.

He waved her in.

"Admiral, I thought you should see this right away."

"Sounds ominous. Divorce papers from my wife?" he grinned impishly.

"That woman loves you more than life," responded the elderly woman, mild rebuke in her eye.

He flipped a hand to the air. "Let me see this," he read the memo.

"Get Adams in here, right away," he commanded, his mood suddenly changing like a raging storm flashing over a calm sea.

31

Colonel Desmond squared off with Special Operations Officer, Raymond Statler as the chopper nearby powered up, it twin blades churning up a whirlwind that chilled them to the bone.

"I've commissioned a ship-load of equipment which arrives tomorrow morning, including cranes and two of the best hydraulic drillers in all of Ireland. You get that thing out of that escarpment in the next 24 hours – clear?!"

"Yes, sir," responded Statler.

"Oh, and one more thing," began Desmond as he stepped closer to be heard over the background din. "Let your team know that their security rating just got bumped up a notch. Anyone so much as whispers about this in their sleep and they'll be seeing the inside of a Naval prison for a very long time."

Statler nodded, turned and trotted off in the direction of the chopper.

Desmond returned to his office where the same G2 men were waiting for him.

"So, gentlemen, what's your take on this?"

One of them raised a brow. "I believe we've just found the UFO the Americans claimed to have shot down eighteen years ago."

32

Before starting their next session, Serena took a moment to quietly observe Kaetlyn, who, in some respects, was becoming even more of an anomaly to her.

She was, to be sure, a contradiction, she thought.

Bright, intelligent, well-spoken – Kaetlyn had tremendous potential.

On the other hand, she was an introvert, intensely private and withdrawn, quite likely the product of the very life she had been forced to live – feeling the need to isolate herself from a world she feared would not accept her, and in fact, did not in a very real sense.

Kaetlyn looked up at her with a bright smile and shining eyes – clearly excited with anticipation over their next session.

"How have you been?" asked Serena.

"Good. Anxious to get on with it."

"Any new insights?"

Kaetlyn shook her head. "No."

"Well, then we should get at it."

"One question before we do," asked Kaetlyn. "Have you ever had a patient where their apparent hallucinations or dreams were in fact real memories?"

"Yes, of course. There are many trauma cases on record who have endured painful experiences and then buried them deep in their subconscious. Hallucinations and delusions have sometimes been traced to such hidden memories. We call them false anchors."

"False – why?"

"Hallucinations are a subconscious recreation of a real event, only with manufactured circumstances."

"Like a fictionalized version of an actual story?"

"Exactly. As I said, the subconscious mind is constantly working to protect us from our own painful past. It's like a buffer, helping us to stay focused on surviving, while reducing exposure to threats we have experienced in the past. It's like a servo-mechanism, not very analytical, and frankly, more push-button than logical, but nonetheless, very powerful in its hold over a person. Sometimes, our subconscious manufacturers things, either to hide things from us, or, possibly to gently coax us into remembering them."

Kaetlyn's brow furrowed. "That's just it, I don't have any bad experiences. I wasn't traumatized as a kid. I wasn't abused. I have never been in a hospital except the day I was born."

Serena jumped on the opportunity to press her point. "I realize that, Kaetlyn, but you must also consider the possibility that such memories are buried so deep in your subconscious, and for that reason you wouldn't necessarily remember them until they were exhumed and presented to your conscious mind."

"So, you're saying that it's possible that there might be some trauma behind all of this – that my subconscious is just screwing with me?"

"We can't dismiss anything at this time – which is why I opted to try regressive-therapy with you."

Kaetlyn grinned. "But you didn't expect it to go this way, did you?"

"I'm not sure what you mean."

"You still don't want to accept that maybe my apparent dream is actually something I experienced in a past life reality."

"I admit, it challenges my professional platform."

"So what, it's not as if psychology has all the answers to human behavior, anyhow."

Serena tipped her head at her. "I know you like to challenge my profession, but the parameters I am bound to do not include past-life regression. I am, professionally-speaking, going out on a limb right now."

"If it works, who cares?"

"It's not that simple. I am answerable to an ethical code as a therapist, and when people read my reports on your case I can be challenged, even barred from further practice if I start dabbling in arts I am not accredited for."

"I don't want to force you to go down a road you don't feel comfortable doing."

Serena drew in a deep breath to quell her frustration. She wanted to help Kaetlyn, but it felt as if she was losing control of the narrative.

She looked her in the face. "Let's carry on, but I'm not making any promises as to how far I can go with this. Okay?"

Kaetlyn nodded as she stretched out on the sofa and relaxed.

"Close your eyes and empty your mind of anything else." She waited a moment. "Now, focus on some aspect of the vision."

After a taciturn moment, Kaetlyn found herself drifting, once again, in the field of blackness.

"I hear something."

"Describe it to me."

"It's a voice, but it sounds muffled, as if I'm hearing it through a wall."

"Can you make out what is being said?"

Kaetlyn's face screwed up as she tried to discern the sound in her head. "No."

"Let's leave that part and go forward to when you spot this object coming at you?"

Kaetlyn did as she asked. "Yeah, I see it. It looks like a small speck ahead, but it's coming at us fast, very fast."

"Keep your attention on it – tell me what happens next."

Kaetlyn felt a growing panic, as sheer trepidation gripped her. "It's getting bigger…" her voice shuddered with a tangible apprehension, "now I can hear the same voice – but it's clearer this time."

"Go on," prompted Serena.

"Someone is yelling…" her eyes opened wide as her face paled and sweat broke out on her brow.

Serena waited in silence.

After a moment she exhaled and looked at Serena with despondent eyes. "We died – again!"

33

Jessie Adams, often referred to as, **SIA**, the Senior Intelligence Analyst at *NMIC*, the National Maritime Intelligence Center, sat across from Rear Admiral, Norman Patterson.

The elderly man's eyes were firmly fixed on a paper in his hand. Finally, he looked up at him and handed it over along with several satellite images. Adams read it and then looked over the photos.

"You're the top intelligence analyst here at NMIC, so tell me, Adams, why do you think the Irish Navy is investing that amount of heavy equipment, backed by two destroyers anchored off the coast of that particular region?"

Jessie's head wagged lightly as he considered the question. "Well, it doesn't appear to be a Navy exercise, judging by these images." He looked up at the Admiral. "Possibly they found something?"

Patterson raised a brow. "Weren't you involved in *Operation Nemo?*"

"Yes, I was on the flag ship for the entire search."

"A search that came up with nothing."

"Yes, sir. May I ask what this about?"

"Do the math, Adams. Just over eighteen years ago, we had three ships combing that region of the Celtic Sea as part of *Op-Nemo*, and we didn't find a goddamn thing. So, why are the Irish back there, in that exact location?"

He looked at the sat-images and then looked up at Patterson. "You think the Irish found it?"

34

"Sir, the logistics vessel is approaching."

Statler turned to see a naval tug, with two cranes and two hydraulic borers aboard, taking advantage of the early-morning calm seas, as it chugged toward them.

The night before, he had his team set up two additional gantries, now suspended to each side of the anomaly, no easy feat considering that his team had to winch up heavy equipment while dangling from ropes several hundred feet above; all the while combating the tempestuous winds that buffeted them about like kites.

It took two hours to get the newly arrived cranes in position and another three hours to raise the hydraulic equipment to their floating platforms, where they now sat securely perched high above.

The entire scene looked so unnatural, tenuous at best, and the lives of his team were at the mercy of the elements which showed no slightest remorse in their determination to defeat them.

Within minutes, the high-powered drills were cutting into the rock, like a knife through cheese.

Shale and all manner of particulates tumbled down the escarpment like a waterfall, as a dark plume of smoke and dust funneled upwards.

The wailing wind, and the screech of the drills, sounded like two dragons in mortal combat. But, in no time at all, the hydraulic drills had bored deep into the rock – and by nightfall, he received the report from his lead engineer. They had reached the end of the anomaly, which now measured some 22 meters in length.

35

Serena sat looking out the window of her small apartment in the *Reenrour Flats* district of Bantry.

It was a charming location, the first floor of a classic Irish cottage, with a small patio surrounded by a brick retaining wall, and beyond that, just down the road, was the center of Bantry itself.

The town was a place of modest activity, certainly not the hustle and bustle of Dublin where she grew up and attended university.

There was a certain charm to it, a confluence of old and new world. With that charm came a certain closed mindedness; a community less prone to accepting change. In fact, in her cursory dealings and occasional meets with the locals, while she found them sincerely friendly, they were also reserved about anything that deviated from the accepted norm, which of course explained Kaetlyn's dilemma.

She enjoyed watching people, not in a judgmental way, but with a compelling curiosity to understand the unknown – the dynamics that drove people to do what they did, and the bonds that held their lives together, or conversely, chipped away at them.

There had been questions which had plagued her in her growing years.

Why people idolized abstractions, such as gods; why people objectified others based on race, color or ideology; why war was normalized, and the sanctioning of murder by another name, in the pursuit of some national agenda, was seen as heroic, and lastly, why people went out of the way to destroy their lives. These were things she could she could not yet reconcile.

She had hoped, as she started her studies, that psychology would provide some closure – but sadly, it had not, because putting labels on people did not provide answers to their problems. And while she recognized certain merits in her trade, in the end, she had to admit that it did not have all the answers about the human condition.

Kaetlyn had cast a cloud of doubt over her. The young rebellious girl, possibly the victim of delusion, possibley this or that, as claimed by her peers, and yet, who seemed to have a better grip on her situation than seemed believable, had challenged her professional platform.

There was something about her that did not fit any of the models, the neat boxes which she had spent so many years learning. Kaetlyn was outside the proverbial box, and if there was a label for her condition, it would have to be, at least for now, *"a paradox"*.

The problem with the subjectivity of her case, she pondered, was precisely that, it was all subjective. Kaetlyn's recent insistence that the dream was, or is, a past-life experience of sorts, was stepping across a threshold into a realm that Serena simply did not feel comfortable dealing with. In fact, she felt that if she went any further down this road, she might well cause harm to Kaetlyn by permitting her to free-wheel herself into a means of escapism, as opposed to facing reality. If she was delusional, at all, then empowering her belief that her dream is some conjuring from a past life might prove to be more harmful than beneficial.

She had a code of ethics as a practioner, and right now, that code was pricking at her conscience.

Serena set her cup of tea to the table, picked up her mobile phone and let her finger idle over the name in her contact list.

Her sense of duty to Kaetlyn, and her responsibility to the profession itself compelled her next move as she tapped the number and waited as it rang.

36

Kaetlyn felt the change the minute she stepped into the room.

Serena had assumed a more authoritative aspect, certainly more somber than her usual casual face, and her eyes betrayed the fact.

"Hello, Kaetlyn."

"What's up, Serena?" she asked as she sat across from the other.

"I'd like to take a different tact today, if it's okay with you?"

"What do you mean?"

"I'd like to administer a mild sedative, one that can help us to navigate better."

Kaetlyn's eyes widened. "Wait! What? We're doing just fine without any drugs?" retorted Kaetlyn, her anger already seeping through.

Serena hesitated. "A light sedative helps the therapy go smoother."

"Oh, I get it. You mean, by drugging me into a stupor you can control my mind."

Serena leaned forward, a mild gesture of control. "Regressive-therapy has limited use, Kaetlyn. Its value is in helping to exhume hidden memories and unlocking encysted trauma. Sometimes, often in fact, the person cannot break through the veil of occlusion and reach those memories without the use of sedatives which permit them to get past their own mental barriers."

"So, now you think my recalls are not real memories, is that it?"

"I'm not saying that."

"You are saying just that. You want to shift onto another method."

"No, I simply want to try all avenues and ensure that we are using the most effective one."

Kaetlyn stood, her head shaking back and forth. "I'm not doing any drugs, and I'm not changing to some other technique."

She turned and promptly left the room before Serena could utter another word.

37

When he received word that the excavation process was completed, and they were ready to lower the anomaly from the cliffside, Colonel Desmond was on a chopper, in fact, he brought another military helicopter along with some twenty-armed military personnel to ensure no foul play.

A part of him argued that it was an overkill, digging deep into the military budget on something that was still an unconfirmed object; while the other side in the debate compelled him to take excessive measures due to the circumstances.

If it was the lost UFO, the one the Americans and the Irish searched for months to find, then any expense was justified.

By the time he stepped from the chopper, the two large cranes had already maneuvered the craft from its cavity high above. He watched with an anticipatory anxiety as the morning gust buffeted the beast, swinging it dangerously back and forth – a momentum, that if too great, would most certainly topple the cranes.

Raymond Statler stood some paces away, radio in hand, while yelling instructions to the crane operators over the howl of a constant wind, as he directed the operation.

Seeing his superior approaching, Statler nodded respectfully without take his eye off the cradle above.

"Sir," said Statler with a nervous twitch in his eye.

"Stay with it, Statler, I just wanted to see the operation for myself."

Desmond turned to look up at the phenomenon, its ghostly silhouette cast against a dimming sky. In all his years in the military, he had never witnessed anything quite like it, and it momentarily mesmerized him as he watched the craft coming nearer, its obsidian-like skin appearing like some creature from another world.

Finally, it touched the ground, sitting there like a giant beached whale.

He turned to Statler. "Get it on the ship and escort it back to base. I brought in more people," he eyed the squadron of soldiers. "Double up the security team to watch over this site and keep nosey locals or tourists away." He took a step closer. "Also ..." he waited for Statler to look at him. "I received a memo, just before I boarded the chopper, from Rear Admiral Patterson, who heads up NMIC in Maryland." He raised a brow. "They're onto us."

Statler cocked his head at the man. "Colonel, I know you're not required to tell me all the details of *Fish Hook*, but I'm not stupid. I happen to remember that just three kilometers out from this very spot, the American Navy was searching for something eighteen years back. Is that what this is all about?"

Desmond grinned. "Just get it aboard that ship, Statler. I'll brief you when you get back to the base."

38

Rear Admiral, Norman Patterson had just stepped into his office when Jessie Adams arrived at the door with a look that betrayed his excitement. Patterson waved him in.

"Sir, they've recovered the object," he handed off the latest images from one of the Navy satellites.

"Damn, it's big," exclaimed Patterson.

"It's over sixty-feet long judging by those pics."

"When did we get these sat-images?"

"About an hour ago."

Patterson's eyes narrowed as they remained fixed on the images. "They'll probably ferry it to their Naval base outside of Cork."

Patterson stood and then paced back and forth for a moment, weighing up all the factors.

He turned to Adams who waited attentively. "Put your top people on this. Bond them up the ass. If they so much as whisper about this to anyone, heads will roll. I want you guys to find out everything you can about it. Surveil dialogues, use search words, whatever it is you guys do in that think-tank of yours. I want solid information, concrete evidence that it is the missing UFO." He paused to look Adams hard in the eyes. "If it is what we think it is, then we're already way behind the 8-ball."

As Jessie Adams closed the door, Patterson pushed the intercom on his desk. "Mary, patch me through to the State Department, right away."

39

Kaetlyn plunked down by the tombstone of Norbert Finnigan, and then stared at the oblique rows of gravestones, many of them now canted and bent with age, crumbling from time and the constant assault of Ireland's coastal weather. She drew in a deep breath as she tapped her mobile phone.

She was on her own now. Serena had shown her true colors, a shrink through-and-through. *Just another drug pusher*, she mumbled aloud.

She cast an eye to the tombstone, "Aye, you're lucky you didn't have to put up with this kind of shite in your day, Norbie boy." She grinned as silence reigned.

Despite Serena's sudden shift, she appreciated the fact that her therapist had helped her dig deep enough to get a foothold on the matter. She didn't feel lost anymore. In fact, it felt as if she had a grip on the thread that could unravel her recurring nightmare.

She held her mobile phone up to her lips. "D-TEKT, search the web for any unusual events that happened in Ireland eighteen years ago."

The avatar nodded with a ghoulish smile as its eyes rotated.

As she waited, a blustery wind swirled through the trees around her, rustling and playing the dying leaves like instruments in an orchestra. She pulled the collar of her coat up to cover her neck.

The avatar spoke. "Would you like the results of my search?"

"Yes."

"I have created a chronological listing of events for the parameters you requested."

"How many?"

"233."

"Eliminate all social events, sporting events, concerts or political events. I just want events that fall outside normal parameters."

"Please define normal?" it asked with a questioning eye.

"Odd, not usual, things that the media reported as bizarre."

"Twenty-one events remain."

"Tell me."

"A dog was born in Belfast with three eyes. A woman in Dublin gave birth to seven babies."

Kaetlyn rolled her eyes. "Anything else?"

"A fisherman off the coast of Kilcrohane reported seeing a strange light in the sky and something crashing into the sea nearby. Another article reported thousands of dead fish washing up on that same coastal area the next day."

Kaetlyn sat up straight. "Kilcrohane – where is that?"

"It is located twenty-four kilometers southwest of your current location."

"Any other noteworthy incidents at that time?"

"There are several articles by *The Irish Times* concerning unusual naval activity in that area," answered D-TEKT.

"Summarize it for me."

"One article mentions that the American and Irish navies were searching for Russian submarines. Another article suggested a salvage operation of some kind. A third article claimed that American Naval ships were searching for an unidentified object."

Kaetlyn's eyes lit up.

"Is there any mention of finding something?"

The avatar's head wagged. "No."

Something had just been stirred in the depths of her soul?

Was it related to the incident in her dream, she wondered?

Was there any slightest chance that what they had been looking for so many years ago, was even relevant to her experience?

Or was she just casting a hook into the sea of possibilities, hoping for a bite, a magical connection that would give her closure?

Despite her doubts, despite all the reasons why the coincidence could not have any significant bearing on her situation, the impulse had already taken grip, compelling her next move without a second thought.

"D-TEKT, when does the next bus leave from Bantry to Kilcrohane."

40

The 23,000-ton, 180-meter-long Irish warship, the *Largs Bay II*, eased into the slip at the naval shipyard on Spike Island.

Several destroyers which had escorted it and its valuable cargo, hovered nearby, including two choppers circling the area, as well as feed from an Irish Military satellite orbiting above.

When the ship finally powered down, Raymond Statler cast a furtive glance at the anomaly strapped to its deck, sighed with relief, and then stepped off the ship. No sooner had his feet hit the dock when several MPs marched up to him and whisked him away.

He was escorted to the main conference facility in the officer's building, where he came face-to-face with more military brass than he felt comfortable with. His eyes rapidly scanned the room, seeing half a dozen civilians intermingled with an impressive array of uniforms. Their somber faces betrayed what was about to come.

Colonel Desmond, standing to one side of the room, directed him to a chair with a wave of his hand and a curt smile.

"Thank you, all, for coming on such short notice," began Desmond. "In the hours it took for the anomaly, the subject of this very meeting, to be transported here, I have had SSO Statler," he nodded at the man, "engage a team of people to take detailed photographs of the object." He pressed a remote, dimming the lights and then projected the images onto a large wall-screen.

"These photos show an object which measures 22.2 meters in length, 5.8 meters at its highest point here in the midsection, which, for those of you who still think in terms of feet, equates to 73 feet long and 19 feet high. Best we can tell, it weighs-in at nineteen tons. As you can see," he pointed to one photo with a laser, "there are no signs of wings or any propulsion system. The entire vessel seems to be hermetically sealed – in other words, airtight. We've not been able to get inside it through what appears to be a portal on the left side."

He pressed the remoting bringing several more images up. A quiet gasp permeated the room.

"Yes, those appear to be the skeletal remains of its crew, we assume. Best estimates put them at roughly two times the height of the average human. Naturally, without getting inside to inspect more closely, it's difficult to say whether they are a different species, but what little we can see of the remains, they certainly appear to be anthropomorphic."

When the lights came up he saw their faces, revealing their stunned looks.

"Statler and his team have done a tremendous job of excavating this object from the escarpment, some 200 feet above the coastline, here," he pointed to a map on the wall. He circled the table, slowly, talking as he did.

"Just over eighteen years ago, an American *Star Wars Class* military satellite shot down an object which came within range of it. The Americans later claimed another story altogether, but nonetheless, whatever it was, fell from the sky and according to their tracking systems, and ours too, it crashed in the Celtic Sea not far from this very place. They promptly launched their fleet, as did we, and after three months of searching nothing was found." He paused, letting that sink in. "We believe that the anomaly sitting on the *Largs Bay*, is that very object."

"But Colonel," voiced someone, "how is that possible? How can an object that size get lodged into the side of a cliff, entirely obscured from view for over eighteen years, without leaving behind any footprint?"

Colonel Desmond sat with a blank look on his face as he answered. "Frankly, I don't have a clue, but that very mystery seems to corroborate our suspicion that it is an alien craft of some sort, and we can only assume that it possesses advanced technology sufficient to permit it to embed itself in solid rock to avoid detection." He paused, a cautionary smile sliding across his lips. "Make no mistake about it, ladies and gentlemen, if that thing is indeed an extraterrestrial craft, we are facing one of the greatest discoveries in the history of the human race; a real game-changer and one that most decidedly will open the door to technology that will change our world."

"However ..." a tone of subtle disappointment resonated in his next words, "the matter has become complicated by the fact that the Americans are onto us. The Foreign Ministry informs me that the State Department in Washington has already sent them a memo concerning our operation. It is just a matter of time before they connect the dots."

"But," asserted a civilian, "the Yanks have no claim to it? We found it on our soil."

Colonel Desmond's lips pinched together as he raised a brow. "Sadly, I wish that were the case." He responded with a sigh. "There is the matter of the 1973 Space Accord, a treaty which we all signed. One of its clauses was that any nation which intercepted a foreign object, of whatever kind, had proprietary rights to it."

"You're suggesting that would include having shot down a UFO?" asked another.

Desmond shrugged. "While I'm sure our government will argue the point, in the end, the Yanks will insist that we turn it over because it was their satellite that intercepted it, and we will have no option but to comply based on that accord."

He paused. "All of that aside, we must act quickly. We must organize our research teams fast if we hope to be one step ahead of the Americans, get inside that thing and get our hands on its technology before all the diplomatic foreplay fails and we are forced to turn it over to them."

"How long do we have?" asked another.

Desmond glanced at a wall clock. "By my reckoning, 72 hours is optimistic."

41

"You can't just walk out like that," the sound of her mum's harried voice cut into her eardrum.

As the bus rolled down Route 591 toward the small village of Kilcrohane, Kaetlyn was now wondering if her impulsive decision was going to amount to anything.

What did she expect to find after 18 years, she wondered?

And to what end would her trip to this small town come?

It was hard enough convincing herself of the merits of her decision, but trying to explain it to her mum, that was next to impossible.

She pressed the phone to her ear as the volume of her mother's troubled voice escalated in pitch.

"Mum, calm down, I'm just going down there to check something out – that's all."

"But, honey, you walked out on your therapist. She sounded very distraught and worried about you."

"I know. We weren't seeing eye-to-eye, that's all."

"Kaet, you have to get back to school and you need to finish this therapy to do that."

Kaetlyn clenched her jaw, calming the ire inside, the encysted emotion she felt about having been exiled from school.

"I promise to fix it when I return. Promise."

"What time will you be home?" asked a restrained voice.

"The bus arrives in Bantry at 9:10 tonight," she said with a quick glance at her ticket.

"Okay, but if anything happens, you call me, and I'll have your dad down there in a jiff."

"Love ya, mum."

Forty minutes later she stepped from the bus in the center of Kilcrohane.

A blanket of heavy gray clouds pressed in from the sea, and a gusty wind greeted her with a slap to her face.

Adjacent to the bus depot was a small taxi agency. Stepping inside, she found a lone man sitting at a desk reading a newspaper with a cigarette cradled between his lips. The stench of nicotine and sweat was almost overwhelming. She tipped her mobile phone at him and pointed on the map.

"Can you take me there?"

He squinted at it and then shook his head. "That's down near Witches' Tit. Nope, can't do it."

"Why?"

"Bunch'a military blokes down there, some kind'a secret operation goin' on. They've closed off the whole area. Best I can do is get ya to Flannigan's Point, there," he tapped her phone with a nicotine-stained finger. "It's a lookout, with those telescopes, you know, the ones you plug a pence or two into. Best I can do fer ya, lass."

"How much?"

"Take ya there and back fer a fiver."

Fifteen minutes later she was standing on the edge of a public observation point overlooking the Irish coast – a magnificent view of the cliffs which scaled down to a narrow rocky beach far below.

The cabbie waited nearby as she dropped a coin into the slot, swiveled the scope and focused on the sight below.

A small contingent of uniformed men and women could be seen on the rocky coastline, with cranes and heavy equipment scattered about. She angled the scope up the escarpment, following the profusion of cables and ropes which dangled there until her eyes rested on the large cavernous hole in its side.

A strange rumbling stirred inside her.

What did they take out of that opening?
Why is it so secretive?
Could it be connected, somehow, to my past?

The cognitive dissonance rumbled inside her like some giant suddenly awakened.

The bitter wind blew in from the sea, snapping at her face like a swarm of angry wasps and a frigid rain suddenly pelted down from the sky, forcing her to return to the safety of the cab.

But now, her mind was a raging fire, as if gasoline had been poured on a smoldering ash.

42

Raymond Statler found himself summarily placed in charge of the second phase of *Fish Hook*.

Colonel Desmond trusted him, and him only, to oversee the team of specialists who were now assigned the duty of getting inside the craft and revealing its secrets.

Nearly ten hours into his newly assigned task, with no less than twenty-one people at his beck and call, not a single millimeter of progress had been made. The portal on the left side of the craft, apparently a door of some kind, proved impenetrable.

Scientists pored over spectrometric-scans, unable to determine the nature of the skin enveloping the ship. A material that seemed lighter than any metal on Earth, and yet, impervious to any attempts to cut into it.

Engineers tried cutting tools – including an industrial laser. Not a scratch. Nothing. A veritable fortress.

Feeling tired and frustrated, Statler was forced to march across the naval compound to the officer's building and appear before Desmond with the disappointing news.

"Sir, we can't get into it. Nothing we have is cutting through that hull."

Desmond's faced manifested both disappointment and incipient exhaustion. "That seems impossible."

"My team has used a spectrometer to analyze it against the Periodic Table and that metal doesn't match anything we know of."

"What are you suggesting then?"

Statler paused. "A controlled Thermite-blast."

Desmond shook his head. "That's a slippery slope, Statler – and it could end up causing more damage than good."

Even as the words passed his lips, Desmond knew that his objection was just so much rhetorical diarrhea. He knew the Americans were already on their way and would show up at his doorstep soon and demand the thing be turned over to them. If they didn't get in fast, they would never get another chance to find out what it was all about, and he suspected the Yanks would not be generously tipping their cards either.

He sighed as he glanced at the wall-clock.

"Do it."

43

Kaetlyn awoke with a deep-seated anxiety pressing down on her, like a weight sitting on her chest.

She stared out the window at the trees which swayed in rhythm to the wind.

Her trip to Kilcrohane the night before had catalyzed some inner sense, a cognitive certainty that whatever it was they had found in that cliffside was somehow connected to her past.

There was nothing to corroborate the feeling, just an indelible prescience.

Was it possible, she wondered, *that she was aboard a craft of some kind? One that had crashed there?*

Tiny pieces of ephemeral nothing floated through her mind, just a vague feeling that something about that coastal region was familiar, *but why, and how?*

While the questions ceaselessly assailed her, she felt as if, by small increments, she was approaching the truth.

The buzz of her phone pulled her back from her thoughts.

"Hi, Kaetlyn," Serena's contrite voice began. "I'm very sorry things went the way they did. It was unprofessional of me to spring that on you. Can we meet again?"

"Why, so you can convince me to take your little blue pills?"

"No, and I'm really sorry I even suggested that to you when we were making progress."

Kaetlyn paused as a rapid debate ensued in her head. "I have something to tell you."

"My morning is clear," responded Serena.

"I'll be right over."

44

Statler, as did the others in his team, stood a good distance away, and watched as the Thermite reached temperatures of over 4000 degrees Fahrenheit.

A cloud of smoke exuded upwards, and of course, the acrid stench of a chemical flash soon reached their noses.

Anxious to see the result, they moved in with hopeful hearts and anticipant excitement, only to find that nothing had happened; not a burn, not a scorch mark, and certainly, not the slightest incision into the surface of the hull.

45

Rear Admiral, Norman Patterson was still asleep when his phone rang. He glanced at the clock – it was 7 a.m.

"Patterson here."

"Sir," began Adams, his excitement spilling over. "I think I have something of interest."

An hour later, with the first rays of dawn peeking over the horizon, RA Patterson stepped into his office with Adams in tow.

"I hope this was worth losing an hour of sleep."

"We've been surveilling phone and email dialogues, using search algorithms that might provide us with more information."

"Nothing too intrusive I hope," said Patterson with a raised brow.

Jessie nodded, but for him, snooping the airwaves, gathering beta-data using search algorithms, and chasing down ghosts was the thrill of the hunt. He knew how far he could stretch the edges of the box before he was stepping into dangerous waters.

"I trained our satellites on two regions. One, the Cork naval base where we know they took the object, and second, around the location where they found it. Our search algorithms picked up two dialogues of interest. The first thread was at the Cork naval base where two people were discussing something about an alien craft and some problem getting into it."

Patterson grinned. "So, the McPaddys are trying to break in."

Adams nodded. "Right. And if we're interpreting this dialogue correctly, they're not having much success at it."

"Good. And the second one?"

Adams tipped his head. "This one is a bit of stretch, sir, but bear with me. Our satellite feed intercepted several conversations between two people, not far from the site of the excavation, in a small town called ..." he paused to check his notes, "Bantry." It was difficult to decipher, especially considering the nature of the dialogue, but ..."

"I'm waiting for the punch line, Adams."

"They were discussing an incident where one of them claims to have been aboard an alien craft."

46

Colonel Desmond stood near the window of his office, his profile framed against the dimming light of a twilight sky.

A heavy brow crested his forehead, while lines of deep concern crisscrossed his visage like furrows in a field.

He turned to Statler, who sat nearby, also consumed in his own thoughts.

"This isn't good, Statler, not good at all. I've just had a call from the Foreign Office. They're getting a lot of pressure from the Americans – and on top of that, the Yanks will have their aircraft carrier – their biggest in the North Atlantic Fleet, parked in our backyard later today.

Desmond turned to look Statler in the eyes. "What other tricks can your engineers come up with? We need something fast or I fear that we will never know the truth hidden inside the anomaly."

Statler straightened before answering. "It's been suggested that we could try cutting through the glass window of the pilot's portal. However, there is a serious downside to that."

"Which is?" asked Desmond, seeing the hesitation in his face.

"The concern is that if we cut through the window, assuming that is even possible, we might unleash something."

Desmond raised a brow. "A viral contagion of some sort?"

Statler nodded. "Aye. We can't assume anything at this stage. The crew of that ship could have died from the impact of the missile, or they could have starved to death, run out of oxygen, or ..."

"Something else."

"Aye, sir."

"You weren't so concerned about that when you used Thermite on the side portal," challenged Desmond.

"It was safe to assume that the ship would have an antechamber which permitted its occupants to pass safely in and out of the ship without compromising its internal atmosphere. But," he nodded at the image projected on the computer nearby, "with the pilots viewscreen, we're opening that ship up directly to our world, and we have no certainty about what killed its crew."

"I get it," said Desmond with a tone of subtle defeat. "What I don't get, given that nothing we have penetrates that hull, is how the hell did an American satellite shoot it down, and for that matter, if there is no damage to the hull, what brought it down?"

"Possibly the Yanks didn't shoot it down, at least not in a conventional sense."

"Are you saying they lied about it?"

"No, sir, I'm suggesting that they might well be misinformed. They think they shot down a craft, but based on our analysis, their missile must have affected the ship's navigational system, not its structural integrity."

"So, the ship lost navigational control."

"That's the most logical assumption," paused Statler. "And if I were Captaining that vessel, I would certainly want to hide it from foreign intrusion while getting a signal out for help."

"But the crew died."

"True, but we have to assume that a ship as advanced as this one will have a highly-developed computer system capable of auto-piloting it; one certainly capable of taking evasive maneuvers in the event that its crew were disabled or killed."

"Like burying itself in a cliff?" said Desmond with a look of disbelief.

Statler shrugged. "As amazing as that sounds, it's the most probable explanation."

47

Serena stared at Kaetlyn long and hard.

"You think I've gone off the reservation, right?"

"That's not what I'm thinking, Kaet."

"Then, what?"

"I'm thinking about the consequences of what you're telling me."

"Meaning?"

Serena leaned forward, a somber look on her face. "You're convinced that this is a past-life experience, and whatever it is they found in that cliffside, that the two are somehow connected."

Kaetlyn nodded, her forehead furrowing as she did. "I can't prove it, but something tells me that's the case. Why is that so hard for you to conceive of?"

Serena sighed. "For the very reason you just stated, there is no proof."

"Except my sense of certainty on it."

Serena tempered the frustration now brewing inside her head. She desperately wanted to help Kaetlyn, but the matter was now freewheeling into an arena she could not control.

"You have to consider the consequences of this."

"Oh, because they'll think I'm weird?" She shook her head. "That boat has already sailed."

"I know that. I'm just saying that this could very easily be misinterpreted and would not act favorably for you."

"I don't care what others think, Serena, I care what I think."

"Okay, but you do want to get reinstated to school, right?"

Kaetlyn's jaw tensed as her eyes narrowed. "I want to get to the bottom of something that has been haunting me for most of my life. I want to know why I am the way I am. I want closure on this. I can live my life without my school accreditation, but I cannot continue to live my life feeling like there are two people inside my skin. That ..." she huffed, "I'm pretty sure will eventually drive me around the bend."

Serena sat in silence, listening to Kaetlyn plead her case.

"I've already been ostracized by the school; and the whole community probably thinks I'm a whack-job by now, so what do I have to lose? Do I pretend I don't know about any of this, bottle it all up and keep it to myself for fear that others will see me as different – as if that isn't already the case? Or do I walk the road I'm obviously already on and bite the bullet? Which one would you take?"

Serena leaned back, crossing her arms across her chest. Her head bobbed as she considered the question. "You have bigger balls than me, Kaetlyn."

"That's not an answer."

Serena sighed. "If you insist on going down this rabbit hole, I will help you, but I cannot protect you if this goes sideways. And ..." she paused, "if someone wants to find out about our sessions, they can, including the school psychologist if he requests a digest. I am duty-bound to provide him with an overview because your treatment was at the behest of the school itself and they are essentially my employer in this regard."

Serena stood and walked to the nearby window – staring off in the distance as she spoke. "I'm taking off my professional hat for a moment – speaking to you as a friend." She turned. "I'm worried about you, Kaetlyn. Putting aside my own doubts on this matter, you must consider the possibilities here. If there is any truth to this story, you could find yourself in the middle of something that is bigger than you realize."

"Why, what do you know?"

Serena approached. "Last night, I did some searching of my own on the internet. Did you know that a Russian source was quoted, some eighteen years ago, claiming to have tracked a UFO that plunged into the Celtic Sea precisely off the coast where you say you saw the Irish military yesterday?"

Kaetlyn nodded. "I've read some other articles that alluded to that."

Serena continued. "Ireland denied it and so did the Yanks."

A grin spread on Kaetlyn's lips. "If they denied it, that's a confirmation that it was probably true?"

"Maybe, maybe not," said Serena as she lowered herself into the chair, shaking her head at the girl. "Nonetheless, you're absolutely incorrigible – maybe even a little stupid, I can't decide which."

"Is that an official diagnosis, doc?"

Serena flipped a brow. "I'm off the record, remember?"

"And what if I'm right, what then?"

"I have no idea. I'm just telling you to be careful who you talk to about this. You could be drawing attention to yourself."

Kaetlyn saw the worry lines spreading on Serena's face – prompting her next question. "And what about you, Serena, how much have you told your Dublin friend about me?"

She hesitated a moment, drawing in a deep breath. "I needed some perspective on your case."

"So, what now?" posed Kaetlyn.

Serena's head shook back and forth. "I think we've gone too far down this particular rabbit hole to turn back, at this point."

48

Kaetlyn heard the voices as she entered the house. *American,* she thought.

Her mother met her in the hallway with a nervous look pasted to her face. "Honey, we have visitors," she said as Kaetlyn continued to the living room and was met by the prying eyes of two people she had never seen before.

"This is Laura Henson and Larry Volk – they're from the American embassy in Dublin."

Kaetlyn trained a suspicious eye at them as they both stood to greet her.

"Hello, Kaetlyn, can we talk?" asked the woman.

Kaetlyn lowered herself to the sofa, her eyes never leaving theirs.

"We've been asked by the State Department in Washington to pay a visit to you and request your cooperation on a very important matter."

"What matter?"

The woman conceded to Volk who opened a brief case, extracted some papers, and put them on the table in front of Kaetlyn and her mum. "We're required to get your consent to complete confidentiality before proceeding," he said.

"That's mental. How are we supposed to agree to something if we don't even know what you're asking us to shut up about?"

Laura smiled, a tactful smile. "It's for your protection, Kaetlyn. The subject we want to talk to you about is both sensitive and a matter of national security."

Kaetlyn rolled her eyes. "Ah, you Yanks, always playing the "national security card."

Larry spoke up. "Sometimes, there are matters that require mutual trust between all parties, and in this case, it is essential. Nothing you say here can be used against you. At the same time, it protects the interests of the US government."

"Which poses the question, why is the US government sitting in our house?" retorted Kaetlyn.

"Kaetlyn, we're not here to attack or harm you or to do anything illegal. We are within our rights to request that in the matter of this dialogue that there be a certain level of secrecy maintained."

Kaetlyn's eyes drifted to her mother's worried visage, the lines on her face were evidence of the troubling storm afflicting her - all of which compelled Kaetlyn to acquiesce, if only to reduce the torment to her.

She picked up the pen and signed. Her mum followed suit, still no less perplexed by the entire matter.

Larry placed the papers back in the briefcase as Laura proceeded.

"Recently, an object was discovered buried in a cliffside, not far from here in fact."

"What kind of object," asked the mother.

"That is yet to be established, Mrs. O'Sullivan," answered the man.

"And where is it now?" asked Kaetlyn.

"In the hands of the Irish navy at their base in Cork."

Volk's hand emerged from the briefcase with several images. He laid them on the coffee table in front of Kaetlyn and her mum.

"That is what the Irish military excavated from the cliffside in Kilcrohane," he pointed.

Claire turned to her daughter. "Is that why you went there?"

"I didn't know what it was at the time, mum. It was just a hunch."

"Then what is it?" asked the mum with a pressing tone as she turned back to the agents.

"We don't know for sure, but according to naval analysts back home," began Laura, "it's quite possibly an unidentified object that was shot down many years ago."

Kaetlyn's eyes skidded upwards to meet Laura's. "How many years ago?" she asked as a cold shock began to permeate her entire body.

"Just over eighteen, to be exact."

"It looks like a whale," said the mum.

Larry grinned. "It's roughly 60 feet in length by our estimates."

Kaetlyn stared at the faint image of the craft as an odd sense pressed into her, as if she had seen it before. She looked up at Laura. "What is it you want from me?"

"We need your help to get inside it."

Kaetlyn leaned back in her chair and stole a look at her mum who now looked considerably more confused.

"Why me?"

"Because," answered Laura, "we've picked up conversations between your therapist and you, as well her and a colleague of hers in Dublin. He's been consulting her on how to deal with your case."

"Ahh," said Kaetlyn with a shake of her head and a look of repressed disgust, "Snowden had it right, you guys just don't respect privacy at all, do you?"

Laura remained silent.

"Why do you think I can help."

"We don't know that for sure. But, given your insights so far, what do you think?

Kaetlyn drew in a breath and pondered it for a time before answering. "I have no idea. I'm just skirting the edges of something I've been trying to reconcile for years."

"Which is more than anyone else has at this time?" stated Laura.

Kaetlyn was silent as her mum reached over and squeezed her hand. "You haven't told me everything, have you?" she said.

Kaetlyn shook her head. "I will, I promise."

Laura pressed on. "You understand the implications of this discovery, right?"

"Yeah, I do. If it's so important to you, why aren't you taking this up with officials in our government?"

Larry answered. "The US State Department is already in dialogue with the Irish Foreign Ministry, and that object will soon be delivered to the USS Gerald R. Ford, an aircraft carrier which is arriving later today."

"So America is claiming it as their property," retorted Kaetlyn.

"It was our satellite which shot it down, so yes, according to the rules of engagement, we are entitled to it."

Kaetlyn grinned. "Is this what your navy was looking for back then?"

Laura stole a look at Larry and then back to Kaetlyn. "Off the record, yes."

Kaetlyn shook her head with a catlike grin. "You're willing to bank on me? Someone who is sitting in therapy and claiming a past-life experience? How can you be sure I'm not just making it all up?"

Laura smiled, a gesture designed to temper the edgy conversation. "When we received a report that you were seen in Kilcrohane yesterday, checking out the location of the excavation, it was considered a pretty safe bet."

"Or maybe just a good guess on my part."

"Look, Kaetlyn, I don't claim to understand everything that is going on here. All I know is that there are people on the other side of the ocean who think you could be a key player."

"Okay, assuming that is true, why not just breach the object yourselves?"

The other man answered. "According to our sources, the Irish military has spent 48 hours trying to penetrate that hull with everything and anything, without success."

"So, I'm the consolation prize, is that it?"

Laura leaned closer. "We know you want answers, Kaetlyn."

"More intrusive surveillance?"

"Can you blame us, considering the potential of this thing, and the answers it might provide about who we are, who else exists in this Universe, not to mention the technology we might learn from it?"

Kaetlyn sighed as she considered the matter. "It depends on who gets hold of that technology. You Yanks have been anything but transparent about past UFO encounters – in fact, you've done everything in your power to discredit the subject and make people believe it's all a hoax. Why should I believe that you'll treat this one any differently?"

"I understand your concerns. I won't promise you that my government will be forthright about what is discovered. At the same time, now that the Irish are aware of it, and have it in their possession, isn't it entirely likely that negotiations between our two nations will result in something more transparent?"

"What do you expect from me?"

"We're asking that you voluntarily come aboard the USS Gerald R. Ford and help us, if you can. There will be no pressure, just a cooperative endeavor. We will fly you there by military chopper tomorrow and you will get the chance to see this object – something I'm sure you want."

"I don't like that at all," said the mother with escalating apprehension in her voice. "You want my daughter to fly to your ship and stay there while ..." she turned to Kaetlyn with pleading eyes.

"Mum," Kaetlyn touched a hand to her arm. "It's okay. I'll explain everything."

She turned back to the two agents. "I'll do it on one condition – that my therapist, Serena Bohannon, goes with me."

49

"I don't know, honey. I just don't like it, not one bit," said Kaetlyn's mum, nervously wringing her hands together as the furrows on her brow deepened.

Harry O'Sullivan hovered nearby, having just arrived as the agents were driving away. His grim solemnity betrayed his repressed anger.

"I know it sounds completely mental, but you were the one who insisted I go to the shrink, and this is where we have come to," said Kaetlyn while stealing a look at her dad.

"So," he began with a stern and rigid face, "you go off to the Yanks' ship, get your brains picked, and what, the Irish get fook'd in the arse?" he raised a challenging brow.

"Harry, language, please," said the mum."

"Dad, it isn't like that, and you know it. You've been living with my issue for my entire life. You haven't understood it and neither have I. Now, it's starting to make some sense to me. If there is a chance in bloody hell that I can finally get the truth about something that has been haunting me, then I must do it – and if the Yanks have that ship in their hands, what choice do I have?"

Harry shook his head. He was battling two fronts at the same time. His own incredulity about the story, about Kaetlyn's experience, all of which was entirely new to him, and, the very idea of letting his most precious daughter fly off to an aircraft carrier in the service of the Americans.

As logic permeated the heated emotion, his frown finally mellowed, as did the look in his eyes. "Kaet, I'm happy if it helps you, lass, I really am, but I'm worried about the Yanks. I don't trust them."

"For the record, neither do I, dad."

Harry O'Sullivan lowered himself to a chair next to her and gripped her hand in his. "You're old enough to make up your own mind now, so saying no to you is likely to get me nowhere. What guarantees do we have that they will let you come back when you want to?"

"It's not a prison-term, dad. I volunteered."

Harry sat there, his eyes suddenly vague and distant. Slowly, his head began to bob as his lips tightened. "I knew this day would come." He turned to his wife, whose sad eyes reflected her own sentiments. Harry looked at Kaetlyn. "You were a miracle in our lives, in more ways than you might know. You filled a gaping hole in our hearts, and ..." he paused. "when you started to show these special talents," he softly smiled, "we both knew then that you would be walking a different path in this world."

He looked his daughter in the eyes. "You know I love you more than life itself, and I'd do anything to protect you."

"I know that, dad."

He sighed. "I also know that if I stop you from doing this, you're gonna hate me fer it. So ..." his head bobbed, "I'm going to give my consent, on one condition."

She smiled at him. "Dad, I'm eighteen, remember? Don't really need your consent anymore."

He waved a dismissive hand to the air.

"Don't matter. I'm coming with you."

50

Colonel Desmond stood on the quay, watching as the *Largs Bay II* eased past the breakwater with its precious cargo sitting on the aft deck.

The naval ship soon disappeared, headed for a rendezvous with the USS Gerald R. Ford anchored in international waters.

He turned and headed back to his office.

The gray dark clouds above pressed down on him, adding to the oppressive mood he felt.

"Sir!" the voice of his adjutant rang through the moroseness now consuming him. The man caught up with the Colonel and skidded to a stop next to him. "We just received this."

Desmond read the memo sent from the Foreign Affairs Department.

"When did that chopper lift off?"

"Twenty minutes ago."

"Fook'n Yanks!" he bitterly exclaimed. "Get the Captain of the *Largs Bay* on the line, now!" Desmond demanded as he marched to his office, pacing anxiously, waiting for his phone to ring and then snapped it to his ear when it did.

"This is Captain, Calhoon."

"Calhoon, I'm ordering you to stay within Irish territorial waters, with the American ship in sight. Do not, under any circumstances, deliver that package to them until you hear from me."

51

Kaetlyn had never flown in a helicopter before, certainly not a military one.

The **HC-6 Chargers Class** chopper powered its way against the constant pound of a Celtic wind with relative ease. Inside, it felt safe enough, but the thrum of the blades cutting the air outside pounded in her skull.

Harry sat quietly solemn – his eyes fixed on the gray mist ahead, with evident anticipation and worry etched on his face.

As she gazed into the misty gray, a wall of rain pelted into the helicopter, like machine-gun fire.

Her mind drifted back to the night before. She had taken a long walk, passing through the graveyard on the cusp of twilight – a place where she could gather her thoughts and calm her mind.

No sooner had she entered the placid domain than she became aware that someone was behind her. She turned and was momentarily surprised.

"You? You're … Shamus, right?"

He nodded with a congenial smile.

Roughly the same height as her, and the same age, Shamus Maguire had a crop of red hair, blue eyes and a friendly face.

"Why are you following me?"

He edged closer. "Can we talk?"

She trained a suspicious eye at him. "You were here the other day, weren't you, watching me from those trees over there," she pointed.

"Sorry 'bout that," he said with a look of mild humiliation.

"Are you stalking me?"

"I'm not stalking you, Kaetlyn. I was trying to get up the courage to talk to you."

"You could have been more direct. Why all the sneaking around?"

Shamus pinched his lips as he gathered his words. "It's complicated."

"Really. You show up a couple weeks ago and drop Tommy in the school yard, then I find you snooping on me the other day, and now, you're following me again. What's so complicated about that?"

Shamus spoke without looking at her. "Do you have dreams, Kaetlyn, I mean, really strange dreams?"

The question caught her off guard.

His eyes drifted off into the darkening realm of the graveyard. "I have such strange dreams – mostly the same one, repeating over and over."

Her brow furrowed as she listened. "Why are you telling me this?"

He turned to look at her. "Because, I know that you have a special dream too."

"First of all, if you know that already, then why are you asking me; and secondly, how do you know anything about me?"

"We share a common friend."

"I don't have many friends."

"My cousin," he answered, a small smile forming on his lips.

"Alana?! She's your cousin? She told you about my dream?"

"In her defense, I dragged it out of her. So please, don't take this out on her."

Kaetlyn felt confused. "You still haven't answered my question – why are you telling me this?"

Shamus drew in a deep breath before answering. "Because ..." he hesitated, "... your dream sounds a lot like mine."

52

The *USS Gerald R. Ford* bobbed marginally, like a toy boat in a bathtub, barely moving to the constant pound of a white-capped Celtic Sea which threw itself into the behemoth without mercy.

The newest in the **CVN-78 Class** of aircraft carriers, replacing its forebearer, the *Nimitz* series, the GRF looked like something from a high-concept science fiction movie as the helicopter ferrying Kaetlyn and her dad swept in for a landing.

Just as it touched the deck with a jolt, uniformed men rushed to meet it. As the door opened, a militant wind greeted them with a cold smack to their faces.

They were promptly escorted to the base of a towering structure which loomed high above the deck of the ship. One of the escorts casually referred to it as *The Stack* as he directed them into a small elevator which whisked them upwards.

When they stepped from the elevator at the topmost floor, Kaetlyn was awestruck by the view. It felt as if she was floating high above the sea, one that seemed to stretch forever.

They were seated in a conference facility which provided an expansive and equally impressive view of the sea, and then provided with sandwiches and hot coffee, and asked to wait.

Moments later, the door opened and in walked Serena Bohannon. The smile on her lips betrayed the fact that she was very happy to see Kaetlyn. She nodded at Harry, who forced a smile to his lips for the first time since boarding the helicopter. "Glad to see another Irish lass, here on this …" he glanced around, "monstrosity."

Serena chuckled. "It's really quite comfortable, once you get used to it."

"When did you arrive?" asked Kaetlyn.

"Few hours ago."

"Did they force you or did you volunteer?"

Serena smiled with a furtive glance to Harry. "Show me an Irish lass that bows to anyone, especially a man, and I'll give up my first newborn?"

No sooner had Serena sat and poured herself a cup of coffee when the door opened once again, and in strode an elderly, but dignified-looking man, wearing crisp naval whites and gold shoulder epaulets, and an impressive array of campaign bars on his left breast. He took off his naval cap as he entered. The woman who followed was also clad in naval whites, clearly an officer but less adorned and considerably younger.

The man strode to the far end of the room, straight-backed and disciplined in his gait, typically military in style. The woman stayed a stride behind.

He turned to face the table. "My name is Jim Harper – I'm the Captain and I want to extend a personal welcome to all of you here on the USS Gerald R. Ford, the most advanced aircraft carrier in the US fleet."

He tipped his head at the woman next to him. "This is Corporal - Lillian Fray – head of Special Operations."

He fixed his eyes on Kaetlyn first. "And you must be our special guest, Kaetlyn O'Sullivan."

Kaetlyn nodded.

The Captain extended his hand to Mr. O'Sullivan, who promptly stood and shook it with a certain humbled respect. "I appreciate your concern for your daughter's welfare and I respect your request to be here with her. I would do the same if it was my daughter."

"I appreciate that, Captain."

Harper turned to Serena. "And you are Serena Bohannon, Ms. O'Sullivan's therapist."

"I am. Nice to meet you, sir."

They seated themselves across the table from the others.

Harper's face morphed from its social ambience, assuming a more business-like sobriety. "I believe we're all familiar with the objective – which is to ascertain as much information as possible, and hopefully, provide us with a means of accessing the anomaly once it is aboard our ship."

"You mean, UFO?" said Kaetlyn.

Harper smiled. "We prefer the term *anomaly*, avoiding incorrect connotations."

"Where is the … "anomaly" now?" asked Kaetlyn, anxious to see it.

"It's being ferried to us by an Irish naval ship as we speak. Given calm enough seas, we hope to be able to transfer it to our holding bay later tonight."

Lillian Fray turned to look at Kaetlyn. "Are you prepared to resume your regression-therapy, or do you need a rest?"

Kaetlyn shook her head. "I'm ready and anxious."

"Good," responded Lillian with an affected smile, followed by a lingering look, a tacit message in her eyes. Something unsaid but certainly tangible.

Harper stood. "Corporal Fray will be your liaison during your time here," he said. "She will report on what you find, and in turn, she will let you know anything that we might require from you. Are there any questions?" he asked, maintaining a congenial, but formal bearing.

Kaetlyn spoke. "What assurances do we have that you will share the information with the Irish? I came here on good faith and the understanding that this would be a cooperative endeavor."

"And it is," responded Harper with certain finality.

53

"How are you feeling?" asked Serena as Kaetlyn dropped onto a cot in the small quarters provided to them, following her first meal in the ship's cafeteria.

"Well, let me see…" she paused, "I'm sitting on top of a floating war machine, about to provide the very people who apparently shot me down from the sky eighteen years ago, with the information about what's inside the ship … my ship."

Serena grinned. "You're really starting to sound as if it was your ship."

Kaetlyn shrugged. "I'm certain I was on that ship – I just don't know why, or how, or from where."

For a moment they were silent.

"Am I betraying my country by agreeing to do this?" asked Kaetlyn in a hushed voice.

Serena offered up a conciliatory smile. "I guess it depends on whether alien technology should be the proprietary right of only one nation?"

Kaetlyn trained an eye on her. "That's the first thing you've said to me that I agree with 100%."

"Then I have truly made progress."

Kaetlyn's gaze drifted off to a nearby portal filled with a gray mantle of darkening clouds.

"I don't want this to disappear into a secret installation in the Nevada desert – covered up the American military who think they have the right to keep alien contact a secret from the rest of the world."

"I agree with that."

Kaetlyn grinned. "Keep this up and I might consider becoming a shrink someday."

"Oh good, I feel vindicated. So, are you ready for a session?"

Kaetlyn pressed her head against the stiff pillow and closed her eyes. "Back to the beginning, right?"

"I'm the therapist here, and yes, let's pick up the incident where it all began."

"Okay."

"What do you see?"

It took several moments for Kaetlyn to relax, to clear her mind of all the recent clatter, and to focus on the vision again.

"The usual. I'm standing by a portal, staring out into space."

"Okay, try to focus on another part of the room. Can you see any detail whatsoever?"

Kaetlyn forced her mind to press through the mental fog and like smoke suddenly clearing, she saw something she hadn't noticed before. "My god, I can see the console in front of me."

"Good. What else?"

Serena watched as Kaetlyn's eyelashes fluttered, signs that she was fighting to claim more territory in the abyss of her subconscious.

Suddenly her eyes opened with a look of mild shock.

"What happened, Kaetlyn?" inquired Serena.

She turned to her. "I saw someone standing next to me."

Serena cocked an inquiring head her way.

"And I recognized him, somehow."

134

54

Colonel Desmond cast an eye at the screen, one filled with the face of the Irish Foreign Minister.

The man's crusty visage, framed by a patina of age and deeply creviced by the stresses of a long political career, glared back.

"This is a shite-storm in the making, Desmond, and I don't appreciate that you've issued that mandate after I promised the Americans it would be delivered to them within the hour."

Desmond took a deep breath – controlling his impulse to tell the man what he really thought.

He was a military man, a naval strategist and an intelligence officer, none of which included the skills of statesmanship. He could have opted to follow a career in politics, but he wasn't good at kissing ass.

"I'm not asking you to agree with my decision, Minister, I'm asking you to tell the American State Department that this matter of them taking several Irish nationals aboard their aircraft carrier before consulting with us, is unacceptable to the terms of your negotiation to return the vessel to them."

The Foreign Minister's head shook, like a petulant principal before berating him. "The Americans have sent their largest aircraft carrier to get this "thing", this is no matter to trifle with, Desmond."

"You're preaching the choir, Minister. Remember, I'm the military strategist here, not you." He paused to temper his growing anger. "Look, if I give them that spacecraft, they have it all, and they have this girl, who, I've now discovered, apparently has some kind of inside information by whatever ungodly witchcraft is at play here, and we have nothing. We have no bargaining chip if we release it without at least negotiating a change in the terms."

"Are you seriously taking this story as creditable – that some eighteen-year-old is claiming to have been on that thing when it crashed?"

Desmond smirked. "The Americans are taking it seriously, that's good enough for me."

"And how exactly is this a bargaining chip?"

"Because, she's an Irish citizen. We could make a stink about it, demand they release her, and if she is what she claims to be, the Yanks will have to play ball with us."

"This could be seen as a provocation, Colonel – a very slippery slope."

"Let's not be so dramatic, Minister. It's not as if they are going to start a war with us over this matter. They'll bluster and scream like they always do when someone says no to them, but frankly, now that they've played this other card, we're holding the ace card. They don't want an incident to hit the global airwaves ... something to the effect that an American aircraft carrier is holding Irish national's hostage."

"That would be a lie."

Desmond shrugged. "Tit-for-tat, Minister. Perception is more powerful than truth – remember - fake news!?" He grinned. "Besides, you of all people should know that after surviving a career in those shark-infested waters you call politics."

The Minister cleared his throat. "What exactly do you expect me to negotiate?"

"Tell them we're holding the craft aboard our ship, in our territorial waters, and that we want this girl to come to the Largs Bay and do her magic. If not, demand they return her immediately before we turn the craft over to them."

The man's head wagged with a distraught face. "That's a tough sell. I'm not sure they'll agree?"

"I'll wager a round of ale that the Americans have been snooping around, that they already know that we haven't breached that craft. The girl is valuable to them – they'll cooperate, believe me."

"You know, I could just go over your head to the General Commander and get the Largs Bay back on track."

"You could, but I just finished talking with him and he agrees with me. Play the card, sir. Make the Yanks kiss our arses for a change – we've got noth'n to lose, but a hell of a lot to gain."

55

Serena and Kaetlyn sat in the officer's lounge sipping on hot tea while staring at an assortment of fresh donuts piled on a tray before them.

Kaetlyn's hand hovered over the three-tiered dish. "I've never seen so many varieties of donuts before, where do I start?"

Serena drew a long smile as she watched her. A week ago, she saw Kaetlyn through a different lens, with incredulous eyes, doubtful ones, hesitant and questioning.

Now, she found herself on a mission to help Kaetlyn get to the bottom of something that Providence itself could barely have dreamed up.

Serena speared her hand into the pile, decidedly intent on taking the very donut that Kaetlyn's eyes seemed to have targeted. She scooped up the thick chocolate and vanilla-cream and scored a bite as Kaetlyn looked on in relative shock.

"That was mine, you bitch," cried Kaetlyn with a playful grin.

"Snooze you lose, right?"

Kaetlyn opted for her second choice, took a bite and then turned to look out the window at the chopping sea. A harsh angry wind tore at the ship, but inside, she felt nothing, not even the blustery wash that screeched against the titan as the Celtic Sea asserted its proprietary right to this domain.

"How are you holding up?" asked Serena.

"I miss it already."

"What?"

"Home." She looked around the lounge. "This ..." she paused, "I feel caged in, like a prison. I can't walk off this ship. Can't just jump on my Tao-Tao and go where I want."

"What's a Tao-Tao?"

Kaetlyn smiled. "My moped. How do these people live like this for months?"

"My dad was in the Irish Navy. He was a tough man, but the stories he related convinced me that I wasn't cut-out for life at the sea. Although," she clipped another donut from the stack, "this isn't all that bad," she snatched a bite.

Corporal, Lillian Fray approached the table where they sat. "Can I join you, ladies?"

Serena nodded.

"What part of the States are you from?" asked Serena as she sat across from her.

"Cambridge, Boston – my dad was a professor at Harvard and my mom taught preschool nearby."

"You didn't exactly follow in their footsteps."

"No, I didn't. I got sidetracked to the Navy," answered Lillian with a reserved smile. "Any progress to report?" she asked, her obvious anxiety bottled up.

"Nothing of importance," said Serena with a glance at Kaetlyn. "We're going to try a different tact."

"Which is?"

"We'll try to redirect the therapy to an even earlier period."

Lillian leaned back in her chair, eyeing the two. "Why?"

"Because," began Kaetlyn, "I can't get past a certain point. I can only go so far before your missile took us out," her rebellious smile spread across her lips.

"Oh, I see. *Our* missile?" responded Lillian. She leaned forward, clasping her fingers and looking Kaetlyn in the face. "I know you don't like being here and there are trust issues between us, I saw that in your face from our first meeting, but hopefully we can learn to work together. We've got the same agenda."

"Do we? Do we have the same agenda?"

Lillian raised a questioning brow.

"Look," began Kaetlyn, "it's not that I don't like you guys. My iconic hero, Elon Musk, lives in America, although, he isn't entirely American. Anyhow ... it's nothing personal."

"Then, may I ask, what is it?"

Kaetlyn leveled a firm gaze at the woman. "I don't trust the American government, it's military or its intelligence community, whatsoever."

"That doesn't leave much room."

Kaetlyn sighed. "I think Americans are no better and no worse than the Irish, or anyone else for that matter – but I do think that America's governance exerts its sense of entitlement under a false banner of democracy." She drew a deep breath before continuing. "I'm here for only one reason, to help unlock the secrets in that craft, assuming I can even do that. Whatever we find, I expect you guys to share it with the world, but, I'm pretty sure that I'm deluding myself into believing that a country that has branded ET as a hoax, isn't going to let that happen."

"Kaetlyn, I can't account for what has happened in the past. My job is to help navigate the process of getting inside that craft and determining what we have on our hands. I don't dictate the terms about what happens next, so you're going to have to reconcile yourself to having helped unlock, quite possibly, one of the greatest discoveries in human history."

56

Rear Admiral, Norman Patterson, had just pulled into the parking lot at NMIC when his phone buzzed.

"Norman," sounded the familiar but distant voice of his contact at the State Department in DC, the one who had helped him fast-track the recent negotiations with the Irish Foreign Ministry.

"Hi Frank. I'm just pulling into NMIC, can I call you back?"

"This is urgent, Norm. The Irish Navy just put a stop-order on the delivery."

"What?!" exclaimed Patterson. "Why?"

"The Foreign Minister is taking issue with the fact that we took those three Irish Nationals aboard the *USS Gerald R. Ford*, without first informing them of our intentions, and that we have violated their trust in doing so."

"That's ridiculous. They're stalling for leverage. Where's the package now?"

"About three clicks from our carrier, on their side of Irish waters."

"What are their demands?"

"They want this girl to go to their ship – they want to be in on the act when we open up Pandora's Box – assuming this girl is even legit."

57

Raymond Statler stood on the aft-deck of the *Largs Bay II*.

In the distance, looming high above the waterline, sat the behemoth, the *USS Gerald R. Ford*. Its towering stack speared into the sky, like a skyscraper coming up from the water.

He turned to stare at the anomaly – which sat tethered to the deck of the ship.

It taunted him. Like a box that no one could open, or the fabled Sword in the Stone of King Arthur's time, it beckoned him to break its grip on his mind.

What the fook are you? He wondered yet again – just one in a stream of endless questions assaulting him.

He'd never personally been a strong believer in extraterrestrials. Having grown up in a small community near Cork, a church-going town, taught to believe in God, to be loyal to the faith, and certainly, nowhere in that picture was he ever told that life existed elsewhere in the Universe, that the hand of God had touched more than just one tiny planet in a universe that contained billions of them.

Ever since excavating the object from the side of the cliff, and all the developments that had ensued, his view on the matter had taken a major shift. If this was everything they suspected, its very existence would change the course of history. It would mean, contrary to many contemporary views, that humanity was not alone in the Universe. It would challenge religious ideology. And it would certainly affect the world of science.

Would the Americans admit that they had an alien spacecraft in their possession – or would they deny it, he wondered?

Would the Irish government make a play to expose their hand, or would they simply acquiesce to pressure from Washington to keep it all under wraps?

In the end, would the world even know this thing ever existed, he thought?

He let out a sigh as his anticipant disappointment ratcheted up yet another notch. Soon, once all the political foreplay was done, he'd oversee the final delivery to the

Yanks – and probably, he would never be able to speak a word of it to anyone, including his own kids. One of the most important finds in the history of mankind would disappear into the caverns of obscurity, only to be raped and pillaged by scientists and engineers interested in revealing its secrets.

The cold damp wind had finally breeched his clothing, bringing his thoughts back to the present.

It was time for a coffee and something to warm his stomach, he thought.

As he turned to leave the deck, an incandescent glow caught his eye.

He swiveled his head in the direction of the light and to his shock and amazement, two spots on the alien craft, one aft and the other forward, were now glowing amber in color – flashing on and off like a street light before turning red.

"Jesus Christ almighty!" he exclaimed as he dashed for the door.

58

Kaetlyn woke to a light rap on her door.

She opened it only to find Lillian Fray, the Special Operations Officer, standing there.

"Good morning," she said with an apprehensive smile. "Are you rested?"

"Aye," answered Kaetlyn.

"Good, because your presence has been requested in the Captain's conference room."

"Is there a problem?"

The look on her face betrayed more than her words. "There's been a development."

"I'll be right there.

Moments later, Kaetlyn arrived at the conference facility where she found Captain, Harper, with Lillian Fray standing next to him, and several other uniformed men and women to one side, and of course, Serena.

Once again, the sobriety on Harper's face was a precursor to something important. "Please, have a seat," he motioned to a chair. Only when Kaetlyn had settled in, did the others follow.

Harper clasped his hands on the table in front of him, his visage reminding her of the Head Master at her school, or rather, former school, when the man was about to chide her for some infraction of the rules.

"There's been a development," began Harper. He leveled his eyes on both Kaetlyn and Serena, "First, the Irish have put a stop-order on the delivery of the anomaly." He paused. "Secondly, and more importantly, the anomaly seems to have come to life."

While the military personnel seemed unfazed by that announcement, as evidenced by their stoic looks, both Kaetlyn's and Serena's eyes were wide with shock.

"What does that mean, "come to life"? asked Kaetlyn.

Harper tipped his head to one side. "Lights are now flashing on the forward and aft portion of the object."

"Did something cause this?" asked Serena?

"The Irish assure us that since loading the object onto their ship, they have not tampered with it."

For Kaetlyn, the news was anything but sobering. She felt a growing elation inside – that her recent epiphany about her dreams, was not her imagination at work. This was real, that craft was real, and it was talking to someone, somewhere.

Harper turned to Kaetlyn. "Young lady, whatever it is you are trying to accomplish in this therapy, and I don't claim to be entirely versed on the procedure nor its efficacy, we need some information and fast."

Kaetlyn tipped her head to the Captain. "What are my Irish brethren saying?"

"They seem as dumfounded by this new turn of events as we are," answered the Captain.

"I'm assuming they're not too happy about the fact that we're here, which is why they've stopped delivery, right?"

Harper raised a brow, a subtle but unspoken acknowledgement. "We don't know exactly what discussions are transpiring, but that isn't the real issue facing us. We need to get in that thing as quickly as possible."

Lillian Fray spoke at that point. "Kaetlyn, we're simply asking you to put as much effort into this regressive-therapy as you possibly can, that's all."

Kaetlyn shrugged. "That's what I came here to accomplish," she said. She sensed that there was something else, some exigent circumstance that must be driving the matter. "Is there something else going on that you're not telling us, Captain?" she asked.

Lillian stole a transient glance at the Captain who subtly nodded. She turned back to Kaetlyn. "A Russian satellite picked up images of the anomaly, in fact, quite a few images as it was being loaded onto the Largs Bay. They've leaked these today through their media channels and it's already going viral."

"And they're saying what?" interjected Serena.

"That the American and Irish military are covering up the fact that a UFO, shot down some eighteen years ago, has now been found."

"How are they even connecting those dots?" asked Kaetlyn.

Lillian answered. "The Russians also tracked the object during its original descent after ..."

"I know," interjected Kaetlyn with a shake of her head, "the unacknowledged military satellite that shot it down."

Lillian accorded her a minor smile. "For all we know, they may have hacked dialogues about it. They probably know as much as we do, and recent events, have probably sparked a lot of interest back in Moscow."

"So, what's the big deal?" said Kaetlyn with a dismissive wave of her hand. "Just do what you guys always do, deny it, call it a hoax, because there is no ET – right?"

Harper's jaw tightened as a raw nerve had been struck by this young civilian. "Ms. O'Sullivan, with all due respect for your views, the matter is not so black and white as you may think."

"Because?"

Harper cast a stern look around the room before answering. "They're forcing our hand by making this public before we even know what we are dealing with."

"Scary proposition for you guys," said Kaetlyn with a suppressed grin.

Harper stood, as did the rest of his retinue. His face was firm and authoritative. "I hope to hear of positive progress today. We need it."

Lillian turned to Kaetlyn before leaving.

"You might consider showing a little more respect for that man, Kaetlyn. Captain Harper is a highly regarded military officer, not some gerrymandering politician, and certainly not someone who would be engaged in a cover up. He's trying to do the right thing, just like you."

Kaetlyn's ego suddenly deflated.

59

The mood had significantly shifted.

Captain Harper's briefing had put an entirely different spin on the matter. The world, to whatever degree people would accept it as fact, was now hearing about the discovery of an anomaly – an alien spacecraft, and the Russian spin on the ball left no doubt about the nature of the images they released.

It was clear that Moscow was forcing America's hand, making it difficult, but not impossible, to hide the existence of the craft.

Lingering over a plate of half-eaten eggs, Kaetlyn wondered if she had made the wrong decision in coming to the ship. And yet, some other part of her, one driven by a compulsion more profound than just political rights and wrongs, screamed at her to press on – to find the truth about who she was and why she was here. Answering that singular mystery meant more to her than anything.

Serena plunked down next to her and scooped up a donut from a nearby tray.

"I'm getting a liking for Yank donuts. Although …" she flicked a brow as she took a bite …"it's not doing my figure any good."

Kaetlyn nodded in silence.

"You seem serious."

"Serious times."

She waved her donut in the air. "Don't let the politics get to ya, Kaet. Our job is to find bottom on this rabbit hole – your rabbit hole."

Kaetlyn smiled. "Aye. But it's more presssure than I thought it would be."

Serena snapped the last bit of her donut into her mouth and then spoke. "You of all people should know that truth isn't always the easiest road to follow."

Kaetlyn shook her head at her. "Keep this up and I might add you to my Facebook friend list."

Moments later they were situated in their small cabin once again. Serena sitting nearby, and Kaetlyn stretched out on the military bed, staring up at the metal ribs that formed the ship's super-structure.

"Alright, close your eyes and clear your mind of all the shite," said Serena with a curt smile.

Kaetlyn complied, letting her inner world empty out. She waited until all the noise abated in her head and nodded.

"Find a time that is earlier than the moment where you usually find yourself standing on that ship," commanded Serena with a firm voice.

At first it felt like she was backing up in a dark room, one that had no finite walls, no limitations, nothing to orient herself. It was an odd and disorienting feeling, as if at any moment she would trip and fall into a deep dark abyss.

"It's hard. I get small wisps of things that just come and go."

"Try focusing on a sound, can you hear anything?"

Minutes passed before she spoke again. "I hear a voice, like before. No, wait … it's two voices, a male and…" she paused, her mouth suddenly dry as sand, "…me." I can hear my own voice. I can see the inside of the ship as if I'm right there. I just can't make out the words we're saying, but I get a sense that we're discussing something important."

Serena said nothing, letting her silence invite Kaetlyn to continue.

Her head shook back and forth as her jaw crimped tighter. "I think he's trying to warn me about something."

"Describe the room to me?"

"It's a different part of the ship – not the same as before. I think …" she turned her head mimicking her movement in the vision, "it's a small dining area, with a counter, some chairs, and work stations."

"Good. Go back to their dialogue. Can you make out what they, I mean, you are saying?"

Kaetlyn's forehead furrowed. "No, but now we're walking toward a door to another part of the ship."

"Okay. Stay with it."

Moments passed, during which Kaetlyn remained unmoving and silent. Slowly, her eyes opened, and she stared at the ceiling without a word.

"What happened, Kaet?"

She turned to face Serena as her smile widened. "I think I know how to get in."

60

Colonel Desmond stared into the thick mist as he spoke to Raymond Statler who stood on the deck of the Larg Bay II several clicks away.

"The Americans are coming your way soon."

Statler pressed a hand over the earpiece to help drown out a constant background wail of a Celtic wind. Behind him, the anomaly continued to flash amber.

"The American State Department has just informed the Ministry of Foreign Affairs that this girl, Kaetlyn O'Sullivan, may have found a way into that thing."

"Do we really believe that an eighteen-year-old girl can actually do that?" asked Statler with a polite yet challenging tone.

Desmond smiled. "Statler, we're both of the same mind. It's a shite-bag from start to finish, and yet, here we are, in the possession of an alien spacecraft, which has just come back to life, and a young woman who claims that she was standing on the bridge of that thing when the Americans shot it down."

"When can we expect them to arrive?" asked Statler.

"Within the hour. Get your team on point, put on some bloody coffee and let's hope for the best. I'll be joining you shortly."

Statler turned to look at the anomaly as a wash of frigid rain whipped down from the dark mantle above.

Its amber lights blinked at him with a hypnotic and mesmerizing rhythm, reminding him that they were from two different worlds.

Book Two

1

Summer was coming to the Antarctic.

Unlike the northern hemisphere, now in the grip of incipient winter, the land to the south of the equator, at the bottom of the world, was reaching its warmest season; somewhat oxymoronic when one considered that temperatures in the Antarctic, though considerably higher during the summer, usually remained below zero, but on some days have been known to go as high as 15 degrees Celsius.

Dr. Beckett and his team, three men and three women, trekked along the surface of the Ross Ice Shelf.

They moved methodically, always wary of changes in the surface, and certainly even more cautious not to build up a heavy sweat, because too much moisture could freeze, and rapidly drop the thermo-balance of their bodies to a dangerous zone in just a matter of minutes.

They pulled two small sleds, one containing the equipment they needed for their mission, the other contained food, medical supplies and emergency stores – including a radio with a sat-com link to a satellite high above in case of emergency rescue.

As he trudged along, his mind worked over the details of their mission.

The drones, deployed several months earlier by the *University of Auckland's Institute of Marine Science*, had been programmed to photograph every square inch of the Ross Ice Shelf, a domain claimed by New Zealand.

The Ross, the largest ice shelf of the Antarctica, measured some 501,000 square kilometers, about the size of France, and rising some 3000 meters in places, most of that below the water line, had become the subject of much concern.

Global warming, despite the denials, was a very real issue which scientists and environmentalists in New Zealand were painfully aware of. While the massive landmass known as the Antarctic seemed intact from the outside, in truth, it was bleeding away every day. The Earth was indeed heating up, as shown in record highs in summer temperatures, raging forest fires and dramatic drops in rain and water tables around the globe.

The big question was just how much of the shelf had melted and how fast was it happening – not whether it was happening, that was a given.

Dr. Beckett visualized the aerial photos provided by the drones, showing a pattern, an apparent rift starting at its south-westerly tip and continuing northeast toward its western edge, appearing like an intermittent road traversing its surface.

Many scientists concluded that it wasn't evidential proof of a rift; possibly a stress point they suggested, where ice had pushed upwards due to the intense pressures within this frozen wasteland. Others argued that it was a definitive sign of imminent rupture.

It was finally decided that the best way to get to bottom of the issue was to send in a team of their best people – and so it was, that Dr. Beckett and the other six specialists who trudged ahead of him, would soon arrive at the first coordinates in the southwest corner.

He hoped for the best, but in truth, he and his team had planned for the worst. As scientists they had to deal in raw fact, not emotion, nor even hope. Bridges maintained their integrity and stayed up because of science and the laws of physics – not hopeful wishing.

The Ross Ice Shelf was no different – it existed because of the temperatures which had wielded it into the behemoth it was today, and if that matrix, that delicate balance, was now changing, which it was, they had to face the fact that it was just a matter of time before Mother Nature would pull the plug.

2

Kaetlyn and Serena sat alone in dialogue with Lillian Fray.

"The plan is to fly you both to the Largs Bay II, where you will …" she paused as if grappling with the surrealism of the situation, "show us how to enter the anomaly."

Kaetlyn listened, feeling, as she did, a nervous tremor building up inside. It was one thing to see something in her mind, a specter that came and went like the wind, but it was quite another thing to pull the rabbit from a hat and perform magic – magic that could change everything.

She exhaled, relieving some tension. "You do realize that I only got a brief glimpse of how she, I mean …I, opened a door, not even the exterior door to that thing," she said with a tip of her head.

Lillian Fray nodded. "We understand the circumstance, but right now, you're the best thing we've got, and given the demands from the Irish, well, they've pretty much got our asses over a barrel."

"At least it's a good show of faith, after which you can get the thing delivered here and sail off into the sunset with it."

Lillian Fray leaned back, eyeing the young girl. "You're a smart cookie, Kaetlyn, I'm not going to sugar-coat this for you. And yes ..." she paused, "there is a certain factor of ass-kissing going on."

Kaetlyn nodded. "I appreciate your sincerity. When do we leave?"

Lillian stood and looked at her watch. "I'll be back in about thirty minutes to escort you to the chopper."

When she had left the room, Serena, who had remained silent the entire time, spoke up. "Are you worried, Kaet?"

Kaetlyn tipped her head with a sidelong glance. "I'm practically pissing in m'pants."

Serena smiled. "Good."

"Good, why is that good?"

"Because I would be concerned if you weren't having an emotional meltdown right about now."

"Oh, good, my shrink thinks I should be traumatized."

3

Having just arrived aboard the *Largs Bay II*, Colonel Desmond stood on the aft deck with his eyes fixed on the fog ridden landscape that shrouded the ship.

Old man Celtic was, as to be expected, delivering up his best weather; thick clouds, fog, a damnably cold wind, and light, but irritable rain. Maybe it was his way of reminding people that this was his domain.

Scattered about the deck were armed Irish naval personnel, a relative show of force, and part of the welcoming party.

A small team of engineers and scientists stood by in a nearby lounge as they waited anxiously to begin their task. Not a soul aboard the ship was anything but ecstatic about the prospects of what was about to be revealed – if in fact, and he was dubious of it, this young girl, Kaetlyn O'Sullivan, could actually access the craft.

A distant thrum cut the ambience.

Desmond squinted into the gray murk, listening as the thumping rapidly escalated. When the **HC-6 Chargers** suddenly emerged from the mist, it looked like a giant prehistoric bird swooping in.

Two men, with neon lamps, stood on the deck, guiding the chopper to its landing position.

As its blades powered down, the doors opened, and people emerged. Desmond approached them.

"Welcome aboard the Largs Bay," he said with an outstretched hand. "You are Corporal Fray, I assume?"

She nodded. "Good to meet you Colonel," she responded as she turned to the others in her party. "This is Harry O'Sullivan, Kaetlyn's dad."

Harry gripped Desmond's hand with a firm shake, only too happy to be back on Irish soil, so to speak.

"And this is Kaetlyn and Serena, both of whom you have already heard about," continued Lillian.

Desmond eyed the young girl who met his look without the slightest hesitation. "Nice to meet you, Kaetlyn," he said with a nod, but already, her eyes were fixed on the craft, sitting not far from where she stood.

Desmond spoke, purposefully breaking her spell. "Shall we go inside from this hellish weather," he said, as he pointed to the nearby door.

In the warmth of the officer's lounge, they nestled around a large table where Kaetlyn found herself facing a group of eager faces – engineers, scientists, military and civilian of different sorts, who looked at her as if she was an alien from another world.

Coffee and sandwiches were laid before them, at which, Colonel Desmond began.

"This is SOO Raymond Statler. It was his team who excavated the anomaly and successfully delivered it to us," he began. "And these folks hovering nearby like vultures," he cast a smile their way, "are an assortment of specialists we called in to assist in this task."

Lillian Fray turned to several others who had come as part of her entourage. "These are naval specialists who will also assist."

"Good!" announced Desmond with finality. "I suggest we warm our bellies with coffee and food and then begin. I'm sure no one is interested in wasting another minute on social foreplay," he grinned.

After a quick ingestion, they moved outside, tightening their jackets against a bracing wind.

Kaetlyn eyed the anomaly which suddenly conjured up images of her final moments alive, before having died inside it.

A shudder coursed her body and with it came a sense of trepidation. Facing her death in therapy was one thing, but standing next to the very craft within which she had expired, that was something to be reckoned with.

One of the engineers began, as he approached the craft. "The door, or what we think is a portal is here …" but Kaetlyn cut him off. "I know where it is," the words escaped her lips even before she had time to consider them.

The others, somewhat astonished by her response, stood unmoving as the dark-skinned girl walked the entire length of the ship, her hand gliding across its smooth contour like the touch of a lover.

Another quaking shuddered through her as something escaped the depths of her subconscious, some cognizance that made her smile. She looked up at Serena who watched on intently.

"This is it. I know it."

Serena stepped from the group and approached her. The others remained stone silent. "How do we proceed from here, Kaet?"

Kaetlyn drew in a deep breath as her fingers gently paused over the slight indentation of the portal itself. "I'm not sure, I think I just need to let it come back to me."

Serena nodded, stepped back, while casting a cautionary look at Desmond, Statler and Lillian Fray who stood anxiously waiting for something to happen.

Kaetlyn traced the outline of the subtle indentation that demarcated an entry, and even now, as she did, dim memories buried deep within, were slowly permeating upwards from the very depths of her unconsciousness.

She closed her eyes, willing herself, despite the drizzle and cold that touched her skin, and the fact that two dozen people were watching her, to go back to that moment, that precise instant where she saw herself reaching up and touching the interior door of the ship.

Small doubts accosted her, like snipers hidden somewhere in her subconscious. She pressed on.

Suddenly the image crystalized, as if she were standing there, in that exact moment.

She watched as the palm of her hand touched the door, as her fingers splayed and then moved in a rapid fashion; quick taps, in succession, followed by a dim blue glow emanating from the spot as the door hushed open.

She visualized the sequence again, and again, her mind consumed in a past-life, a brief fleeting moment in time as the crowd stood in abject silence, with only the sound of the wind and sloshing waves to be heard.

Without opening her eyes, she moved her hand to the door, poised her palm on its smooth surface and then tapped, as best she could recall, the same sequence she had envisioned.

Nothing happened.

With an anxious sigh, she repeated the procedure, again, nothing happened.

Feeling a sense of desperation, she opened her eyes and stole a look at Serena who nodded at her with a tacit look of reassurance.

Once again, Kaetlyn closed her eyes, locked on the image of herself in her past life and then pressed her hand to the door, and it struck her then, that the position of her hand was wrong.

She hadn't factored in her height; she was much taller in her former life, and the position of her hand was actually toward the top left corner of the door, not the center, where she currently had it placed.

That was it, the portal was built for a taller person, easily several feet taller than herself.

She slid her hand upward, stretching it high above her head, sliding it along the burnished surface until she couldn't reach any higher. Once more, she tapped her fingers in the same sequence and heard the gentle hush as the door whooshed open.

A collective gasp emitted from behind her.

Kaetlyn opened her eyes and found herself staring inside a dimly lit entry – a small antechamber.

In that instant all her trepidation, her encysted emotion, her doubts about her sanity, the wail of her questioning mind, all of it seemed to evaporate, replaced by relief, a relief so profound that tears pooled in her eyes and coursed down her cheeks.

Someone made a move to approach, but Serena stepped in front of the group quietly motioned everyone to remain exactly where they were.

Serena watched Kaetlyn, who stood facing the open portal, her chest heaving and tears quietly falling to the deck, like spots of rain.

It was a surreal moment for all, waiting anxiously for the young woman to do something.

Finally, Kaetlyn wiped her eyes, turned to Serena as a smile crested her lips and then without hesitation or word, she stepped into the ship as the door hushed to a close behind her.

4

Dr. Beckett and his team had pitched camp and started their procedural research.

On the surface, and by eye, there was no apparent distinction to be seen anywhere. The Ross Ice Shelf stretched for hundreds of kilometers. But of course, the human eye was not equipped with the delicate sensors which the scientific drones possessed; an ultraviolet spectroscope that could detect geological layering, unseen contours below the surface of the ice, fissuring and provide density readings.

The sequence involved drilling a series of deep holes, then lowering special sensors which emitted a high frequency. Up top, they would measure the response, much the same as radar detects depth and contours of an ocean bed. The frequency emitted by the sensors could detect the consistency in the ice, changes in mass - even cavities. It was a tedious process, drilling, measuring, and noting results, all the while being accosted by the frigid hand of the Antarctic, even now, in its summer-period.

For the first several days it seemed as pointless as any venture could be imagined, but on the fourth day, after having drilled and sounded-out no less than fifteen separate holes, something rather astonishing happened. The frequency they received back revealed that just 280 meters down, the wall of ice, as manifested by the measurements on their computer, seemed to have disappeared.

They repeated the procedure, moving another twenty-five meters further along the surface, following the image-pattern as closely as possible, and this time the sensor response showed the same thing, only at a depth of 133 meters.

That night, beseeched by the angry wail of an Antarctic wind, they congregated in their tent - their only refuge against the cold.

Beckett's mind was busily at work, calculating depths for each change in density noted, and then plotting these on a computer graphic. Soon, the picture was clear.

He leaned back and eyed his companions who sat huddled around a small heater, their hands pressed tightly against the warmth of coffee cups, but their eyes firmly fixed on his.

They all knew what it meant.

Deep down below the surface, pockets had formed in the ice shelf, which confirmed their worst nightmare – the Ross Ice Shelf was melting away from beneath, and at those depths, and given the gargantuan pressures invoked by such a mass of ice, it was clear that they were facing an inevitable crisis – it would start to break apart, sooner than later.

5

At first, Kaetlyn felt an embryonal fear forming in her gut, not unlike the feeling of suddenly being locked in a dark room – but then it quickly passed as she realized that the same procedure that got her to this far, would probably work for other doors.

She approached the next portal, placed her left hand high above her head and repeated the sequence of taps, precisely as she had done before. The door silently swept to one side, disappearing into the wall.

Stepping forward, it hushed back into place behind.

She found herself standing in the mid-section of the ship, which she immediately recognized from her sessions.

Things were strewn about the floor, broken or bent or crushed, evidence of the crash.

As her eyes adjusted to the dim interior, she began to see the actual proportions – everything was so much bigger.

She stepped toward the nearest chair – nearly twice the size of a normal one. The lip of the counter which ran the length of the room, came up to her chin.

She turned to face the door to her left, as if she knew exactly where it led, repeating the same sequence, the code, and then stepped into the bridge as lights came up, illuminating the room.

With a gasp she looked down at the skeletal remains silently entombed in this place for years, and it suddenly occurred to her that one of them was her, another her, from a former life.

6

While a team of specialists carefully analyzed and catalogued the skeletal remains, Kaetlyn, Serena, Colonel Desmond, Lillian Fray and Raymond Statler sat in private conversation inside the dining area of the Largs Bay.

Desmond was momentarily silent as he considered their situation. Now that they had access to the ship, something he doubted would happen because of this young woman's "therapy" – he had to move fast. Lillian Fray, his American counterpart, had already contacted her people and informed them of the fact.

Desmond leaned into the table, looking Kaetlyn in the face. "Young lady, what you have just accomplished is nothing short of amazing."

Kaetlyn nodded, but she didn't share his sentiment in the same way that he meant it.

"Once the forensics team have catalogued the skeletal remains and moved them from the ship, are you prepared to go back in and explore the ship's computer?"

Kaetlyn drew in a deep breath. "Of course."

Desmond turned to Serena. "I will arrange a room for your sessions."

Kaetlyn's head wagged vehemently. "No, I want to do the sessions inside that ship," she turned an eye to the craft, its aft portion sitting less than five meters from the window next to her.

Desmond cast a look to Lillian. She shrugged.

"I see no problem in that."

"And, I don't want anyone else inside the ship during our sessions. Between sessions, that's up to you, but when Serena and I are inside, no one else is."

Once again Desmond nodded. "I'll go brief the others. The sooner we get you in there, the sooner we find out what this thing is all about," he said with a glance at Lillian.

Lillian turned to Kaetlyn.

"What did it feel like when you first entered?" she asked with a girlish look of curiosity on her face.

Kaetlyn raised a brow. "Strange, bizarre, shocking, a relief, and yet, entirely familiar in a way I cannot explain."

Lillian smiled, her eyes glazing over as if she had maundered off to another place. "I can only imagine how it must feel to see something like that – the place ..." she paused for the right words.

"It's okay, Lillian, just say it. The sensitivity-ship has long sailed," said Kaetlyn.

"To remember a past life, that's one thing, but to actually connect to it, in a real sense, that's, well, kind of a mind-fuck!"

Kaetlyn chuckled. "That was the word I was looking for, a mind-fuck, says it all." She grinned.

The others left the room leaving Kaetlyn and Lillian alone.

Kaetlyn looked at the other, sensing the same tacit, yet unstated message in her eyes.

"Why are you really here, Lillian?"

The woman's head swiveled toward her with questioning eyes. "What do you mean?"

"Since the first day we met I've sensed that you had two agendas – you're working for the American Navy, but it seems as if there is some other theater happening in your mind."

Lillian was taciturn as her eyes idly drifted about the small lounge. She drew in a breath. "This is off the record, of course,"

Kaetlyn nodded.

"When I was eleven, my family and I were camping in the McKenzie Mountain Wilderness area, you know, up by Lake Placid. One night, as I sat out by the fire alone, stoking it with wood …" she paused, her eyes glazing over once again, "… I saw a flash of bright light streak across the sky, and then it swept down over the trees. I thought at first that maybe it was a falling star – but it was too low, and when it stopped and just hung there, hovering over the trees just across the lake from where I was sitting, I knew it couldn't be." Her eyes rose to look at Kaetlyn. "The light moved toward me, getting bigger and brighter as it did, and within seconds it was hovering over the water right in front of me."

"What was it?"

Lillian shook her head. "Well, I can tell you that it was nothing from this Earth."

"How could you know?"

"I just knew. The shape, the light. It wasn't spinning or moving, it was just hanging there. As I watched it, more astonished than afraid, it moved even closer. That's when I felt it."

"What?"

She shrugged. "The connection. I felt as if they were watching me, like I was watching them, and even though I couldn't see them, I felt them, I sensed their presence."

"Wow!"

"Yeah, it was a wow-moment."

"How long?" asked Kaetlyn.

"To be honest, I lost track of time."

She sighed with a lingering look of nostalgia in her eyes.

"That experience changed my life. I went on to study astrophysics, eventually finding my way into the Navy where I signed up for a program to study UFOs."

Kaetlyn leaned forward. "No way! You mean the US Navy acknowledges ET as a fact?"

Lillian grinned. "Of course they do, but not publicly. Why do you think we're here? Why do you think I was assigned to this mission?"

"I knew it," lightly exclaimed Kaetlyn with a look of mild victory in her face.

Lillian drew nearer. "I told you my story, one I have only told a few close friends, because I wanted you to know that you are not alone in this endeavor, Kaetlyn." She paused to study the other. "I had my doubts at first, wondering if you were just some over-stimulated hyper-imaginative girl, but now … I'm on side."

"Good to know."

Lillian assumed a more authoritative posture. "I know what you're battling with, Kaetlyn. You want to know what's inside that thing, you want closure on this shadow that has followed you your whole life, and at the same time, you don't want to see it all disappear." She tipped her head at her. "I know how something like this can change you. I was changed by my experience. And I'm sure there are thousands of people who have had similar life-changing experiences just like mine. So, I want this discovery to be public domain just as much as you do."

She paused to cast an eye around the room.

"I have no idea how this will end, but I'm certain that my government will put this craft in a deep military installation somewhere and issue its standard shore story."

"Why are you telling me this," asked Kaetlyn.

"To protect you," she answered with worried eyes.

Lillian leaned back, casting another cautionary eye around the lounge before continuing.

"Be careful, Kaet, there are vested interests at work here, people who do not want to share the secrets inside that thing and if you step on their toes, you could become an obstacle to them. Do you understand?"

7

Rear Admiral, Norman Patterson waited as the President of the United States, along with several of Patterson's peers, sat and fixed a gaze at him.

"Let me get this straight, Norman," began the nation's leader, "you're saying this ..." he paused as if still reconciling the matter, "eighteen-year-old woman, through some past-life memory, was able to figure out how to get into this thing, where no one else could?"

Patterson nodded. "Correct, sir."

"And now we're dependent on this same young woman to access that ship's computer?"

"Yes. Our technicians have, along with the Irish, tried every known means of interfacing with the computer. We flew in our best data-hackers and they couldn't get a beep from it. We need the girl, that's the bottom line."

The President leaned back, eyeing Patterson, and then looked to his right at Anne Lansing, the Secretary of State. "What do you think, Anne?"

She cocked her head to one side. "To be honest, Mr. President, it's quite bizarre."

"Yes, of course it is, but what do we do with it? On the assumption that if she figured out how to enter that thing, she will do the same with the ship's computer system, then what?"

Patterson offered up an answer. "Mr. President, this isn't entirely unprecedented."

The President turned to him with a questioning visage. "Meaning what?"

"It's not the first time we've recovered alien artifacts of this nature."

The President's eyes widened. "So, the stories are true?"

Norman Patterson grinned. "Some are true, some are hyperbole – but essentially, we've managed to deal with this kind of thing in the past. It takes time and a good shore-story, that's all."

"Time, we don't have, Norman, not with the Russians stirring up a shit-storm about this thing."

"Which is why we should get it out of sight as quickly as possible and get control of the narrative."

"You mean, put a lid on it?" said the President.

170

"Unfortunately, to not do so would create havoc, sir," answered Patterson with a tacit nod to the Secretary of State.

"I think, Mr. President," she began, "what Norm is trying to say is that if we let this news continue to go viral, especially if this girl manages to access this ship's mind, we are opening the door to quite an avalanche of media exposure we don't need or want."

The President drew in a deep breath, his head lightly bobbing as he did. "You're suggesting hushing it up until we find out what it's all about?"

"No, sir," paused Patterson, "I'm suggesting we counter the Russian campaign with one of our own, deny the whole thing. It's the easiest way. Otherwise, as Anne says, we're heading for a shitstorm of media exposure which will compromise the operation."

"And you think the Irish will agree to that?"

Patterson shrugged. "We'll find a way to appease the Irish."

The President was silent for a time. He had just barely scratched by on the mid-term elections and was on his way to starting a new run for his second term in office, and he certainly didn't need conspiracy theories about alien spacecrafts muddying up the perception of the electorate.

He waved a dismissive hand to the air. "Do what you think is best, Norman," he said with a sober visage. "But, if this goes sideways, I need to know about it."

8

Kaetlyn felt very alone.

A sense of nostalgia and longing had crept into her world, coming from a place she knew not of, but with a depth that was consuming her.

Sitting by the portal of her small cabin aboard the *Largs Bay II*, with her chin resting in the palm of her hand, she stared at the sea, feeling like the impossible victory of having penetrated the occlusion of her subconscious mind was so anticlimactic, considering what now faced her.

Lillian Fray's covert warning still played in the back of her mind.

An obstacle. Hmm! She chimed aloud. Her sense on the matter had been correct. There were other's with a different agenda to her own. She wanted transparcency, but there were those who wanted power and leverage – and this ship, hers no less, was a potential weapon in the wrong hands.

And while it made her feel a little better knowing that Lillian was on her side, it didn't change the fact that the result would be her responsibility – good or bad.

Was it right to crack that safe, she thought?

Was it meant to be exposed to Earth?

Was humanity even capable of dealing with its secrets without turning it into a shite-storm – more war, more greed, more theatrics to leverage power in the hands of the few?

Then again, what purpose could have made their trip so important? she wondered?

She ached to know the truth. Every step along this path so far had opened doors to her, and presented new ones, fueling her passion to get closure on a life once lived, before her sudden demise.

Why had her past life haunted her, and why was it beckoning her now, she wondered?

Was it just the mystery of it all, or was there a reason, some import that her subconscious mind was compelling her to know, tapping on her consciousness and demanding that she wake up to its call?

A light knock came to her door. "Come in."

Harry O'Sullivan stepped in and sat next to his daughter with his usual fatherly smile, while squeezing her hand. "Proud as shite of ya, lass" he said.

"Thanks, dad."

"You don'a look so happy 'bout it."

She sighed. "Just worried."

"What's got your locks in a curl, besides the fact that you just opened a fook'n alien ship for everyone to nose about?"

"It's not that. I want to know what's in there just as much as they do."

"Then what's troubl'n ya?"

Kaetlyn turned to him. "I'm worried that whatever is in there won't see the light of day."

"You're mean'n they'd cover it all up?"

She nodded.

"Look, Kaet, you can't take all of this on your shoulders. The world's a complicated place, governments have agendas and you can't control what might or might not happen."

Desperation formed on her face. "It feels like have to, dad. If I open it, I must be responsible for what happens. Besides ..." she paused to reflect, "...I was on that ship. I had a role to play and until I know what it was and why we were sent to Earth, I can't just abandon my responsibility."

Her father raised a brow. "Yer talk'n 'bout another lifetime, Kaet. You aren't accountable for somethin' you ain't."

Her head shook. "That's just the thing, dad, I'm accountable. It was me then, it's me today, just different circumstances." She turned to face him. "If you knew you could prevent something really bad from happening, wouldn't you?"

"Course I would."

"That's how I feel."

Her father stood and paced the room for a moment before speaking. "I don'a think I ever told ya this, but when the opportunity arose to adopt you, I was hesitant at first."

"Why, because I'm black?"

The father flicked a brow. "I'd be ly'n if I didn't say yes. A black girl in a predominantly white community, especially here in Bantry." He paused. "I ain't racist, you know that, lass. But the moment I saw your face I fell head over heels in love with ya. I was worried that I'd be bringing you up in a world where fair ain't always accorded everyone. I wasn't so sure I'd be giv'n you the life you deserved or that I could protect you from what was com'n."

Kaetlyn was silent.

"Course, your mum came to the rescue. She sat me down one day and told me, in no uncertain terms, like she can do sometimes, that destiny doesn't pick the person - the person picks their own destiny. And by god, I'm glad she put her foot up my arse, because you turned out to be the best thing in my life." His lip trembled as the words parted his mouth.

He turned to her. "I believe in you. I always have. I haven't always understood your circumstances, but I trust your judgement, Kaet."

Kaetlyn felt tears pooling in her eyes, and something else too, a sudden resurgence in her determination to stay the course.

She stood and hugged him.

9

Refreshed by sleep and a hearty breakfast of bangers and beans, Kaetlyn and Serena briefly met with Colonel Desmond, Raymond Statler and Lillian Fray – all of them eager to get on with it.

"Have you managed to find anything useful during the night?" asked Serena.

Desmond shook his head. "Besides picking apart the bones of a few aliens and trying to hack into an impenetrable computer – nope." His sense of frustration seeped through. "I hope you do better," he said with a nod to Kaetlyn.

Moments later, Kaetlyn and Serena stepped into the silent domain of the ship's control room.

By now, the skeletal remains had been removed and the chairs stood empty. Kaetlyn climbed up on one.

"Feels weird?" said Kaetlyn.

"Just another weird thing in a series of them," said Serena as she looked about, acclimating herself to her surroundings. "Are you comfortable with this, Kaet? We can always move inside."

"I'm fine." She paused. "I wanted to do it here because I think it will help me remember things faster if I'm inside the ship itself."

"That's a logical assumption."

Kaetlyn's eyes wandered about the room. The semi-circular control panel in front stretched the entire breadth of the ship, a polished black obsidian-like surface. The walls and floor were steel gray in color, and yet, to the touch, they felt soft. The lighting exuded from ceiling and wall units, inset flush to the surfaces, emitting a soft hue.

Kaetlyn turned to look out the massive portal. Like tinted glass, it curved around the front of the bridge, and for just a moment, it conjured up dim memories of standing in this very room, watching as the object streaked toward them and ended their lives.

She exhaled and turned to Serena.

"I have one question before we get started," began Serena. "When you first stepped inside this ship, didn't it occur to you that you might be compromising yourself, exposing yourself to the possibility of some deadly pathogen?"

Kaetlyn shook her head. "Raymond Statler actually warned me about that possibility, but to be honest, when the door first opened, I had an out-of-body experience on the spot. It was like I suddenly jumped out of my head and was floating several feet above. It was a wonderful feeling, total ecstasy, and frankly, I just didn't care about anything else."

Serena's head bobbed. "Well, okay, then. Shall we get on with it?"

Kaetlyn nestled into the chair, closed her eyes and waited until the small storm in her head abated. She nodded.

"Let's go back to that moment when you saw the woman ..."

"You mean me," interjected Kaetlyn with a wry smile on her lips.

"Yes, of course. Tell me what you see."

It took a while to navigate through the mental morass and the dialogues that echoed, like faceless voices in a fog. "I can see him now."

"Who?"

"The one I'm talking to as we walk toward the door."

"Describe him."

"Tall, with skin as black as mine." She smiled. "His hair is a black with silver highlights and braided on the back." She paused. "His eyes, they're ... like a deep blue Grecian sea."

"You said that you're talking, can you make it out?"

Her head wagged. "No, I still don't understand the language. But I sense we are talking about something important by the look on his face. He seems alarmed."

"Okay, what happens next."

"We step into the bridge and..." she paused as her face flushed with excitement... "I see another male now – he's sitting at the console. We're talking to him. The dialogue is fast and heated."

Kaetlyn tensed as her breathing hastened.

"What's happening?"

"The pilot, I think he's warning us that something is coming at us. I can see him pointing to the view screen."

"And?"

"The other one turns to me, says something and tries to push me into the nearby seat ... but ..."

Her eyes popped open.

"It was too late. Whatever it was, it exploded, and everything just went black."

Kaetlyn shakes her head. "Obviously it was the missile from the American satellite that hit us, but I can never get past that point."

"Let's pick it up when you are standing in the other room."

Kaetlyn shuts her eyes and refocuses. "It's getting really old watching myself die over and over."

Serena grinned.

They repeated the process again and again, each time coming to the same impasse, the dark oblivion of death.

Kaetlyn felt the taste of defeat – it was exhausting.

10

Shamus Maguire found himself immersed in a growing obsession for someone he hardly knew, or did he?

He'd barely had a chance to reveal his dreams to Kaetlyn when she had to dash off home, and then, the next day, she had disappeared.

He'd checked her usual haunt at the graveyard, he'd passed by her home several times, he'd even walked the streets of Bantry, checking out coffee shops and pubs with no sign of her anywhere.

Maybe it was stupid, he thought, *to have told her about his dreams. Maybe it had spooked her.*

In their short meet in the graveyard days before, he had only managed to skirt the issue, during which time

Kaetlyn was reserved, silent, watching him with suspicious eyes.

He had revealed his deepest secret to her.

Would she reciprocate and reach out to him, or would she feel compelled to avoid him out of fear, or some other dark calling?

The questions assailed him.

And the draw, the feeling he sensed for her, pulled him inextricably forward.

Now that their paths had crossed, he knew that their inexplicable connection was, somehow, indelible – and if he ever hoped to understand the strange haunting, the visions of a woman he was certain he loved, and the deep dark abyss of oblivion that followed, she held the key to unlocking it all.

The question that plagued him now was how to gain her trust and how to bridge the gap between them – if that was even possible.

11

After much discussion about their last session, and with the anxious eyes of all concerned watching them as they approached the portal, Kaetlyn and Serena re-entered the ship the next morning.

Within minutes they were back at it, and like soldiers, they trudged through the battlefield of Kaetlyn's past life, assaulted by transient images, a language that she could not remember, nor fathom, the fleeting faces of people she once knew, and the dreaded instant just before death took them each time.

It was a painstaking and brutal exercise, one that required perseverance and taking each small detail remembered as a victory, another step toward achieving full closure.

But now, they had reached an impasse.

With her limited skills in past-life regression, Serena had tried every angle, pressing Kaetlyn to search out small wisps of memories, the keys to the anchor that held it all in place – but death's grip on her past life was not giving up its secrets easily.

Kaetlyn hung there, her eyes drifting about the interior of the ship.

Scant feelings, token memories, ghosts of her past touched her like playing a game of tag.

Each time she tried to grasp onto something tangible it seemed to disappear into the murk of her vaulted subconscious.

Serena felt her disappointment.

"I'm sorry, Kaet, I don't know where to go from here. We've hit my limitation using this technique."

Her eyes rested on the smooth obsidian-like console before her. "I know, you've done your best," said Kaetlyn as her mind desperately searched for an answer. There had to be a way to get past the mental barriers of her past life.

As she stared at the console, a small spark suddenly flashed, an idea, one she had not even considered before now.

Kaetlyn placed the palm of her left hand on the console, splayed her fingers and then tapped in the sequence, the very same one she used to gain access to the ship.

The console lit up like a Christmas tree, rippling with hues of blue and green, and then suddenly, a hologram appeared above them with a face – the three-dimensional image of what appeared to be a woman – but certainly no woman she had ever witnessed before.

They watched in utter shock as its voice echoed off the walls.

12

Colonel Desmond had never spoken directly with his counterpart in America. The two men had never had the occasion to speak.

Although, Rear Admiral, Normal Patterson had a prestigious career as the commander of the American North Atlantic Fleet, and technically, out-ranked Desmond, in truth, their functions were on a par – both engaging in Naval intelligence for their nations, simply on different orders of magnitude.

When the screen came to life, Patterson's visage appeared, a man who was easily ten years his elder.

Desmond nodded respectfully.

"Colonel Desmond," began Patterson, "it's good to finally meet you face-to-face."

"Likewise, Admiral."

"This is a secure line, so let's speak candidly, shall we, military man to military man, and leave the fucking politico's out of the equation for now, agreed?"

"Agreed," answered Desmond.

"This matter with this," paused Patterson, "alien craft, has the potential of going sideways on all of us."

Desmond refrained from smiling at the man's dissimulation. He knew that this call was intended to bend him in favor of letting the Americans control the narrative with regards to the anomaly.

"What's your meaning, Admiral?"

Patterson cocked a brow. "Well, if this young lady continues, as she is, to open the door to the mind of that thing, who knows what secrets we'll find." He grinned. "My concern, which is shared by most at this end, is that we must get this matter put into the right context, so that others do not portray it inappropriately."

"Others as in, us, or are you referring to the Russians?"

Patterson crimped his lips. "I'll be more direct. We can't let the world know that we just dug up a fucking alien craft. And frankly, Ivan has already started the dominoes falling with the leaks from Moscow."

Desmond leaned back in his chair, eyeing the other. "I'm going to be candid too, Admiral. Are you and your superiors more concerned about the backlash created by news of having discovered an alien spaceship, or, are you more concerned about controlling the narrative because America wants to keep it under wraps for its own purposes?"

Patterson pinched his lips as he considered his answer. "I expect a little of both."

"And you want us to acquiesce to your demands."

"Colonel Desmond, we appreciate what you've done, and personally, I'm impressed by your work, but let's be straight – it was our missile that shot that thing from the sky, so yes, we are in a position to dictate the terms. That said, we want and need your cooperation to make this work."

"And, what, we get a pat on the head for our part in it?"

Patterson was silent.

Desmond leaned forward. "Admiral, I'm quite familiar with your operative policies when it comes to such matters, and your government's propensity for cloaking things under the mantel of "national security" to protect your domain, but over here in Ireland, we're not in that same frame of mind."

"What's your meaning, Desmond," answered the man, a thread of ire evident in his tone.

"We have cooperated with you in this matter, in all regards, except in terms of delivering the craft. That," he waved a hand, "was your un-doing, because you played a few cards behind our backs."

"Come now, Desmond, let's not act like the politicos and throw derisions and point fingers. You and I are made of the same clay, we're military boys, we fight wars and we are strategists in a whole different arena. It was our intelligence people who discovered the girl, and frankly, we would be nowhere with this thing if I hadn't played that card. That said, I can't tell you what we're going to do with it, not yet, because we don't know what we are dealing with."

"How about a simple agreement that you'll share what you find?"

Patterson's head wagged lightly side to side. "I can't negotiate that at this time, Colonel. It's simply not my place. But ..." he cast a quick glance over his shoulder, "there's nothing stopping you from taking as much information as you can between now and the time you deliver that thing to us."

"And you wouldn't consider that a violation of your intellectual property?"

"Personally, I don't give a rat's ass about proprietary rights, Desmond. My job is to get that thing on our ship. Just be smart about it. Don't advertise it. Keep it under your belt and play along with whatever narrative we give the world."

Patterson leaned closer to the computer. "Here are my only terms, Colonel, backed by the President of my country. That thing gets delivered to the Gerald R. Ford by tomorrow night, 18:00 hours local time. Whether or not this girl breaks the computer code."

13

Harry O'Sullivan sat at one end of the table in the officer's lounge of the Largs Bay II.

In all his life he'd only been on two ships – one that sailed from Dublin to England, the other, from Ireland to Iceland. Both times his stomach had proven to him that he was a landlubber, through and through.

The Largs Bay, though not a small ship compared to many, was nothing in comparison to the American behemoth. On the Gerald R. Ford, he barely felt the hand of the Celtic, whereas here, aboard the LB, it rolled and bobbed like a bottle in a frothing sea, and that rhythm was being replicated in his stomach.

He forced his attention back to the conversation at hand, as his daughter related the details of her most recent visit inside the craft.

"It was definitely talking to us," said Kaetlyn.

"How can you be sure it wasn't just a recording of some kind?" asked Lillian.

Serena spoke up. "The hologram, I mean, the face, it turned and looked at us as it spoke, as if it was real, present – it felt sentient, definitely not a recording."

Kaetlyn's head bobbed. "Yeah, definitely sentient. It was talking to us, or at least, trying to."

Raymond Statler spoke. "How do we crack the language it spoke?"

"I don't know," answered Kaetlyn as she looked to Serena. "I suppose we try to focus on getting me to remember it. I don't see any other way."

One of the American computer engineers standing nearby stepped closer. "I have a suggestion," he said looking to his superior.

Lillian Fray nodded her consent.

"Assuming that the computer is an advanced form of Ai, wouldn't it be reasonable to assume that is possesses cloning capability?"

Several other technicians lit up, their eyes growing wider.

The American pulled a mobile phone from his pocket, placed it on the table in front of everyone and pointed. "Right now, if I wanted to, I could clone the information in all your phones with just a simple tap, using anyone of a dozen apps designed to transfer digital information from one device to another, providing they are compatible."

"You think an alien computer system would be compatible to an android?" asked someone.

The man shrugged. "If the laws of electro-magnetics are the same in this alien world, then their computers will be able to interface with ours."

"Get to the point," demanded Corporal Fray of her engineer.

"The point is," he turned to Kaetlyn, "… if you can get that computer to connect to your mobile phone, maybe it can learn about us. Maybe," he paused, "it can even learn our language in a matter of seconds."

14

Wasting no time, they went straight back to the ship and settled into their oversized chairs. "It almost feels familiar now," said Serena with a crooked grin.

"Yeah, if only it wasn't the same place where I died," responded Kaetlyn.

"Does it upset you if I speak so candidly?"

Kaetlyn's head wagged. "Not at all. Your humor helps me to deal with it."

Serena assumed a more professional stance, her face sobering as she spoke. "We haven't had much privacy outside of these sessions. How are you doing?"

A deep sigh escaped Kaetlyn's lips. "I'm okay. Personally, I find the whole thing both exhilarating and exhausting. Every time I go back to my past life, it's like poking into the realm of the dead."

"It's understandable, Kaet. When we set high expectations for ourselves it can be a two-sided sword. The ecstasy of accomplishing our dreams, and the pits of depression if we fail."

"Wow, spoken like a true shrink," responded Kaetlyn as she pulled her mobile phone from her pocket. "Let's hope this works," she said as she placed it face down on the console, and then tapped in the same code as previously.

Once again, the hologram sparked into view, a three-dimensional image of the face, a face that Kaetlyn sensed she knew, but could not yet fully grasp.

It, she, whatever, was definitely the personification of a female of the race, her skin as black as the night sky, silver hair braided like dreadlocks, deep green eyes, and what appeared to be glitter on the skin.

She turned to look directly at Kaetlyn, its lips moving and the strange language reverberating off the interior of the room.

Kaetlyn picked up her phone and held up to the holographic image, and then placed it to her ear, mimicking talking.

For a brief second, the holographic image stopped its strange utterances, then it nodded as if it understood.

Thrilled that she had made a connection, Kaetlyn once again placed the phone face-down on the console and waited.

The hologram faded to nothing.

Minutes passed with nothing happening.

She turned to Serena with a raised brow. "Am I doing something wrong?"

Serena shrugged. "I'm a shrink, Kaet. I wasn't trained on the art of talking to HAL."

Kaetlyn turned back to the console, when suddenly, an intense white light appeared beneath her mobile phone.

In silence, they watched, unsure what was happening. A moment later the light vanished.

"Shite!" exclaimed Kaetlyn. No sooner had the expletive escaped her lips when the hologram appeared once again.

The face turned to look her in the eyes and its voice permeated the room like sweet honey.

"Hello, Kaetlyn."

15

The sound stirred Kaetlyn from her sleep.

She rubbed her eyes and stared at the low ceiling and the austere surroundings of a naval sleeping quarters, embraced by darkness.

The familiar buzz came again.

She fished under the blanked, found her mobile and tapped it. D-TEKT's avatar was waving at her. "You have a message, Kaetlyn" it said.

"From who."

"Shamus Maguire."

"Read it."

A light whistle emitted from the avatar.

> *"Kaetlyn, I hope you don't mind, but I asked Alana for this number. I was worried about you – you disappeared. Are you okay? Can I help you in any way? Please get back to me. Shamus"*

16

News of First Contact, that is, if talking to an alien computer could be categorized as such, spread like wildfire aboard the *Largs Bay.*

Both Colonel Desmond and Lillian Fray wanted to set up cameras inside the ship to record the entire process, but Serena Bohannon insisted on her entitlement as the therapist, to maintain a code of privacy as dictated by her professional protocols, and demanded that she be permitted to perform one final session to confirm that Kaetlyn was entirely satisfied with the results of her therapy before making it a matter of public domain.

They argued against it, but the 29-year-old Irish lass held her ground and walked away uncompromised.

As they approached the alien craft not less than an hour after their last encounter, two dozen anticipatory eyes were fixed on them, like gold diggers waiting to pounce on the chance of plucking nuggets of wealth.

It was no longer a matter of "if" or "when" – the fact is that Kaetlyn had breached the computer's interface, and for the first time in known history, humans were talking with an alien intelligence, even if only, an Ai.

There was a tangible sense of anxiety in the air and written on the faces of every person who quietly watched on.

Colonel Desmond nodded at the two as they approached the portal. "Good luck," he said with a small grin on his lips.

Lillian Fray and several of her team stood off to one side. Her eye caught Kaetlyn's and she too nodded.

Whatever came of this next encounter would no doubt be the start of a new chapter in human history – the question on everyone's minds was *what?*

17

Jessie Adams waited as his superior, RA Patterson, sipped on his coffee and then straightened in his chair, fixing him a firm look.

"Personally, I don't give a rat's ass if this girl makes more progress. It's better for us if she doesn't. Once she's back in our hands, and we have that thing aboard the GRF, we'll be controlling the entire narrative."

Adams nodded. "There is another issue, sir," he said.

"The Russians?"

"Yes. They're not letting up on the story." He handed over a brief.

Patterson read it and then tossed the papers to the desk. "Fucking, Ivan, stirring up shit as always."

Again, Adams nodded.

"So, what's your take from the intelligence angle – why are they holding our feet to the fire?"

"There is only one plausible explanation, sir, the Russians want whatever is inside that ship, whatever knowledge or technology it possesses. They're making it go viral so that in effect, there is no way for us to hush it up."

"I told the President that we needed to launch a counter-campaign of our own, to dead-agent Ivan, but the White House PR machinery is slower than a snail crawling through a pile of shit," declared Patterson with an annoyed huff. "It's not your problem, Adams. Keep your people nosing around, keep me informed on what you find, meanwhile I'll get with my contact at the State Department and see if I can get the sand out of the wheels."

Adam's stood – pausing momentarily.

Patterson noticed his hesitation. "What is it?"

"Sir, I have one other concern."

"Which is?"

"No one seems to be troubled by the fact that those lights are still blinking on that craft."

"What's your meaning, Adams?"

"What if that ship has a transponder, what if it is signaling back to its home world? Have we considered the possibility that its rightful owners might now be alerted to the fact that we have their property and that maybe they might come for it?"

A lopsided grin formed on the Rear Admiral's lips. "You know, I've let my incredulity be stretched a long way over this whole affair, and that's quite an accomplishment for an old sea dog like me. But, having to worry whether ET will show up to claim their missing star ship, that's pushing it too far. Let it go, Adams."

"Yes, sir," said Jessie as he turned and left the office.

Stepping from the building, Jessie looked up at the night sky, countless stars blinked at him from galaxies far far away.

He couldn't shake the disturbing cognitive dissonance that stirred deep inside; *what if they had poked the beast – what then*? he wondered.

18

Shamus stared at the text message he'd just received from Kaetlyn.

He was happy that she had finally opened-up to him, but at the same time, he was completely perplexed by its cryptic content.

What was happening to her? And where was she, and why?

The questions pounded the inside of his skull like a jackhammer.

Finally, he donned his jacket and braced a cold Irish wind as he trudged through the rain. Arriving to the house, soaked and frigid, he knocked on the door. A hall light illuminated as it opened.

"Yes, how can I help you?" asked the woman.

"Ma'am, I'm sorry to disturb you at this time of night. My name is Shamus Maguire. I know your daughter, Kaetlyn."

Claire O'Sullivan pushed the door open, looking him in the face.

"Why are you here, Shamus?" she asked, her brow furrowed with sudden concern.

"I apologize for showing up this way, but I think the lass is in a tight spot."

Her eyes widened. "Come in, you'll catch a cold standing in that rain."

She sat him at the kitchen table, prepared hot tea and some of her fresh-baked scones, and then lowered herself in the chair across from him.

"Now, please, tell me about this matter."

"Ma'am, how familiar are you with your daughter's ..." he paused, searching for the right word.

She smiled. "No need to be coy young man, I am quite aware of my daughter's circumstances."

Shamus felt relieved at hearing this.

"Well, then there's no point in mincing words, is there?" he said. "The truth is that Kaetlyn and I barely know one another. The last time I spoke to her she seemed very harried about something."

"May I ask what you spoke about?"

He flicked a brow. "We share the same experience."

Claire's face betrayed her sudden shock. "Are you saying that you had the same dream, I mean, experience, as her?"

"More or less - yes. I don't know all the circumstances of her dream, just the little that my cousin related to me."

Claire cocked her head.

"Alana is my cousin and Kaetlyn's best friend."

"Oh, small world."

"I've been having this recurring dream for years now. I never talked to anyone about it, until one day I opened up to Alana, and that's when she told me about her friend who had a similar recurring nightmare."

"What did Kaetlyn say about all of this?"

Shamus shrugged. "Our conversation was brief, me talking and her listening ... and ..." he paused, "I don't think I made a very good first impression to be honest. In any case, after I tried to explain my situation to her, she insisted she had to get home and that was the last time we talked before she disappeared on me."

A nervous twitch came over Claire as she hesitated with her next words. "Shamus, my daughter hasn't disappeared. She's ..." she drew in a breath and exhaled, "on a rather bizarre mission if I may say so."

"Doing what?"

"I'm afraid that I have been bonded, for security reasons, and cannot say. I spoke to her yesterday, she seemed fine." She tipped a worried look his way. "You implied that she might be in trouble, what gave you that idea?"

Shamus placed his phone on the table so Claire could read the latest message from Kaetlyn.

Claire leaned back, the furrows on her brow suddenly deepened with worry. "Why would she ask for your help?"

He shook his head. "I don't know. I was hoping you could shed some light on the matter."

She wrenched her hands as her anxiety rose to a new level. "I'll tell you what I know, but you mustn't say a word of it to a soul."

19

Jim Harper sat perched on his elevated captain's chair, providing him a clear view of the entire deck of the Gerald R. Ford far below, as well as a 360-degree view of the horizon, one where the gray clouds had turned into a dark and ominous mass.

"How long before it reaches us?"

"Roughly three hours, Captain," answered the Navigation Officer.

"Force-value?"

"On the Beaufort Scale, it's expected to be at least 9, sir."

Harper drew in a deep breath. Force 9 meant winds upwards of 90 kilometers and high seas. Although his carrier was designed to easily withstand such a gale without any real threat, it still meant they had to batten down the hatches, get all the aircraft off the upper deck, and secure the ship to ride out the storm. It also meant that there was no way possible to transfer the anomaly from the Largs Bay to his ship that day, as ordered, not with waves breaking as high as fifteen feet or more. They'd have to wait until the storm abated, something he knew his superiors would not be happy to hear.

"Issue general quarters," he said to his second in command and get Lillian Fray on the line."

20

After the initial shock of hearing the holographic image greet her in English, Kaetlyn answered. "Hello. What do I call you?"

The face paused, as if considering the question. "You may call me, LIN."

"Does it mean something?"

"It is the equivalent of an acronym in your language and closely approximates my name in the tongue of my creators."

"Who are your creators?" asked Kaetlyn, excitement racing through her veins like electricity.

LIN smiled. "Aren't we jumping the gun, as you people like to say?"

"I don't understand."

"You are not exactly the same individual I remember from my memory banks although I do recognize your signature."

Kaetlyn stole a look at Serena and then turned back to LIN. "Well, it's kind of complicated, LIN. Apparently, I died in a crash, in this very ship ..." she pointed to herself, "and this is the new me."

LIN's face sobered slightly as she weighed up the information. "I see."

"Do you, because I've been tremendously confused about it for years." She turned to Serena. "Serena helped me, using therapy, to figure out that I died on this ship some eighteen years ago."

LIN looked at Serena and then back to Kaetlyn. "That explains the oddity."

"What oddity?"

"That you could not have otherwise accessed this ship, nor its computer system, me, unless the ship's security system recognized your signature."

Kaetlyn's brow furrowed. "You mean the code I punch in each time we entered?"

LIN's head wagged lightly. "No, your signature, Kaetlyn. Every individual has a unique frequency or vibration, the differences are subtle, barely perceptible, but to the ship's sensors, and to my software, they are as clear as night and day."

Serena spoke. "Are you saying that we emit a unique vibration different from others?"

LIN smiled. "It's a poor use of terms, but in an over-simplified sense, yes. You are, as you've obviously realized through the therapy, non-corporeal in nature."

"You mean, we're spirits."

LIN raised a brow. "I find your language to be terribly lacking in this regard. You do not have the proper terms to define who you are beneath that façade you wear."

"Who are we?"

"You are, to put it simply, an unquantifiable entity, a non-physicality, but one with immense potential. In the same way that your world uses finger prints or DNA to identify people, we use the vibratory signature emitted by each life force to indentify them, as opposed to physical form."

"You mean like an electronic frequency?" asked Serena.

"That is a fair anology, but not an accurate platform. The life force, which is you, in essence, is not a *something*; it cannot be measured on a level of physicality like electromagnetic waves as you know them to be."

"So, it's something entirely different?"

LIN nodded. "Yes, of course, because life essence is the source of everything – it is something of its own and quite superior to the physicality around it. We utilize special sensors to detect the subliminal vibration that resonates from you, which is why you were able to enter the ship despite the *new you*, as you said.

"That explains why others have not been able to replicate the access code."

"Correct. No one, but the crew of this ship, can enter it. As the other crew members have expired, that seems to mean that you are the only person remaining with security clearance to enter and go as you please."

"Well," began Kaetlyn with a flick of her brow at Serena, "I guess that throws a wrench into one of the theories of our origin."

LIN raised a brow. "I am not familiar with all aspects of your culture, not yet at least."

"A lot of people in our world still believe that we all came from one matrix - created by the hand of some god – as if we are all just pieces of some whole."

LIN smiled. "Similar belief systems exist in other galactic systems, but most of them have come to realize that their existence is not predicated in such beliefs."

Kaetlyn's mind was exploding with questions. "Gawd, I want to talk to you for days and pick your brains."

"Strange term, but I think I get your meaning," responded LIN.

Kaetlyn was momentarily silent as she considered her next question. "Can you tell us what happened, why the ship crashed?"

LIN nodded. "I can. And better yet, I can show you," at which a parallel hologram appeared with a lucid visual projection, like a film. "I record everything that goes on in the ship. At the time, as you can see from this recording of the bridge, yourself and the other two members of the crew had become aware that the ship was in danger." The visual shifted to the viewscreen, showing the approaching object. "It appears that we underestimated the technology of this culture. One of their satellites fired a weapon at our ship, and, as you can see … it exploded nearby."

Kaetlyn and Serena watched as the visual rocked and suddenly went blank. A strange sensation pressed against Kaetlyn's chest, as if reexperiencing the pain all over again.

"So, we died?"

"Yes, unfortunately. Your crew was killed by the impact of the crash the ensued when we struck water."

"And me?"

"You survived for a brief period. In fact, it was you who directed me to camouflage the ship and hide it from detection."

"What was my role on the ship?"

LIN smiled. "You are, or were, the Captain and head science officer. As to the other members," she flashed an image of each to the screen, "one was the ship's pilot, the other was the chief engineer, a specialist in planetary terraforming." She paused. "He was also your mate."

Kaetlyn felt a lump in the base of her throat as a wall of emotion suddenly unleashed itself from some encysted bubble. It took her like a storm, as tears suddenly welled in her eyes.

"I'm sorry if this upsets you, Kaetlyn," said LIN.

Kaetlyn wiped her face, trying to stem the flow as she did. "It's okay."

LIN continued.

"The explosion didn't compromise the structural integrity of the ship, but it did render my navigational system inert at the time. I lost control of the ship and we plummeted into the atmosphere, crashed into a body of water, and using what little reserve power I could muster from the reserve banks, we were able to resort to emergency tactics to hide the ship from detection."

"In solid rock?!" said Serena with a raised brow.

LIN smiled.

Kaetlyn composed herself, quelling the sea of emotion that had been stirred inside. "Where did we come from? Who sent us? Why?

LIN answered. "You have many questions, and I have many answers for you which I will happily provide, but let us first consider why you were sent here?"

"I don't have a clue, LIN."

"You truly do not remember the purpose, the task you and your crew were meant to perform?"

Kaetlyn's head wagged. "No."

"LIN cocked her head. "Your mission was to terraform the planet."

"Terraform it, why?"

"Because, Kaetlyn, unless circumstances have drastically changed since your death, this planet was listed as a Category Five."

"Meaning what?"

"A CAT-5 world is one on the brink of a cataclysm, and in the case of Earth, that disaster is being brought about by global warming; and unless that trend is reversed, many or most of its inhabitants, whether human or animal, will largely perish in the wake of events to come."

Book Three

1

Dr. Beckett sat next to a string of notable people, at a table that stretched nearly half the length of the stage.

Luminaries from not only his scientific circles in New Zealand, but no less than ten other nations, including Australia, Japan, Germany, Sweden, Canada, Britain, China, Russia and America – were in attendance.

Facing him was a crowd-filled hall, easily five hundred people, including media.

The precursor to this gathering in Auckland, New Zealand, was a press-release by the BBC, headlined: *"Ross Ice Shelf split is imminent, announces Auckland research team."*

The Chairwoman of the *University of Auckland's Institute of Marine Science,* Leslie Fontane, sat three seats down, with her hands neatly clasped before her as her eyes remained fixed on the burgeoning crowd. Beckett sensed that while her body language said one thing, her mind, like his, was in quite another place.

Finally, the doors closed, and Leslie Fontane approached the podium.

"Thank you all for coming to this rather impromptu brief. The matter at hand is of course quite dire, so in the interest of permitting us to deliver a full and vivid presentation, I ask that all questions be kept to the end when we open the floor for such."

She smiled, amiably, yet reservedly.

"Some months ago, our department of the University launched a DSM, a fancy term which means *Drone-Surveillance-Mission*. Essentially, we sent out several drones to systematically survey the entire surface of the Ross Ice Shelf. The drones were equipped with the most advanced spectrometers, capable of reading to depths of several meters, providing not only a 2-dimensional picture of RIS, but also a 3-dimensional one, revealing what is going on beneath the surface to a limited degree."

The room was silent, pin-drop silent as she paused.

"As you may well know, The Ross Ice Shelf is the largest ice shelf of the Antarctica, measuring roughly 500,809 square kilometers, or 193,363 square miles for those of you still measuring physicality by old-world systems," she paused to let the chuckles abate. "RIS varies in height, in some places it measures 50 meters above the waterline – however, as we all know, 90% of its depth is below sea level." She paused, gathering her thoughts. "The images, and the information which we received from the drones took some time to analyze, but when we did, we discovered a very troubling picture." She motioned her hand to an operator who dimmed the lights as a large wall-screen illuminated behind her. "These images, taken at that time, show what appears to be a fissure along its surface. It's difficult to get a perspective on the proportions, but when those images were laid out, the picture it formed showed that there was, very likely, a massive rupture – one extending along this line," she traced it with a laser pen, "starting somewhere in the southwest corner, here, and heading northeast, possibly as long as a couple hundred kilometers." She paused, letting it sink in.

"We debated the matter for several weeks; some argued that it was not a fissure at all but the symptoms of pressure points within the ice field. However, in the end, the consensus was the same – the phenomenon was far too startling to leave to speculation, and potentially an omen of something worse." She turned to Dr. Beckett. "We dispatched Dr. Beckett, who heads our R&D department, and a team of specialists, to analyze the RIS at select coordinates where the imagery seemed most conspicuous. His team returned just last week, and after exhaustive review, well..." she smiled tremulously, "I won't take the thunder from his brief. Doctor..." she conceded with a nod.

Beckett took the podium. He had no notes. No papers. Just a somber look on his face which betrayed the message he was about to deliver.

"Thank you, Leslie."

He fixed his gaze on the audience. "For once, the media got it right with their headlines. The Ross Ice Shelf is indeed melting ladies and gentlemen, and the rift captured by the DSM, is a fact, a shocking one."

He paused. "I will provide you with all the details of our mission, and I will be happy to answer any questions too; but let me frame this talk appropriately - make no mistake about it – the rift is irreversible at this point."

A small rumble emitted from the audience. Beckett raised his hand.

"The rate of melt, is beyond repair, no matter what we do in the foreseeable future. The sea water, beneath the Antarctic has been warming. We knew there was a threshold, we just didn't know for sure if it was a 1.5 rise in global temperatures, or higher, but now we know without a doubt that below the surface of RIS, and presumably the rest of the Antarctic, the ice has been melting away at an increasing rate." He trained a somber face at them.

"The implications of this event are clear. Ocean levels will inevitably rise quite markedly. Coastal areas around the globe will be flooded, affecting nearly 50% of the world's population and massive tracts of farmland which feed them, and us. Weather patterns will change dramatically, affecting food production and other aspects of our lives, even the species we depend upon for our survival. Mother Earth has just played her ace card and we are facing an event which goes beyond apocalyptic. In fact, if the results of our research are accurate, and I have no reason to doubt them, the impact of polar melting could result in an extinction event for many or most of us."

The auditorium exploded in a turmoil of voices.

2

Leaving the relative safety of the alien ship, as ironic as that sounded, Kaetlyn and Serena stepped out onto the deck of the Largs Bay II as a violent wind smacked into them like a sumo wrestler.

They went directly to the officer's lounge where they met Colonel Desmond and Lillian Fray who sat anxiously in wait, and plunked down across from them, poured some hot coffee and took a sip to warm their bellies.

"So ...? asked Lillian with a raised brow, her excitement oozing out of every pore of her face.

"Well, it appears that we were sent to save the world," said Kaetlyn with an impish grin.

Desmond lowered his head, leveling his eyes at her. "Save the world?"

Kaetlyn nodded.

"From what?"

"Our stupid shite, as usual," she answered. She eyed the ship through the window. "Our mission was to stop global warming, if possible."

Lillian Fray twisted her head with a confused look. "You're saying that an alien race sent you guys here to stop global warming?"

Kaetlyn shrugged. "I know, mental right!? ET is supposed to be a violent and rapacious bunch, intent on our demise, but it's quite the opposite; they wanted to save our sorry arses."

"I don't understand, why global warming?" asked Colonel Desmond.

"I don't have all the details yet," tiredly responded Kaetlyn, "but according to their drones and their technology about habitable planets, like ours, there is a threshold beyond which the planet resets itself."

"But, why would they even care?" asked Lillian, now ultimately fascinated.

"I don't know. I don't know if they are our secret landlords, if they have another agenda, or if they're just a nice bunch of altruistic people."

The room was silent for a time, only the sound of a howling wind could be heard.

"How exactly is this supposed to happen?" asked Desmond.

"You mean, stop global warming?"

He nodded.

"She didn't get into the details yet," answered Kaetlyn. "And frankly, I was so exhausted after listening to her, that I needed a break before continuing."

A smile formed on Lillian's lips. "You keep referring to this computer as a she, why?"

Serena answered. "The holographic image is that of a female."

"How can you be so sure – she's an alien?"

Serena tipped her head at Lillian. "Oh, I think a woman of one race could easily spot a female of another."

Kaetlyn stepped into the fray. "The physiological parallels were undeniably female in nature. Her eyes, the shape of her body, the whole package ..." she paused, "not to mention the fact that she had breasts."

"Well, I guess that settles that issue," interceded Desmond with a grin.

"And she's black, like me, with long silver hair. Quite stunning in fact," added Kaetlyn.

"So, you spoke nothing of technology or science?"

Kaetlyn's head wagged. "No. With the introductions now more or less out of the way, I think LIN will be quite happy to answer my questions about how exactly we were meant to accomplish our task."

Colonel Desmond leaned back in his chair. His mind was fast at work. The deadline from Norman Patterson, to deliver the anomaly by 18:00 hours this very day, was weighing heavily on him. He needed information. He needed Kaetlyn to dig into that computer, and fast.

"Are you prepared to go back in there soon?" He asked.

Kaetlyn nodded. "Soon as I eat and take a short rest, yes, of course."

"Good…" he answered when the door to the lounge opened and a cold wind washed in as Raymond Statler stepped in.

"Sir, we've got a gale com'in our way."

"How big?" asked Desmond.

"At least a Force 9 – but more likely to be a 10."

"When?"

"Two hours, maybe sooner."

"Fuck," the expletive escaped his lips. "What does the Captain say?"

"He wants to take us back to the naval yard until it passes," answered Statler as he eyed the anomaly on the deck. "We didn't prepare for this contingency, sir. We strapped it down for a one-hour trip, during calm seas, not a gale."

3

The storm clouds roiled and blackened the sky, like smoke spewing out from a massive fire as the storm hit them faster, sooner and harder than expected.

Winds surged over 60 kilometers, driving towering waves that pounded into the Largs Bay with angry determination to break it apart.

Hail pelted into the window of the bridge, like machine-gun fire, obliterating his view of the ocean ahead.

"What's taking so long?" growled the Captain into the receiver.

"Sir, the aft anchor is snagged," answered his Supercargo.

"Fook me!" he exclaimed as he turned to his First Officer. "Get out there and get that fook'n anchor up – now!"

Minutes passed as the pounding waves continued their assault and the moan of the wind became the roar of some bestial juggernaut.

"Sir, it's stuck. We can't get reel it up," announced the First Mate over the receiver."

The Captain's mind was fast at work. A snagged anchor, in this storm, would make them a sitting duck.

"Cut it loose!" he ordered, thinking to himself that losing an anchor was certainly better than losing his ship.

The ship heaved, like a cork, as white caps drafted as deep as ten meters from crest to trough as the storm grew.

The crew desperately fought to release the chain, but the sea fought back even harder, smashing into its hull, spinning it like a top, as it pivoted around the snagged anchor, while tossing men across its deck like mere chips.

Finally, the chain, unable to sustain the dynamics of a mult-ton ship pulling at its links, snapped free of its linchpin and the ship lurched upwards, like a rubber band suddenly released.

The Largs Bay groaned as it fought the forces of nature, heaving up and down, prow to aft, like a glass bottle caught in a violent stream.

Raymond Statler steadied himself against the rail, waiting for a momentary lapse in the violent pitch, just long enough for him to skid across the deck and catch a flailing rope.

Hail and rain pelted into his face, but with the help of another crew member he managed to secure the tether, a meager restraint around the anomaly, before another wave washed over the ship, sending them both crashing against the rail.

Soaked to the bone, bruised and shaking from the cold, Statler held on, waiting for the ship to right itself so they could continue the process of securing the alien craft. He knew that the momentum, the steep cants and the violent attack of the waves, was a disaster waiting to happen.

The wail of the wind, the roar of the sea, was suddenly accented by another sound.

He turned to look at the anomaly and watched in horror as the straps holding it to the deck, strained and screamed, followed by a loud crack which echoed into the night as one after another snapped away, like mere string holding an elephant.

"Get back!" he screamed as the ship plummeted yet again into a deep trough, skidding downward like a rollercoaster; and in that instant, they heard the screeching sound that caused each and every one of them to freeze where they stood.

4

Lillian Fray stood in one corner of the officer's lounge, gripping a hand rail, trying as she did, to prevent herself from being tossed across the room.

Her eyes were transfixed on the maelstrom just beyond the window, as men and women struggled against a raging sea.

She pressed the sat-phone to her ear as she waited for the Captain of the Gerald R. Ford to answer. He needed to know just how serious things were at this end.

Just then, the ship's prow rose high up into the air, riding the crest of an immense wave. Instead of breaking through, it teetered on the crest and then it began to slide backwards, falling downward into a trough that looked as ominous and terrifying as anything she had ever witnessed in her naval career.

She braced herself for the impact she knew was coming.

The ship plowed into the sea, tossing her into a nearby wall, her head striking it hard and painfully, but that pain was nothing compared to the shock she experienced as she righted herself and watched in horror as the anomaly broke free of its restraints and skidded across the deck of the ship, smashing through the rail and then disappeared into the maws of a furious sea.

5

As medics tended to the injured, and the storm continued to rage outside, Colonel Desmond, Raymond Statler, members of his team and the American contingent, squeezed into the crew dining area.

Their clothes were soaked, and the cold touch of the wind and sea still shook them to the core.

"We've got a shite-bag of trouble here, lads and lasses," began Desmond, feeling a surreal sense of shock at having just lost quite possibly one of the greatest finds in the history of the race.

Lillian Fray, still teetering from the blow to her head, eased her way toward them as she spoke. "I just got off the sat-phone with Captain Harper," she said as she eased into a chair next to Statler. "The GRF has several submersible drones which can be deployed to help locate the anomaly. Probably all we can safely deploy at this time, at least until that storm abates."

Desmond cocked his head. "I'll have to discuss the matter with my superiors."

Lillian nodded. "I realize we're still in Irish territorial waters, but we shouldn't hesitate, Colonel. This storm could easily push that thing kilometers away, or for matter, deep into the trenches where it could take weeks or even months to find."

6

The Alexander Nevsky, a *Borei Class Russian Nuclear Ballistic Submarine*, measuring 170 meters long and carrying a crew of 130 men and women, cruised below the surface of the Celtic Sea, while a storm raged above, pitching towering mountains of waves that ravaged anything audacious enough to brave it.

Captain, Pavel Ivanov, stood silently watching the screen as several dots were reflected on the range-finder, a highly sophisticated radar sensor that could detect shapes, both small and large, within a radius of several kilometers both above and around the Nevsky.

One dot, he knew, was the American battleship, the Gerald R. Ford. Two other dots represented smaller fishing vessels. And the fourth dot was the Largs Bay, the Irish military ship. Identifying vessels was easy, because transponders provided frequencies, codes in fact, which any ship, or sub, could utilize to identify others in their vicinity.

Deployed from the North Sea, its usual haunting grounds, the Nevsky and its crew had a new task assigned to them, one which had no precedents.

Russian military intelligence had picked up communications over the past several days, showing that the Irish and the Americans had discovered an unidentified object of some kind, probably the very one the Americans had lost years before.

Pavel's mandate was to stay out of range, to observe and to await further instructions. What exactly those orders were to be, he had no idea, but right now, they had to skirt the edges, ghosting the other ships, while hopefully remaining undetected.

"Sir!" snapped a communicator to attention next to him. He handed Pavel a print-out.

The Captain read it and then turned to the pilot. "Set a course for these coordinates," he said as he pushed the paper into the man's hands.

Pavel's head reflexively bobbed, a gesticulation that afflicted him whenever faced with a serious problem; and even though he had no idea what their task was to be, the very fact that he was sitting near the seabed, with the largest and most deadly aircraft carrier in the American fleet hovering above him, suggested that his new task was anything but trivial.

7

The matter of the "missing anomaly" had now struck a chord, a discordant one at that, amongst senior officials in Washington – the President being one of them.

Up until now, the matter, which seemed a little far-fetched for the tastes of most, had been left in the hands of NMIC and the Captain of the Gerald R. Ford. It seemed a simple enough operation. Get delivery of the object from the Irish and then move it to a secure location in the naval yards in Virginia, and then let the think-tank people take it from there.

The matter was now complicated with news of its loss. Moreover, and the very catalyst for heightened concern, was the fact that a Russian sub had been spotted in the area, and while those were international waters, it posed a sudden threat.

The President himself called for an emergency meeting in the Oval Office.

Rear Admiral Norman Patterson entered the room, ringed with numerous military officials and suits, feeling somewhat abashed that the operation had suddenly escalated to a crisis.

The President trained them with a displeased look before breaking a somber air. "This whole business of recovering this "thing" was never particularly high on my agenda. I have more pressing matters here at home. However, when I heard that we just lost it …" he cast a tentative glance toward Patterson, "and that the Russians are prowling those waters, it seemed pretty clear to me that we couldn't let this fall into their hands."

He paused, shaking his head with a certain manifest disbelief still imprinted on his face. "Whatever that thing is, whatever knowledge or technology it might contain, it cannot be absconded by Ivan. Is that clear?"

All heads nodded.

"Now," he turned to Norman, "I'm not pointing fingers, Norm, and I realize you didn't exactly anticipate this storm, but since NMIC has the most insight, I want you to sit down with all these people and stir up a plan that ensures we get that thing back in our hands, and fast."

Patterson nodded. "Yes, Mr. President."

The President stood. "And one more thing. No incidents. No shots fired. Nothing. This is a race, and whoever wins gets the prize, but I'll be damned if I'm going to lose to them."

8

Even before the gale had subsided, submersible drones had been deployed by the *Gerald R. Ford*, as well as another contingent of drones in the air above.

Following a pre-programmed matrix, each SD moved to its prescribed coordinates and started systematically scanning for signs of the anomaly. It would be a difficult and tedious process, and for obvious reasons. The object was dark in color, not easily distinguishable, especially now that old man sea had stirred up sediment into a soupy mix, and particularly if it had sunk to the bottom.

Moreover, the Celtic ranged in depths as much as 300 meters in parts, with rising sand ridges and yawning troughs. In effect, the anomaly, presumably having sunk, could be wedged deep in some dark trough, or hidden in a sandy ridge, or lying hundreds of meters in the pitch black.

Captain Harper, under direct orders from his superior at Naval Command in Virginia, had no delusions about the task now facing them. It wasn't like tracking a military asset which was usually equipped with a transponder. This was an alien craft – so all bets were off. It would be a time-consuming job gridding out hundreds of square miles of sea and combing each square inch of it.

To the southeast, the horizon was no longer a black singularity, as it had been during the storm. A crimson line now announced the coming of dawn, and finally, the passing of the tempest.

"Get Lillian Fray on the line," he said to his communicator.

Moments later they were connected through a at-com.

"How's your head?" he asked, seeing the large bruise on one side.

Lillian offered a transient smile. "I was dropped several times as baby – seems to have prepared me for the occasional bump."

Harper nodded without a smile. "What's the current status over there?"

"Desmond has a search team in play, smaller boats equipped with sonar, two reconnaissance planes and three choppers. He's determined to find it."

"Damn, I hate to point fingers," began Harper, "but they really fucked the duck on this one - not having that thing secured properly."

She raised a brow. "In their defense, sir, the anomaly was never intended to stay on the deck of this ship for more than an hour before being delivered to us. The storm caught everyone off-guard and they didn't have the proper restraints on-board for something that big. And..." she paused with a shake of her head, "Murphy's Law struck once again."

"You mean the anchor?"

She nodded.

"We couldn't see it from here because of the storm, but my radar people told me that at one point the Largs Bay spun nearly 360 degress on that tether."

"Yeah, it was pretty frightening actually."

"And what about the girl?"

"She's resting in her quarters."

Harper leaned closer to the screen. "My orders, directly from the Admiral, are to retrieve that thing, without complications and get it aboard the GRF. They also want the girl back here in preparation for when we recover it."

"In other words, we move the entire operation to our end."

"Exactly. We're not leaving it in their hands a minute longer."

She nodded. "I understand, sir."

"One more thing, Corporal. Ivan has a sub cruising these waters. No doubt, they've heard the news. Tell Colonel Desmond to double-time the search at his end."

9

Kaetlyn hung over the rail of the *Largs Bay*, staring down at the sea as waves, now reduced to a fraction of their height during the storm, gently lapped against the side of the ship.

A frosty wind braced her face, blowing her long black hair into a trail behind her head.

It felt good to be outside the cabin, to see the sky, to smell the sea, and to sense freedom again. Being cooped up for hours during the gale was as close to claustrophobic as she had ever experienced.

She sensed that now, more than ever, while she still had a chance, that she had to do something. She knew when they found it, that everything would go into overdrive. The Americans would press the issue and get the her shipt aboard their carrier, and no doubt, they would demand her presence too. There would be no more negotiations or deals – just enforced property rights.

More convinced than ever that she had to protect the contents of that ship, her ship, from being monopolized, and now, vaguely aware of the mission which she and her comrades had been sent to accomplish, she simply could not let it fall into the wrong hands.

A light footfall caught her ear as Serena slipped up to the rail, her freckled white face reddened from exposure to the cold and her auburn hair flailing about her head. She pulled the collar of her jacket up to block the cold.

"So, how you hold'n up, Kaet?"

Kaetlyn sighed. "You're the mind-doctor, what do you think?"

"I think you're haunted by something else now."

Kaetlyn turned to face her.

Serena continued. "When we started our sessions, you were trying to figure out the nature of your dream. I think that haunting is over and has been replaced by a new one."

Kaetlyn nodded. "And what would you recommend for it?"

"Well," she tipped her head into the wind, "I can't use therapy to fix it. I could subscribe some pills to numb you – but then you'd refuse those." An impish grin formed on her lips. "I'm probably putting myself way-out on a limb for even suggesting this, but you can always go public about it."

"Meaning?"

"If you really want to protect the intellectual property contained in that ship, and whatever other secrets it may offer up, then maybe your only option is to make it impossible for the Americans, or even our own government, to cover it up."

"But, how? I'm stuck on this ship?"

"What about Shamus? You told me he wants to help you, right."

10

Prowling through the lower trenches of the Celtic seabed, The *Alexander Nevsky* resembled a massive shark in search of its next meal.

Captain Pavel Ivanov and his crew at the helm, were glued to the screens, checking and rechecking every shape that might reveal the presence of the sunken treasure.

Since beginning this phase of their task, Moscow had upgraded it to top priority, all of which meant one thing to Pavel – he couldn't fuck it up.

Hours had passed, with strained and tired eyes following the gridded matrix of this subterranean world. On several occasions, he had ordered the submarine turned back in the direction of some questionable shape, but each time, as they glided near, disappointment set in.

The concern was that the storm above had abated, and doubtless it was that both the Americans and the Irish would intensify their search.

As Captain, the burden of responsibility was not only in securing "*the asset*", it was critical not to be spotted in the process.

"Sir," a man pointed to a screen. Pavel turned to look. Whatever it was, it was large, but it was also partially buried in the side of a trough.

"Take us in closer and deploy a drone," he commanded as he rubbed his tired eyes, hoping that this would not be a waste of time.

11

A blustery wind ripped into Shamus as he stood on the cliffside, overlooking the sea.

Angry dark clouds swept across the sky, but there was a patch of blue in the distance, the precursor, he hoped, to better weather.

Throughout the night he could think of little else than Kaetlyn.

Despite their brief encounter, Shamus was certain that what they had shared so many years ago, still transcended everything, as if love itself could permeate the very dimension of time.

The question was, did Kaetlyn feel the same?

He turned from the cliffside and began his trek back home, feeling an apprehension gripping him, a sense that all was not well with Kaetlyn.

As he stepped through the door of his home, his mobile phone buzzed. The message read:

> *Thanks for offering to help me. I can't talk over the phone for fear that someone might be able to pick up the conversation. I am sending you an encrypted file from a secure website. Use my name to open the file. Kaetlyn.*

12

Like a flock of gulls in search of fish, the Irish *AW139* Navy helicopters glided over the sea, each working a quadrant in search of the lost prize.

High above, surveilling a broader section of the Celtic, was the Irish *CASA CN-235* – a twin-prop Naval aircraft used for maritime patrol and reconnaissance.

Several other crafts were situated equidistant between where the Largs Bay was anchored, and the coastal region of southwest Ireland.

Colonel Desmond anxiously watched from the aft section of the ship as his small army tackled the problem of finding a relative toothpick in a haystack. He turned to look at the marks left on the deck of the ship, where the anomaly had literally torn free of its tethers and then skidded through the railing into the gaping maws of the sea.

Raymond Statler and several of his team stood off at a distance. Statler looked worn and tired, probably just as exhausted as Desmond now felt.

He couldn't help but think whether this entire matter was an omen. He wasn't particularly religious nor a church-going man, but maybe a higher power was telling them to let this thing go – maybe the human race wasn't ready for the secrets it harbored.

Then again, his pragmatic side argued in favor of doing everything possible to recover it, because certain it was that if neither he or the American's found, the Russians probably would.

He shook his head and returned his gaze to the sea.

Somewhere out there, an alien craft had sunk, and a Russian sub was crawling the seabed in search of it.

He prayed that the alien craft had sunk in Irish waters – but he knew better than to get his hopes up too high, especially when Murphy's Law was tapping him on the shoulder at that very moment.

13

Shamus responded to Kaetlyn's message and within the hour he received an answer from her that was several pages long, providing explicit details on what she had recalled from her therapy, and her dialogue with the computer, LIN.

Not only was it shocking, he suddenly felt freed of that subtle, yet always present dark visitor that had lurked nearby all these years, forcing itself on him more nights than he could remember, taunting and poking at him, challening him to penetrate the obscurity of his subconscious mind and reconcile the mysteries it held. Moreover, he now understood why he felt compelled to find her – that cognitive awareness that if he was here, alive in this place, then she must be too. And he was right – Kaetlyn is, or was, his soul mate aboard that ship.

Compelled by her desperate call for help, Shamus promptly emailed the Breaking News Editor at *The Irish Times*.

An hour later, he received a call.

"Is this Shamus Maguire?"

"It is."

"I'm Donovan O'Neil. I got your email. This better not be a prank."

"It's not."

14

Pavel and his crew watched as the drone moved closer, its camera zooming in and then scanning laterally along the length of the object.

"Stop," commanded Pavel, "go back."

The drone operator swiveled its camera to the left.

"There," pointed the Captain, "go in closer."

"What the hell is that?" he said in a hushed voice, as they stared at something blinking, on and off, a barely perceptible glow coming from beneath the sand."

Feeling a sense of growing excitement, that maybe they had just found the asset, Captain Pavel ordered a team to go out and investigate.

15

Lillian Fray rubbed the tender spot where her forehead and the ship's bulkhead had met the night of the storm.

"Still hurts, does it?" asked Desmond.

She nodded, then took another sip on the Irish whiskey he had provided. "This certainly helps to numb the pain," she grinned.

"Aye, it does. Did ya know that whiskey was invented by us, and the Scots, but us first," he winked, "to help endure the hellish weather we have."

"Sounds like a tall tale, but I'll buy it for now."

Desmond leaned back, taking a casual pose as he spoke. "Whilst I know we're players on two different sides, you and I don't have to be distanced. In the end, it's not going to be us that makes the final decisions about that thing, anyhow," he paused.

He rolled his eyes around the inside of the officer's lounge and rested them back on her.

"Ever since I got my first pubic hairs," he grinned, attempting some humor to lighten her mood, "... I wanted to be in the Navy. My granddad and dad were both sailers. Loved hearing their tales, some of them tall no doubt since sailers love to spin a good yarn. I started off in Scouting Ireland, ya know, a club like your Boy Scouts in America, then I joined a youth sailing club to earn my sailers stripes, all with my sights set on a career defending and protecting the realm." He sighed. "And yet, after over twenty years at this game, no matter how high I manage to scale the ladder, there's always someone above me who calls the final shots."

His head shook. "If it'd been my call, Lillian, I would have kept that bloody thing in our naval yard and eventually popped its cherry, and not all this nonsense we've been put through, and now," he cast a look to the sea, "losing it to the Ol'man himself." He grinned. "How's that going to read in the history books, uh?"

"I understand your frustration," responded Lillian with a slight look of despondency. "When I got these," she flicked an eye to her shoulder bars, "I figured I had become someone important, but I'm so far down the pecking order that I'm still just a drop in the water."

Desmond topped up their glasses and then raised his to the air. "Well then, here's to fook'n drops of water, Sláinte," he exclaimed as he gulped the whiskey away.

Lillian followed suit, her face screwed up as it burned her throat.

"So ..." he tipped his head at her, "how about it, let's work together, you and I, and leave the final decisions to the brass, eh?"

"Off the record?" she asked with a raised brow.

"Off the record."

She stole a glance at the diming light of a twilight sky. "It's irony, isn't it?"

Desmond raised a questioning brow.

"We've stereotyped ET as the evil villain in our plots; *mankind against the terrible invaders from space*; and yet, here they are, taking the high road as watchdogs over us, making sure we don't destroy our world."

"Maybe they think it's their world?"

"Maybe they're our secret landlords," she chimed back with a shrug, as visions of her own encounter, so many years ago, flashed into her mind. "We're so arrogant as a race. It's utterly ridiculous to assume we are alone in a universe this big, and yet, so many want to believe that's the case. We're just one species on an island of billions. And yet ..." she turned her eye to him, "we're fighting over property rights to something that really doesn't belong to us."

"I wondered the same thing, maybe it's not ours to take."

Her head wagged as a look of worry coursed her face. "We haven't even considered the possibility that its rightful owners might not agree with the intrusion. What if they decide to come for it."

16

Donovan O'Neil, the Breaking News Editor at *The Irish Times*, sat within the confines of his small cubicle, staring out the window at *McCabes Deli* across the street. He needed a coffee, a strong one at that, to combat his most recent call with Shamus Maguire, who had provided even more details about the alleged story, one which sounded as bizarre as any he had heard in his eighteen-year career.

Being the frontline editor he tended to get a lot of hot tips from people, some as bizarre and farfeteched as imaginable, such as Mermaid sightings off the coast, serpents, dragons, ghosts stalking people, banshees and more – but never this, never an alien ship and the story that went with it.

The only reason he had responded to the lad's email, being one of hundreds he received in any one day, was his statement that he had information about an event that had happened eighteen years before, in fact, something that Donovan himself had investigated in his first year as a novice journalist, but which had come to nothing.

Back then, he had investigated reports of naval ships, off the coast of Ireland, allegedly engaged in a military exercise, which in fact, was clearly a cover-up for something else. Something big, involving three American naval vessels, and several of the Irish flotilla.

As he Sherlocked the trail, he came across a weather-beaten fisherman who had been out on the Celtic one early morning, and over a shared bottle of Irish whiskey, the man related having seen something streaking down from the sky and plunging into the ocean.

Donovan could have dismissed it entirely as a hoax, but the harried look in the man's face, the tone in his words, and the shaking of his hands were testimony that only a fool could dream up such an account. His story, along with local talk of hundreds of dead fish washing up on the shore the day after the fisherman reported his sighting, convinced him that something else was going on – something the military was hiding. And yet, after several months, the ships disappeared and along with it disappeared the story.

Sparked with renewed interest, he wondered what to do with this latest tip. He had nothing but the word of this lad, Shamus, and some mystery girl whom he would not divulge information about, but who apparently, like him, had remembered some past-life experience involving an alien craft, which had crashed back then, and had recently been excavated from a cliffside near Kilcrohane.

If it was true, it would be the most important news release in modern history, if not the history of mankind, for it would change countless paradigms and theories about existence, creation and the nature of the Universe.

How could he prove it? That was the question. And without proof, his editor and chief would kill the story before he got past page one.

17

A cacophony of engines cut the sky above as Kaetlyn and Serena settled into their normal routine, this time, inside Kaetlyn's cabin. Small as it was, she could stretch out on her bunk while Serena sat nearby.

Nobody seemed very concerned with Kaetlyn and for that she was happy and relieved.

"So, has your stomach settled since the storm?" asked Serena, her usual positivity reflected in her bright eyes, reddish cheeks and a sea of freckles that somehow gave her a girlish look.

"I'm fine." Her eyes drifted about the room, as if distracted by something.

"Fine or "fine"?" Serena lightly challenged with humor in her voice.

Kaetlyn sighed. "What if they don't find the ship? Or worse, what if the Russians find it first?" She looked up at Serena. "I overheard Colonel Desmond saying that there was a Russian sub nearby and he was very concerned about not letting it fall into their hands?" Her head wagged as a somber look washed over her. "I have to talk to LIN. I have to know how we were meant to stop global warming."

"But, surely, you don't still feel responsible for the mission?"

"Why not? Just because we died doesn't mean the mission died. And besides," she cast a worried eye to the sea. "Our world is dying, Serena. Despite the repudiations of the elitists and one-percenters who don't give a shite except their bloody bank accounts, the planet is warming up, and it's predictably heading us for global disaster in ways we have never experienced in known history."

Serena raised a questioning brow.

"I know, you're thinking that I've gone from being delusional to some hero-obsession; the eighteen-year-old girl who's going to save the world – right?"

Serena tilted her head to one side. "Actually, I love Marvel comic characters," she smiled disarmingly. "But no, I wasn't thinking that at all. Fact is, I think it's high time that women stepped in and cleaned up the mess created by our patriarchal dickheads, but that said, I'm concerned that you might be expecting too much of yourself. You've already accomplished what most people thought was impossible. You've even taken the "if" out of past-lives, proving beyond reasonable doubt that they are a fact, and not just hypothetical or paranormal phenomena."

"I appreciate the vote of confidence, but what if the narrative were different, would you have the same perspective?"

"I don't get your meaning."

Kaetlyn turned to her. "Well, let's say for example that the ship had nuclear warheads on board, or some weapon of mass destruction – something that could kill off millions? What if I was the only one who could disarm it or stop it from happening, even now? Wouldn't that be within my moral purview?"

Serena acquiesced with a nod.

Kaetlyn drifted for a moment before speaking. "Remember, when we first started our sessions and I told you that I have had this feeling of guilt shadowing me for most of my life?"

"I do."

Kaetlyn sighed as she looked at the other with pleading eyes. "I may have died, Serena, but my mission didn't, and for first time in my life I understand the source of that haunting guilt. Every day my subconscious mind was reminding me of my duty to this planet, a duty which I had failed at, and that guilt has been eating away at me ever since."

18

The mini-sub, large enough for two, slipped quietly from the side portal of the *Alexander Nevsky*, washing out into the waiting arms of the sea in a cluster of bubbles.

The pilot deftly navigated it towards the object buried in the side of the trench ahead. Slowing its speed, he approached with caution, to within a meter and then moved horizontally, following its sleek form until the aft portion disappeared into the sand.

After a moment, the pilot reported. "I would say it is twenty-meters long, maybe five meters in height and a bit more in breadth. I can see a light blinking on one end, and the other, just barely from under the sand."

"Is there any sign of an opening, a door?" asked Pavel.

"No," responded the man. "I see no way in, but I do see what appears to be a windscreen of some sort." He swung the craft over the object and hovered there with the sub's full beams aimed at it. "It's black inside. I can't get a clear view – there's too much sediment stirred up in the water."

"Nudge it, see if it moves at all?" said Captain Ivanov who watched the entire process through the sub's outer cameras.

The pilot eased the sub forward, extending two mechanical arms and pressed into it, nothing happened. He pressed harder, still nothing.

"It's lodged in the sand, and I would say, quite heavy too."

"Pizdets!" The expletive issued from the Pavel's lips and echoed off the interior of his control room, the Russian equivalent of "damn it!"

"Okay, come back."

Pavel turned to his communications officer. "Send a message to Moscow. Tell them we found the asset, but it is too large for us to move or ferry. Give them the coordinates and the depth, and request they send a ship, one that has deep water winches aboard."

He swiveled his chair and stared at the object on the screen.

Something about it sent a shiver through him.

19

It had been over 48 hours since the object had disappeared into the sea and there were no sightings and no slightest footprint to be found.

Nerves were on edge.

Tempers were short.

And sleep was even shorter.

Between Naval Command in Virginia, and the repeated calls coming through from Rear Admiral Patterson at NMCI, in Maryland, Captain Harper felt the intense pressure on him to get a result.

The *Gerald R. Ford* had been dispatched almost a week ago, a simple enough mission, it seemed, to pick up an object from the Irish. It was supposed to be cut and dry. Sail in, anchor near Irish territorial waters, receive the package and sail home. What could go wrong?

Being a sailor most of his life, Harper understood two things about life at sea. Plan and prepare for the worst, and that old man sea, given the slightest opportunity, would find your weak points and leverage them to his advantage. That was the way of things when you lived and worked for months at end on a floating piece of steel, with miles of ocean beneath, just waiting to take you as its next prize.

He had every able-bodied man and women aboard engaged in all-out-search for an alien craft, buried somewhere at sea.

Harper knew the terms of engagement and he'd been around long enough to know that a similar operation was carried out 18 years ago, one that ended without success.

If he recovered the anomaly he would close an old wound.

If it was taken by the Russians, the wound would be opened and fester.

Was he doomed to the same end, he wondered?

Would this be the swansong of his long naval career – the Captain who lost a spacecraft from another world?

Or worse, would Ivan slip in and take it from under his nose?

He gulped down the last of his coffee, just one in a long train of such, and then put the binoculars to his eyes, picking up the outline of one of his helicopters coming in for refueling.

"Sir," the voice of an adjutant said to his right. He turned as the woman handed him a paper. "This just came in from Naval Command."

Harper read it and felt his heart suddenly sink.

"Urgent: Satellite footage has detected a Russian trawler, The Lubov, heading your way. The Lobov usually works waters northwest of Irish territorial waters. Intelligence here suggests they are rendezvousing for a pick up."

20

A light knock sounded at the door of Kaetlyn's cabin.

"It's open."

Lillian stepped in to find Kaetlyn sitting on her bunk.

"Am I disturbing you?"

"Nah – kind of bored to be honest."

Lillian eyed the mobile phone in Kaetlyn's hands, and the image of the avatar on its screen.

"Seriously, an alien?"

Kaetlyn grinned. "Ironic, I know. This is D-TEKT, the newest generation of search apps.

"Interesting name for an app."

"D-TEKT, say hello to Lillian."

The avatar's eyes blinked. "Hello, Lillian. How are you?"

"I'm good, and you?"

A light whistle emitted from the avatar. "Answering subjective questions isn't part of my neural-programming."

Lillian raised a brow and then turned an eye back to Kaetlyn. "May we speak for a moment?"

"More bad news?"

Lillian drew in a breath and exhaled. "I'm sure you've already picked up on bits and pieces of it, the Russians seem to have located the alien ship."

Kaetlyn's eyes illuminated. "I heard they were in the area."

"Seems they found it about five clicks from here, right on the edge of the international waters."

"That storm really pushed it far away."

Lillian nodded. "It did."

"So, what does this mean?"

"That is the topic of the day. The Russians are bringing in a trawler to draw it up from the seabed."

Kaetlyn saw the frustration written on her face. "Oh, I get it, you guys can't do shite about it without creating an incident – right?"

"Right. Technically speaking, a Russian fishing trawler operating in international waters does not violate any maritime laws. We can't do anything aggressive or even appear to be so, because then the Russians would claim military intervention which would be a provocation. It's simply a worst-case scenario for us."

"So, your hands are tied?"

Lillian shrugged. "It's in the hands of our State Department right now, but so far the Russians are playing the denial card."

"But, wouldn't you be able to see if they took the ship aboard this trawler?"

"No, the Lubov is designed for hauling in the carcasses of whales which are as large, or larger than the dimensions of the anomaly. They could pull it into their hull and be off without a single confirmed sighting."

"Shite! Then we lose it forever," a sober cloud suddenly moved over Kaetlyn's world.

Lillian was silent for a moment, and then continued. "Do you trust me?"

The question caught Kaetlyn off-guard. "In a relative sense."

Lillian smiled. "Still worried that we'll hide it away from the world?"

"I trust you, but I don't trust the people you work for."

Lillian's head tipped to one side. "I guess we deserve that, given our track history."

"Why are you here?" asked Kaetlyn.

"I figured you deserved to know what was really going on."

Kaetlyn smiled. "I appreciate the transparency."

A look of repressed guilt rippled across Lillian's face, betraying something unsaid.

"What is it?" asked Kaetlyn.

"I'm concerned that you are not being entirely transparent with me."

"What makes you think that?"

"Maybe it's my 6th sense, but quite honestly, I see it your eyes."

Kaetlyn drew in a deep breath. "I've told you everything I know so far."

"And yet, you still distrust us."

Kaetlyn nodded. "Yeah, I do."

Kaetlyn watched the other for a moment before asking the question. "Why didn't you reveal your alien encounter with others?" she asked.

Lillian drew in a deep breath and exhaled. "I guess I was afraid of what would happen if I went on record claiming an encounter."

"You mean what others would think of you, or how it might affect your life if you went around telling people that you had a close encounter with ET?"

The tacit look in her eyes was her answer.

Kaetlyn flicked a hand to the air. "I don't have an ambition to be the sole proprietor of what's inside that ship. But like you, I'm worried about the consequences of just flinging open the doors. My moral compass is clanging so hard in my head that it sounds like a bell ringing."

"You're not exactly throwing it open to anyone. Right now that ship's computer won't let a single person interact with it unless you're sitting in there doing the talking."

Kaetlyn shrugged. "We both know that can probably change. Now that I've gotten it to learn our language, I could probably just as easily instruct LIN to interface with others, and my role would become redundant."

"But you don't want that to happen?"

"No. Not until I understand the nature of the mission we were on, and everything contained in that computer's data base."

"Why, because we can't be trusted with that knowledge – is that it?"

"You of all people should know better than to play that card. Your nation is the only nation to ever use atomic warheads against civilians. America struts about the world, claiming its proprietary right to nuclear warheads, and maintains the largest nuclear arsenal in the world, and then accuses other nations of their untrustworthiness to possess such. It's not only arrogant, it's hypocrisy." She paused to let some of her angst funnel off.

Lillian was silent, inviting Kaetlyn to get it all off her chest.

"The only way to ensure that no one monopolizes it is to make sure that everyone has access to it – not just your government, nor even mine."

"So, what are you prepared to do?"

Kaetlyn's eyes idly drifted before answering. "Whatever I have to."

21

Captain Pavel, of the *Alexander Nevsky*, listened as his counterpart, the captain of the Lubov, the trawler floating on the surface some 150 meters above, related the surgical details involved in pulling the object nearly 200 meters upwards, into the holding bay of his ship.

"Yes, of course," Sergei answered with a thick accent that betrayed his roots in Siberia, "I have plenty of cable. The problem, Captain Pavel, is we do not know how much it weighs. We know nothing of how it is balanced or it's center of gravity." He paused, a crackle replacing his voice over the secure line. "I fear that the currents here could also pose a problem."

"I'm aware of the factors involved, Sergei, my question is, can your pulleys deal with the unknown margins?"

"I think so, but there is no certainty, not until we hook up to it and test it free of that sandbar."

"Okay, now here's the next problem," began Pavel, "the object is entirely smooth – shaped like a cucumber, but without a single extrusion that would allow us to attach a grappling hook, or moreover, grip to. So, here is how this will go. You will lower tethers to my divers. They will wrap them around the forward section of the asset, and then you will ease it from the sand bar just enough to expose the aft section which we will then tether. At that point you can pull it up to your vessel. Sound simple enough?"

Sergei was quiet a moment as he weighed it up. "Very tricky, Captain. Lots could go wrong in that scenario."

"We don't have time for anything to go wrong. The Americans are watching your every move now, and the Irish are patrolling their territorial waters within a stone's throw of your boat.

"I know," said Sergei, "I can see them from where I'm standing. What if they approach us?"

"Don't worry about them, or the Americans, you are not violating any maritime laws. You are a fishing vessel operating in international waters, that's your official status.

If anyone approaches, stick to that story – they cannot stop or board your ship under such circumstances."

"Okay."

"Any other questions," asked Pavel.

"Nyet," answered Sergei, but as the line went dead, he mumbled, "We just need a fucking prayer."

22

Donovan O'Neil poured through the archives of *The Irish Times* in search of anything that might have happened since the events of nearly eighteen years before, something that might add credibility to the story offered up by Shamus Maguire.

As with most journalists, he wanted to believe the stories that came his way, the bigger, the more sensational, the more outrageous the intrigue and corruption and scandal involved, the better – but like most other hounds in his trade, prudence was both a virtue and a safety net.

He didn't put the food on the table for his family unless he kept his editor happy with his work, so time spent exploring the nebulous, if not even, the unorthodox stories such as this one, was time taken away from something else that paid the bills.

Rubbing his tired eyes, he continued entering search words and scrolling through the results, but all to no avail. No additional evidence whatsoever had surfaced since the event that had first sparked his journalistic blood years before.

The only evidential proof that Shamus was not making it all up was the fact that there were, in fact, ships off the coast of Ireland, exactly where he said they would be. In fact, when Donovan checked the Coast Guard records, which were less secretive than those kept by the military, it confirmed that in the past two days, several military boats, planes and choppers had been spotted scouting the seas off the coast. No mention was made of their purpose, just the usual ambiguity, a *"Military Operation"* – the favorite mantra of the military when attempting to camouflage the true nature of their operations.

The question remained, how to corroborate the story.

Returning to his desk, he found a note from his assistant. "Check this out," said the tab appended to a print-out. Donovan read the short memo, a tip sent in by a worker aboard an Irish fishing boat:

> *"Been fish'n these waters for years, ain't never seen a Russian trawler, a whaler in fact, anchored so close to Irish waters. They was winchin' sometin up, sometin big and it donna look like no whale I ever seen. Figured you boys might find it interest'n.*

23

After a sleepless night, Shamus crawled from his bed just as his mobile phone buzzed.

"Hi Donovan."

"Shamus, I've done some checking around. Your story is holding up so far. Not only is there an American aircraft carrier off those shores, but it's the biggest in their fleet. Not to mention two Irish naval ships and a covey of search vessels, helicopters, reconnaissance planes; and according to a tip we received from a civilian fishing vessel, a Russian trawler was spotted at anchor near Irish waters, hauling something very large into its holding bay – and it wasn't a whale, but certainly as large as one."

"So, what do we do?"

"We can't prove anything yet," answered Donovan. "We've got nothing in terms of footage, or evidential material, but there is one thing I am willing to do."

"Which is?"

"If I can speak to your source, even if only by phone or a chat, I am willing to tell her story."

"So, you want her to publish her story?"

"Assuming my editor doesn't think I've lost my mind, yes."

"If she does that, it'll put her directly in the line of fire."

Donovan paused. "Unfortunately, yes."

24

The first time Kaetlyn had taken the elevator to the top of *The Stack*, the hub that towered high above the deck of the Gerald R. Ford, a vessel with over 6000 crew aboard, two and a half times the number living in her home town of Bantry, excitement had coursed her veins. But now, as the elevator whisked her upwards, she had nothing but butterflies in her stomach.

It was a brilliant day, with a few fleecy clouds and a rather awe-inspiring view of the sea as she stepped from the elevator.

Entering the conference room, its tone certainly did not parallel the panoramic painting beyond the windows.

Captain Harper offered a tentative, yet polite smile as he motioned her and Serena to their chairs.

"Okay, let's get started," he began. "I don't need to elaborate for anyone in this room," he glanced at Colonel Desmond, Raymond Statler and his own officers, including Lillian Fray who sat next to Kaetlyn and Serena, "the importance of this operation. We've confirmed that the Alexander Nevsky, a *Borei Class Russian Nuclear Ballistic Submarine*, found the anomaly, and called in the Lubov, a Russian trawler that Ivan, I mean, Moscow, uses for undercover operations in the North Seas."

"Do we have confirmation that they have actually started the process?" asked Colonel Desmond.

"According to video footage provided by our submersibles, they've already hoisted that thing into the Lubov." He paused. "While Washington haggles with Moscow over ownership rights, our instructions from Virginia are to hem-in the Lubov until the talks are completed." He pressed a remote in his hand, causing a wall screen to illuminate. "Our tactical team has devised this assembly. The red dots represent the GRF and the Largs Bay, the smaller green dots are the Irish vessels, and the blue ones demarcate our submersibles." He clicked on the remote. "The orange dots represent two of our subs which are speeding our way as we speak. We expect them within the hour."

"A show of force, is that it?" said Desmond.

Harper nodded. "A bit of psychological warfare too. We're sending a message to Ivan." He turned to Kaetlyn.

"The next step, part of the on-going negotiation process happening on other levels than ours, involves you, young lady."

Kaetlyn felt a lump in her throat, making it hard to swallow.

"If the Russians won't agree to turning the object over to us, assuming they get it all the way to Russian soil, there is little we can do to the force the matter, short of a military confrontation. Frankly, I'm not so sure that Washington is willing to go that far. However," he fixed his gaze on all, "as we already know, that object is impenetrable without you," he nodded at Kaetlyn, "and furthermore, it's computer apparently won't parley with anyone without you there." Harper struck a silent pose.

So..." he paused in his step and turned to face Kaetlyn. "We are asking you to step up and engage yourself even further, Ms. O'Sullivan. This matter is no longer what it once was, we are now dealing with the potential of serious security issues, potentially a threat to our way of life if this technology falls into the wrong hands."

"What do you expect of me?" she nervously asked as the eyes of the entire room watched on.

Captain Harper tipped his head at her. "We can only assume that Ivan will come to the same impasse we did, and that's when we play our ace card, you. We need your help to be the bridge, so that we can force their hand in cooperating with us, if it comes to that."

Kaetlyn felt her sense of triumph suddenly deflating, replaced by a growing sense of dread. The closure she had so desperately been seeking to achieve from a dream that had haunted her for years, had now been relegated to a mere chess move in some political power-play, one where she had been reduced to a pawn and the gate-keeper, the one who would let the others pass into the castle and lay siege to it.

25

"I am sorry that our lack of acquiescence to your demands is causing you upset, Ms. Secretary," answered Anton Kobylkin, Russia's Minister of Foreign Affairs – addressing America's Secretary of State over a secure chat line.

Anne Lansing, certainly no novice to the complications and intrigues of diplomatic intercourse, a graduate of Harvard Law, mother of two daughters, and survivor of a twenty-seven-year marriage, had navigated more than her share of troubled waters. A month ago, she had brokered yet another peace accord between Israel and the Palestinians – not that she thought it would last, because it seemed that both sides were intrinsically opposed to lasting peace, and for that matter, sanity, and would do anything in their power to upset the accord eventually. However, it was good for public relations, aggrandizing a positive image of America's role in the Middle East, as well as bolstering Presidential ratings and more kudos for her party.

"Anton, we both know this is bullshit. You're treading on thin ice by confiscating that object – and it violates the Space Accord of 1973."

"Hmm," he hummed, his face revealing not the slightest emotion. "Anne, the object which you claim is yours and yours alone, was found by our submarine, in international waters, showing no markings or indications whatsoever that it is property of the American government, and for that matter, not the slightest indication of damage which you also claim to have shot down over 18 years ago, but cannot corroborate whatsoever. So, please," he paused to tip his head at her, "how exactly are we violating your rights to this thing?"

"What I am trying to tell you is that the reason you don't see any marks, or damage or signs of a missile strike on that thing is because whatever foreign material that ship is made of, is relatively impenetrable."

"And yet you still claim to have shot it down?"

"I can't explain the discrepancy," she paused. It was time to play her ace card. "Up until a few days ago, we couldn't get into it. Our engineers, the Irish, no one, using no means known to us, could penetrate that hull."

"We have good engineers," he said with a smirk.

"I don't doubt that for a minute, but what you don't have is the key to the front door."

Anton leaned into the camera. "What exactly are you getting at, Anne?"

"We have a girl aboard our aircraft carrier who knows how to get inside that thing. She's the one who broke the code. In fact, without her, no one can ingress this craft or interface with the computer, and I mean, no one."

Anton's face screwed up in obvious confusion. "Is this a joke, Ms. Secretary?"

Anne shook her head. "No, Anton, it's not. As bizarre as this may sound, this young woman claims that in her past life she was aboard that very alien craft. No one believed her at first, but when the chips were down, she turned out to be the key – the only key to the door."

Anton stared at her, a vague nuance of incredulity sweeping over his face.

26

"Jimmy, listen to me," pleaded Donovan O'Neil, watching as the editor and chief of *The Irish Times* shook his head vociferously. "This is big – possibly bigger than anything we have ever run. People won't give a shite about political scandals, Brexit, or anything else once this news hits the airwaves, and we have a chance to be the first to release it."

"Big trouble, big nothing," responded the editor who leaned forward with a finger pointed at Donovan. "You're going out on limb here, Don – a thin one at that. The last time we took on this elephant we wasted a lot of time and money. The Americans found nothing. The Irish navy refused to cooperate and gave us some shite about military exercises. All we had was the word of a single fisherman and some locals who saw dead fish wash'n up on the damn shores." He paused, shaking his head more vehemently. "We took this one in the arse, we're not doin' it again, Don, not based on these sketchy facts – and certainly, not based on the word of two eighteen-year-olds."

Donovan felt himself sinking into the vortex of editorial rejection. "Jimmy, I just know there's somethin' to this."

"How do'ya know that, Don? Because there are ships out there? How do'ya know they're not just flim-flammin' about, play'n the usual war games, some cock fight between the Yanks and the Ruskies?"

"We don't, of course, but we have …"

The editor cut him off with a firm wave of his hand… "The word of an eighteen-year-old woman and her associate, who supposedly is the gate-keeper to his thing, based on some past-life experience? Come on, Don! You can do better than that."

The editor tipped his head at the other. "Look, Donnie, you normally bring in the bacon. You been doin' a hell-of-a job for nigh-on eighteen years – but unless you can give me somethin' solid, you know, potatoes and gravy, at least a banger or two, then I can't afford to have you goin' off chase'n ghosts-stores, or, aliens. We're already walking a thin line today, getting our bloody arses kicked by independent news agencies – I can't afford to have one of my best men skipping a beat right now."

Tail between his legs, Donovan trudged back to his cubicle, despondent, but not beaten.

27

Kaetlyn watched the rhythmic roll of the sea as she mused over a new element that had entered the spotlight on the stage of her mind.

Did death remove the right of ownership?

The question had been bouncing around her skull for hours now.

Her therapy had helped to prove that past-lives was not a matter of "if" anymore – it was a reality. Subjective or not, recent events had shown that people were not finite, they were immortal, living successive lifetimes – not just one.

And the more she thought about it, the more she began to see that the very structure of the society was based entirely on just one paradigm, that death was a finality.

There were no laws or rules of convention that permitted someone to come back and claim ownership rights regarding a former life. The only conventions provided by law were the rights of bequeathment – giving over one's property and wealth to others.

What would happen if past-lives was an acknowledged fact, and not treated as paranormal, she wondered?

What if people had a way of proving their past-life identity?

What if death was viewed, not as the end, but as a new beginning?

How would the world be different today if Tesla had been able to come back in his next life, pick up where he left off and finish the amazing technological breakthroughs he had been working on?

What if Martin Luther King had come back in his next life to continue to champion the rights of people?

Then again, what if Hitler or Stalin claimed their previous calling and resumed their heinous acts?

The very platform of society would most certainly change, she thought, *but surely the greater truth was more important to the future of the culture than holding people prisoner inside a false box of ignorance about their true identity.*

Her thoughts drifted back to Shamus – the mystery man in the plot, one who had turned up on her doorstep just the night before she left Bantry – announcing his bizarre dream, the same one she had been experiencing all these years.

Was it possible, she wondered, *that Shamus was the person who had stood by her side on the bridge of that ship when the missile struck?*

Was he there when they died?

Was he, as LIN had said, her mate, her lover from a past life?

The coincidence of their past and then present, within the same geographical region, was bizarre to say the least.

Moreover, she wondered, *was it even possible that by having shattered the amnesia about her past, that her feelings, her love, and her passions at that time, could also endure?*

Was it even likely that the love shared between two sentient beings, a life time ago, or even ten life-times ago, could now be as actual and real as any?

She sighed. So many questions and no answers.

As a gathering of gulls squawked and fought over a fish, she turned to see if anyone was near before slipping her mobile from her pocket, and then dialed his number.

"Hi, Shamus, it's Kaetlyn. Can we talk?"

Book Four

1

Hannah Weber watched the eastern tip of the Antarctica glide into view.

Travelling at an orbital speed of 27,000 kilometers, the *International Space Station* afforded her a similar sight no less than 15 times a day – in fact, the grandest one of all, as if she were God looking down upon the Earth.

Generally referred to as Ginger Rogers by her American crew mates, because of her ginger-colored hair, milky-white skin and rouge lips, Hannah actually hailed from Munich, Germany.

As a specialist in the seismic and geological fields, she had been inducted into ESA, the *European Space Agency*, and eventually drew the winning lottery ticket for a stint aboard the ISS.

Her crew mates included two American scientists who were executing studies on the physiological effects of prolonged duration in space, in preparation for America's next big venture, a manned mission to Mars; as well as two Russian scientists doing geological studies of the Siberian domain.

Her French co-partner, Vivian Dubois, was similarly trained as her, affording them a 24-hour operation; while one slept, the other performed their tasks, back and forth for the duration of their 90 day mission.

Under pressure from many groups and government agencies, ESA had put together the team with the mandate of providing irrefutable proof that global warming was heading the world toward an unprecedented debacle if not curbed.

NASA had already provided satellite footage showing the marked reduction in the polar caps around Greenland, but Hannah's job was specifically to analyze the Antarctic, using the most sophisticated equipment available.

While the public outcry on global warming and environmental declination was on the rise, the obvious was still being missed by many, if not most; if the indigenous population of wildlife on the planet had been reduced by some 40% in the last 50 years alone, where did that leave humans in the next decade or two? Certainly, our existence would hit a threshold too – considering that we were systematically wiping out other life forms.

If the coral reefs died, and the natural plant life that kept the oceans oxygenated, thereby providing the means for fish to spawn and grow; and if the polar regions melted, the result was inevitably and irreversibly catastrophic for humanity – and yet, fake news, fake leaders, fake politicians, and certainly, greedy corporate mongrels, refuted the obvious because of their personal agendas.

Hannah watched as the vast continental sheet of ice rolled toward her. It was an amazing sight, one that never failed to cause her to pause – because here, in juxtaposition to landmasses which supported life on Earth, was a mountain of ice that seemed to be a contradiction. And yet, she knew from her training that the Antarctic, and its brother in the north, were a critical piece of the pie. They were anchors, keeping the planet in balance climatically. And like a ship, if the anchor drifted or shifted, so did the ship.

She tapped the hand-held pad, bringing up a control module, and typed in the coordinates, waiting as the signal reached Apex, the name given to the highly sophisticated spectrometer fixed to one arm of the International Space Station. The screen came to life as Apex's cameras zoomed in on the location 406 kilometers below, and seconds later she was looking at the eastern edge of the Ross Ice Shelf, as if she were merely hovering ten meters above it.

Now, began the task, a diagnosis of hundreds of square miles of ice, because she knew there was a sickness there, it was just a matter of finding it.

2

With its precious cargo safely secured in the holding bay, the Captain of the Lobov received orders to head north, through the Barents Sea, to the nearest Russian naval base in the Okulovsky district.

Nervous and yet intrigued by his catch, of which he knew nothing, Sergei plotted the itinerary, passing them northwest of Ireland, by the Faroe Islands, and then up the coast of Norway to their destination.

The *asset* turned out to weigh in just under the limit of his ship's capacity to winch from where it sat on the edge of a sandy trench. Fortunately, the sea was kind that day and offered up no serious challenges as they pulled the object through the aft-cavity into an open bay where it now sat.

While he had been told nothing about why it was so important to retrieve, the timber and tone of the orders were such as to convey the direness of the mission. *"Get that thing aboard your ship, Captain,"* he recalled the voice of the

Naval Commander. *"This is more important than you can possibly imagine."*

He wheeled his trawler, nosing it north-eastward, with a five-knot wind at his face, and moderate white-caps kissing his bow.

"Captain," a voice broke his mental solitude.

He turned to the lookout. "There's an American ship following us, not more than three kilometers."

Sergei clutched his binoculars, strode through the door to the starboard observation deck and focused on the object in the distance.

"Good fucking Christ, it's an American aircraft carrier." As his eyes scanned the ship, he gasped. "That's the Gerald R. Ford, the largest in their fleet?"

The lookout nodded as pointed. "Captain!".

Sergei turned to see five fighter planes approaching in a V-formation from his port side, their altitude was so low that their afterburners displaced the surface of the sea. They swooped upwards, passing so close that it sent a tremor through his body.

"Pizdets," he exclaimed. "Get Moscow on the line."

3

Shamus was beside himself.

He'd just hung up with Donovan O'Neil at the Times; they were not about to run the story.

His frustration mounted by the minute.

He paced the living room of their house while his mother sat at the kitchen table, casually watching him with an amused smile on her lips.

"You're wear'n out my rug, Shamus. What's got your knickers in a knot?"

He stopped and looked up at her and then dropped in a chair next to her.

She offered him a motherly smile. "Maybe it would help if you talked to your ol' mum?" she ended with a raised brow.

Shamus stared at the table for a time before answering. "It's just too fook'n bizarre, mum. You wouldn't believe me."

She grinned. "It wouldn't have somethin' to do with those dreams you get?"

He looked up at her. "You know about my dreams?"

She tipped her head at him. "It's my job to know what's happen'n with you. I'm your mum." She paused. "Besides, I've heard you talk'n in your sleep. It's been pretty routine."

"You never mentioned before."

"Never thought it was important until now – see'n you all worked up." A smile crept across her lips. "It can't be worse than see'n a Banshee."

Shamus flicked an eye her way. "A Banshee!? That's mental."

"Mental or not, I seen one in the woods up the road, 'bout twenty years ago."

"You're fook'n with me, right?"

"See, that's exactly what happens when you try to tell people shite that doesn't fit into their ideas about normal." She tipped her head at him. "What's on your mind, son?"

He played with a spoon for a time, debating how much he should say, if anything. Finally, he looked up at her. "This is going to sound so mental…"

4

"You're following our trawler?" asked Anton Kobylkin, Russia's Minister of Foreign Affairs, with a soured demeanor that echoed his indignation.

Anne Lansing, America's Secretary of State, nodded. "You haven't gotten back to me about my offer, Anton. So, yeah, our Navy will be following your trawler all the way to Russia if that's what it takes to get you guys to play ball."

Anton's head rocked side to side. "This isn't good, Anne. You are provoking us. The Lubov is a civilian vessel."

"That's bullshit, and you know it. The Lubov is a cover ship, which you use when it serves another agenda, such as now."

Anton's brow furrowed. "Having an American aircraft carrier and several of your planes following a Russian trawler isn't going to bode well with Moscow."

"Don't forget about the two subs we have shadowing your ship," she added with a lopsided grin.

Anton huffed. "This is outrageous, Anne."

"Is it? Is it any more outrageous than you guys stealing something from under our noses, when you knew full well that we had lost it during that storm?"

"It does not justify a military provocation."

"Then get me an answer from the Kremlin."

"I have presented your proposal to them. It's under consideration."

"Then our ship, subs and planes remain as they are," she answered with a firm eye.

"And if we don't accept your proposal?"

"That's not my decision, Anton. I'm the messenger, like yourself."

"So, you would fight us over this?"

She paused to draw a breath. "You must impress on Moscow that we have no intentions of allowing this thing being taken from us. Please, make that very clear to them."

5

Having left the Largs Bay, Kaetlyn and Serena sat alone in the dining area, having agreed to return to the Gerald R. Ford in the hopes that the Russians might strike up a deal, or, if necessary, Kaetlyn would be used as their ace card to force their hand.

"We talked," said Kaetlyn in a hushed voice.

"I'm glad you reached out to him – you seem calmer now," answered Serena with an innocuous smile. "What was his reaction?"

Kaetlyn shrugged. "Hard to tell over the phone."

"You think Shamus is the same one as on the ship?"

"It makes sense, I guess, about as much sense as everything else."

"What did you tell him?"

"Everything I remembered about our final talk just before we went down." Her head shook. "I mean, how should someone react to being told that in a past life he was in love with me and I with him?" She sighed with obvious growing frustration.

"How do you feel about it now?"

"Confused as shite." Her eyes drifted a time. "Is it possible that a lifetime later, under entirely different circumstances ..." she glanced at her hands, "that we would still feel the same about each other?"

Serena smiled. "I guess that depends on you."

"You're not helping with your cryptic remarks."

"This is new territory for me too, Kaet. Can I offer some advice, off the record?"

Kaetlyn nodded.

"I'm no expert on the subject of love. Believe me, I've had my ups and downs in relationships and right now I'm taking a sabbatical from the whole thing." She paused. "Do you want to know why I decided to make psychology my career?"

"Because it pays well?"

Serena shrugged. "A definite perk, but no."

"Okay – then what?"

"Love."

Kaetlyn's head cocked to one side with a confused look washing across her visage.

"My parent's relationship was the matrix for my career-decision."

"Why?"

"When I was young, they seemed so in love. We did things together as a family and our home was a happy and peaceful place. By the time I was in my early teens, it was a very different picture. They had become distanced from one another, cold and bitter even. What love existed between them seemed to have been buried deep inside, if it was there at all." She sighed. "It puzzled me, and I thought about it a lot. At one point I wondered if it was my fault, but then I realized the same thing was happening to other kids I knew in school or in the neighborhood. Love seemed to be transient with far too many families, and that made no sense." She wavered a moment before continuing. "How could something so powerful, a bond so tenacious that it could bring two people together in a lifetime of devotion to one another, suddenly, and quite inexplicably, have the glue holding it together, come undone?"

Kaetlyn listened in rapt silence.

"By the time I was your age, just about to jump off the boat of high-school and swim out into the world, I decided I would take on this subject. I figured that psychology might help me understand the complexities and vicissitudes of human relationships, and that maybe I could help others navigate these waters."

"I had no idea."

"When I have asked my patients *what is the most important thing in your life*, do you know what they often answer with?"

Kaetlyn's head shook.

"You'd think it would be security, happiness or money, but it's rarely ever one of those. Most people want love, and in so many cases, the source of their trauma, and their mental afflictions sources back to lost love, broken relationships or the longing for the love they once had, leaving them feeling empty, depressed and and unfulfilled."

"So, did you find the answers you were looking for?"

Serena shook her head. "No, unfortunately not. However, this development in your situation fascinates me. It's made revisit the whole issue. In fact, I'm beginning to think that maybe love is so potent that it transcends time and physicality in ways we do not yet understand – like gravity; and if love can do that, it must be the most powerful force in the universe."

So engaged in conversation, neither of them noticed the Naval MP approaching until he snapped to an abrupt stop and stared down at Kaetlyn.

"Ms. O'Sullivan, I've been asked to escort you to see the Captain." His deliverance had the timber of seriousness which his face already betrayed.

"Now?"

"Yes, please."

6

Shamus' mum sat in silence as the last words rolled off his tongue.

Glancing at the wall-clock, he noticed that an hour had passed since he began disclosing the details of his and Kaetlyn's story.

She had remained silent the entire time, revealing nothing of the storm, he reckoned, that must be brewing inside her head.

For him, it was a relief to finally open the door to his deepest secret, a dream, a past-life experience, which had been visiting him most every night for years now.

His mum let out a deep breath as she raised a tentative brow.

"Well, now, you've outdone yourself with that one, Shamus," she said as she stood and walked to the kitchen counter, filled the teapot with more water and waited as it boiled – her silence was testimony that she was still processing it all.

Finally, with two hot cups of tea in hand, she sat back down and looked her son in the eyes.

"Where is Kaetlyn now?"

"In her latest text she told me she's back on the American ship – which is now following the Russian trawler."

"Good fook'n Lord, sounds like a damn Ludlum novel in the making," exclaimed his mum as she gingerly sipped on the hot brew. "And this Donovan, the penner with *The Times* – anything more with him?"

Shamus shrugged. "He seems to have run aground. His editor doesn't buy the story."

Her brow twitched. "It's understandable, this tale is right up there with Big Foot and alien abductions."

Shamus leaned forward. "Do you believe me?"

"Course I believe you. If I can see a banshee I guess you can have your past life – seems par for the course."

Shamus sighed with relief.

"So, I guess the question is, what to do about it, right?" she said.

He nodded.

"I do have a suggestion for you."

"Which is?"

"I say fook the lot of 'em. Make a video and post it on the internet. Tell the whole world what's going on. Tell 'em about Kaetlyn and this thing, this ship, and what the Yanks and Ruskies are up to."

7

As she stepped into the conference room of the *Gerald R. Ford*, it felt as cold as the air outside; and each face she looked at carried a grim and churlish aspect, a precursor to what was about to come.

Captain Harper, not particularly a warm and friendly personality, had lost what little geniality he had shown as his eyes bore into hers.

"You've not been honest with us," he began. You've been in touch with someone on the outside, telling them everything you know, in direct violation of the secrecy bond you signed," he announced, like a judge passing down his sentencing.

The air chilled even more as silence reigned.

Harper raised a brow. "Do you have anything to say?"

Kaetlyn cast a furtive glance at Colonel Desmond, Lillian Fray and several other officers who stood nearby and then turned to face him.

"I agreed to come here to help gain access to that ship."

"You also agreed to keep the matter secret."

"That means nothing now that the Russians have it."

"It means everything, Kaetlyn," he said, bearing down on her. "You've shared this information with someone who has gone public with it. Do you realize that?"

"That was bound to happen."

Harper's hand struck the table with a firm smack. "That was not your call, young lady. This matter has become complicated…"

"Because the Russians have it instead of you?" she retorted angrily.

Harper pressed his lips together, stemming his anger. "I'm quite aware of your distrust of our government and our intentions, but I assure you that whatever we do with that thing will be far more positive than what the Russians do."

"Based on your history, I'd say that's hypocrisy," responded Kaetlyn defiantly.

Lillian Fray, seeing the temperature rising, interceded with a calm voice. "Kaet, listen to me, please. You must see the bigger picture here. This isn't a question of the good guys and the bad guys, according to anyone's definitions, this is really matter of security on a global basis. And now, by releasing that information, you've involved your friend…"

"So what, he's not bonded and certainly free to say his mind."

Colonel Desmond stepped into the fray, rising to his feet as he did. "He's an Irish citizen, lass, as are you. Neither of you are in any danger or trouble, despite the bond you signed. Such a bond has no legal bearing in Ireland and isn't enforcable, unless of course you plan to hold Kaetlyn prisoner on your ship," he said as he cast a disdainful eye at the Captain.

Harper sighed, "Of course not. I apologize for my anger."

Colonel Desmond continued. "The point here is more about the narrative no longer being in our control. Not only do the Russians have the anomaly in their possession, the internet is spiking as news of its existence goes viral; and let's not forget, it was Ivan who started that ball rolling, not Kaetlyn or her friend."

By now, Captain Harper had regained his equilibrium. "Kaetlyn, you know that we're following that Russian trawler, and that we're attempting to negotiate with Moscow to play ball with us."

She nodded.

"Are you still willing to help, even if it means…"

She cut him off. "Captain, I'm committed to finding out the truth of what is contained in that ship. If I have to fly to a Siberian to do it, I will."

As dialogue resumed amidst the others, Kaetlyn's eyes drifted to the gray horizon. Her nightmare had morphed into something else entirely, and in some ways, the new trepidation she felt was far greater, because now she was worried about what she could be unleashing into the hands of less provident men, and certainly, those with an obsession to leverage power.

8

Shamus was glued to his computer screen, watching as the views on the video continued to escalate at a maddening rate.

When he had posted the video the night before, following his talk with his mum, he had no idea of the domino-effect he would set in motion.

In the first hour, there were nearly 2,000 views. When he woke up in the morning, there were 28,000 views, and now, several hours later, it was nearing half a million

His mum entered his room and laid a plate next to him with a sandwich, and a cup of tea. She looked over his shoulder, shaking her head as she did. "Well, I guess your 'ol mum was right."

Shamus nodded as he scrolled down the thread of comments, hundreds and hundreds of them, from people all over the globe. "There are so many questions and comments – I can't possibly answer them all?"

His mum smiled. "Just let it take its course. Now," she nodded at the sandwich with an authoritative look, "eat up. You can't live on those "*likes*"."

9

Rear Admiral Norman Patterson sat watching as the President paced back and forth behind his desk.

It was not exactly his finest moment, watching the man he served ratchet up in stress over something that he, Norman, should have dealt with days ago.

Across from him sat Anne Lansing, the Secretary of State and the Secretary of Defense, James Bidwell.

The President finally stopped, turned, and gripped the back of his leather chair – a dour look was carved into his face.

"This is fucked up, guys. You're putting me in a real shit pile here."

"Sir," began Anne."

The President flicked a hand. "Go ahead."

"The Russians will concede, they have to."

"Why would they?!" he exclaimed. "Just because the fucking Irish couldn't figure out how to get into that thing doesn't mean the Russians won't. It's too big a variable to assume that this girl ..." he paused.

"Kaetlyn O'Sullivan", she offered.

"Right, her. Everybody's thinking that she is the key."

Patterson spoke. "In truth, Mr. President, she is the key. We didn't think so at first. In fact, our original plan was to simply use her as bait, to help leverage the Irish, but now, she's turned out to be the fulcrum."

The President came around from his desk and sat between them.

"Seriously, I don't care about the girl. The bottom line is we can't let the Russians take this thing into their territorial waters, whether or not they agree to use the girl to help, doesn't matter. The point is, that thing, whatever it is, had the technological ability to penetrate solid rock and embed itself there. It remains impervious to every attempt to penetrate it, and based on the information you're telling me, the fucking thing doesn't have a scratch on its surface. Not to mention the skeletal remains that were recovered. Am I correct so far?"

"That's correct, sir," answered Patterson.

"Whatever we can learn from that ship is probably more valuable than anyone can possibly imagine, so I'm not letting the Russians steal it from us," said the President with a firm jaw. He turned to Bidwell. "Jim — what options do we have, short of firing shots over the bow of that Russian trawler?"

266

The Secretary of Defense tipped an eye at the other two before answering. "We don't want to provoke the Russians, and we're certainly not going to start a war over this, but I think there is one way we could buy some time for the negotiators."

"I'm all ears."

"A blockade."

"Isn't that the same thing as provoking them?" asked the President.

"Mr. President, the Lubov will pass through the strait between the Faroes and the Isles of northern Scotland, and then up along the Norwegian coast before making it to the Barents Sea. We can deploy enough ships and subs from our northern fleet to form a fairly conspicuous blockade."

"What's the point of doing that?"

"It buys us time," answered Bidwell as he turned an eye to Anne Lansing. Bidwell continued. "It'll be a stand-off, for sure, but I'm quite sure that the Russians won't engage us. They'll see it as a sign of our resolve and will concede to negotiating the matter."

"And what if the Lubov forges through?" asked the President.

Bidwell tipped his head, "Then the bluff is up."

Patterson spoke up. "There is another factor that could be in our favor. A friend of Kaetlyn's posted a video to the internet which has gone viral, with nearly a million views in less than a day, and in that video, he tells the story, including the bit about the Russians sneaking into our backyard and taking the craft aboard their trawler. We can use that leverage against Ivan, because now, the world knows what they did."

"That won't stop the Russians," offered the President.

"No, it won't, sir," Patterson said with a shake of his head. "It just lessens the chances of a nasty confrontation while Anne and her people try to massage the whole thing."

10

"Donovan," the voice of authority echoed through the large room, one filled with many cubicles scattered about the media floor of *The Irish Times*.

It was a voice that everyone knew.

It's timber and tone denoted whether the calling would be a happy one, an approved editorial, or if it carried the potential for an ear-bruising.

Donovan had endured his share of brow beatings, and some praising too, but there was no doubt that the first was disproportionately larger than the second, a way of life in a business where the editor and chief had the power to sanction or end one's existence as a journalist.

He made his way through the sea of dividers, the occasional curious eye looking up at him. As he entered the editor's office, the man was standing, glasses twirling in one hand with a sheet of paper in the other, which he waved in the air like a flag in the wind. He tipped his head at Donovan.

"Do you know what this is?" he asked.

"No."

"This is what you've been look'n for, proof that maybe that arse of a story you been pitch'n my way is worth the cost of a cup of coffee."

Donovan took it and read, his eyes growing wide as they did. "Fook me," he exclaimed.

"Yes, indeed."

"The Americans have redirected their entire northern fleet to the straits between the Faroes?"

"Aye," answered the editor with a smile. "So …" he tipped his head at Donovan, "maybe you best find a way to turn this into a real story, before that punk, Shamus Maguire, steals the wind from our sails with another video, which …" he turned to his computer, tapped the keyboard, and then looked at Donovan, "… now has close to two million views," he finished with a disgruntled shake of his head.

11

When Lillian Fray caught up with Kaetlyn, following the meeting with the high brass, she found her sitting in one corner of the dining area along with her dad and Serena.

"May I join this somber party?" she asked with a disarming smile.

Kaetlyn waved her in.

"So, is this a private discussion or can I partake?" she asked.

Harry O'Sullivan spoke up in the absence of any other immediate response. "We're talk'n about Kaet's next move."

Lillian raised a brow. "Maybe I shouldn't be here for that?" she half joked.

"No, I think ya should," responded the man, as he fixed a firm eye on Lillian. "My daughter has done everything you folks have asked of her. She's not the one who lost that thing at sea. She's not the one who let the Ruskies slip in and take it from under your noses. And she's not the one who created this mess."

Lillian offered a tempered smile. "No one is accusing Kaet of those things, Mr. Sullivan. The specific upset …"

He cut her off. "I know what yer all upset 'bout, and maybe, given yer circumstances, I'd feel the same, but Kaet's got her reasons for what she did."

Lillian offered a tacit glance at Kaetlyn who sat in morose silence.

It was Serena who spoke next. "Do you even know the entire background on this …" she waved a hand about the large dining area.

Lillian shrugged. "I'm not sure I understand what you mean."

"Kaet was sent to me by her school because they figured she was uproarious, troublesome and such, in need of a little behavioral adjustment. No sooner had we started talking when she revealed to me her recurring dream … which you now know all about."

"I understand that, but is there a point here?"

Serena leaned forward. "The point, Ms. Fray, is that while I agreed to come here on Kaet's behalf, I am, first and foremost, a therapist, and Kaet is my client, and the entire purpose of this process was to help HER, not you. The regressive-therapy was meant to give her closure on something that has been troubl'n her for years. This was intended for her benefit, and now, as she attempts to navigate it her way, she is being singled out as a turncoat who has committed treason because she exposed her personal insights to someone who also shared that same experience with her." She paused to look at Kaetlyn whose eyes remained fixed on the table. "Kaetlyn has every right, security waiver or not, to do what she wants with the information she has obtained through the course of her therapy. You do not own her mind and you do not have a monopoly on her intellectual property which is protected by the laws that regulate my profession. So, yes, there is another platform to all of this, a higher one, and if Kaet feels the necessity to dictate her own terms, you're going to have to listen to her."

"Did Kaet tell you about my personal experience with ..." began Lillian.

Kaetlyn suddenly piped up at that point. "I did."

"Then you know that I'm caught between a rock and a hard place here. On one hand, I am championing her cause, because I have lived with something similar, an experience that was so profound that it changed my life. On the other hand, I'm duty-bound by my vows to my employer, the Navy and the US government."

Harry O'Sullivan smirked. "Aye, then you're in a shite-storm of your own, aren't ya, lass?"

Lillian smiled. "I am."

Silence reigned for a moment before Lillian continued. "Right now, the North Atlantic Fleet is sailing around the horn of the Faroe Islands, intent on putting up a blockade to prevent the Lubov from reaching Russia."

"Shite," exclaimed Harry.

"The Russians are already threatening to send their own naval forces. It's going to be show of force guys and I have no idea how it's going to end, but I suspect that the entire matter has gone too far for me to do anything effective to help change the course of events. But ..." she paused, tentatively reaching over and squeezing Kaetlyn's hand, "I'm on your side, more than you can know, and I think, as evidenced by the video your boyfriend posted ..."

"He's not my boyfriend," retorted Kaetlyn.

Lillian smiled, sensing something much deeper between them. "As I was saying, judging by the massive response to that video, I'd say the world is on your side too."

12

It was a dreary day in Moscow, which was not particularly unusual for November.

Thick clouds pressed down, threatening inclement weather, maybe snow, but certainly nothing less than the sobriety that now engulfed the city.

For Anton Kobylkin, Russia's Minister of Foreign Affairs, the solemnity was aggrandized by affairs developing in the North Sea.

He had just finished a meeting with no less than the Supreme Commander-in-Chief, the President himself, as well as the Minister of Defense and the Chief of the General Staff – a discussion which felt as surreal as the very subject upon which it rested – an alien spacecraft.

The President, firm and resolute as always in his manner, sat in silence as the three constituents of his government argued back and forth about the best means of dealing with the Americans.

In the end, despite his urgings to avoid a confrontational approach, Anton's platform was stopped short as the President broke his taciturnity.

"You are right, Anton, this is a show of force from the Americans, and while I am quite sure they are not about to start a war over this matter, I will not permit the world to see us as weaker."

He turned an eye to the Minister of Defense. "Match the Americans with the same number of ships, planes and submarines, no less, no more. I want them there in hours – ready to escort the Lubov home."

The man snapped to his feet, saluted and left the room.

Anton sank deeper into his chair, like a deflated balloon. His job was to negotiate agreements, and whenever the military was called in, it was a slap to his face, because bullets were not ambassadors of peace - they were killers.

The President turned to him, cocking his head as he did. "I value your advice, Anton, and I know you did your best to convince the Americans to stand down, but this matter is far too important to us, and we cannot permit that craft to become their exclusive domain."

Anton put on his best affectation and smiled. "I understand Mr. President," but deep inside, he felt that they may have just crossed the threshold, beyond which lay only disaster.

13

The *Cessna 172P Skyhawk* cut a path east by southeast, on a tangent that Donovan O'Neil hoped would put him directly over the theater which he knew was now unfolding in the North Sea.

He turned to the pilot, in fact, an old friend of the family who owned and operated several seaplanes which they used to ferry tourists, oil company workers and others to and from the Faroe and Shetland Islands.

As he peered down into the gray froth, the sea was spotted with vessels, large and small, even the occasional oil rig.

The pilot kept their altitude under two thousand feet to remain just below the thick mantle of clouds, affording Donovan the view he needed.

"Somethin up ahead there, laddie," said the pilot.

Donovan brought the binoculars to his eyes and focused on a string of objects, barely perceptible against a sea of black.

"Can you go lower?"

"A mite, not much though – don't want to get in the middle of a shite-fest."

The Cessna dropped a few hundred feet, leveled out and continued ahead. With minutes the view became clearer. Donovan drew a deep breath as he contained his excitement.

He grabbed his mobile phone and started videoing. "Fook'n Christ almighty!" he exclaimed as the shapes morphed into battle ships, flying American colors; a string of them, running diagonally across the face of the sea.

"How far is the Lubov from that line of scrimmage," he asked.

The pilot shrugged. "bout a hundred and fifty clicks, less or more.

"Can you come around one more time ..." began Donovan when his words stuttered to a stop, like an engine suddenly cutting out. He sat there in abject shock, watching as a V-shaped formation of ships emerged from the mist beyond, heading directly toward the Americans.

14

Captain Harper had his feet firmly planted against a powerful northerly, as he stood on the observation deck of the *Gerald R. Ford*.

The frigid wind slashed at his exposed skin, like an angry bear, as he peered through the binoculars at the *Nikolay Kuznetsov* – the Russian aircraft carrier and lead ship for the flotilla in the distance.

There was no doubt in his mind that the Captain of the Kuznetsov had a similar strike force at his disposal. In fact, if memory served him right, the Russian aircraft carrier housed 41 fighter aircraft and a sizeable array of long-range ballistics. Not to mention the other five ships, and who knows how many subs the Russians had called into play.

At no time in recent history, not since before the Communist bloc had toppled back in 1989, had the two powers gone toe-to-toe. There had been incidents of course, brief confrontations, none of which had ever escalated to the point where a line of scrimmage had been drawn like this.

He turned and focused his binoculars on the Lubov, the Russian trawler with its prize in its hold.

"How long before we reach the trawler?"

"Thirty-eight minutes at our current speed," answered the pilot.

Harper shook his head. His orders were to remain where they were and do nothing that would or could provoke

275

Ivan; somewhat oxymoronic considering that this much military force was provocation of the worst kind.

15

Ever since returning to their base outside Cork, Raymond Statler had been fretting over the turn of events, so much the case that he had barely slept the night before.

He felt cheated, like having found the woman of his dreams and then having her taken from him before he could enjoy the victory.

Before joining the navy, he had boxed, a popular sport in Ireland, and had earned some victories of his own. Boxing, besides permanetly disfiguring his right ear, had taught him a valuable lesson, when you're down, get up. Simple as it sounded, there had been several times in his short pugilistic career when he had tasted both blood and imminent defeat, only to remind himself that standing up was a lot easier than giving up, and on at least three occasions, he had returned to the fight triumphantly.

Now, was one of those times, on bended knee, apparently beaten, when those words, *stand up*, echoed in the back of his head.

Colonel Desmond had also flown back to the base just the night before, finding it no longer useful, nor necessary, to remain aboard the US aircraft carrier – especially considering the circumstances.

Statler knocked on his door. Desmond waved him in.

The man looked tired, and worn, as if he hadn't slept in days – which was probably the case.

"What is it, Statler?" asked Desmond with a weary voice, his eyes locked on small pile of papers.

"I may have an answer to our dilemma," said the man with a humbled voice.

Desmond's eyes rolled up to meet his. "Come again."

Statler took a cautionary step closer, realizing that his superior might not be in the best of moods to receive such a flamboyant and outrageous suggestion as the one he was about to make. "I think I might know a way to defuse this situation and give us another shot at the anomaly."

Desmond peered at him. "What the fook are you chatter'n about, Raymond."

"Give me five minutes of your time, sir. If you think I'm off kilter, I'll leave."

Desmond motioned him to the chair with an irritated nod.

"I've been reviewing all the factors surround'n the anomaly and something struck me."

"Which is?"

"When the American missile originally knocked it out of orbit, some 18 years ago, no obvious structural damage was done to the ship itself. In fact, Kaetlyn's dialogue with the ship's computer confirms that her navigational system was the only thing nullified at the time."

"We already concluded that it must have been an EMP, and I have it on good advice from Lillian Fray that that was the case," said Desmond with a dismissive yawn.

Statler nodded. "Aye. An Electro-Magnetic-Pulse explosion within proximity of the craft, could explain why it crashed as it did."

"We've been over this ground before, Statler, get to the point," said Desmond, his ire manifesting through a tired visage.

"It occurred to me that if we could replicate that pulse in the vicinity of the Lubov, that is, before it reaches the line of scrimmage and the shite really hits the fan, it's entirely possible that the on-board computer might interpret it as another threat to the ship and respond in a similar fashion."

Desmond leaned back in his chair, his tired mind suddenly awakened by some strange possibility. "Even if that was possible, what good does it do us if that thing flies off somewhere? Maybe it buries itself deeper into the seabed, or a mountain where we can never find it?"

Statler leaned forward, feeling more empowered by Desmond's interest.

"Yes, that is possible, sir, but not likely."

"Go on."

"I think it's more likely that the computer, now that it is aware of what has happened with Kaetlyn, that it might attempt to reach out to her."

"Because?"

Statler shrugged. "She's the captain of that ship, remember?"

Colonel Desmond shook his head, but Statler carried on.

"If we can replicate a scenario which forces the computer to act, it could accomplish two things; first, it might take evasive actions o fits own and get out of the hands of the Lubov, and secondly, as I said, attempt to contact Kaetlyn."

"It's a wild idea, Raymond."

"Yes sir, it is, but given that LIN has a mandate to fulfill the mission, it could work, and at the very least we'd have neutralized a conflict between America and the Russians; and because we're prepared for it this time, hopefully, we'd be able to track where that ship goes, giving us a chance to get control of that it again."

"And how do you propose to deliver the EMP?"

Statler's grin widened as he handed over a sheet of paper.

"Fook me," exclaimed Desmond as he stared at the schematic. "Of course, the *Man of War* - our underwater line of defense against a Russian assault from the north," he uttered as he looked at the schematic showing the location of nearly 50 submerged EMP devices, stretching across the North Sea between the Faroe and Shetland Islands.

"Those EMPs were specifically engineered to release a powerful enough electro-magnetic force to cripple a naval incursion, even submarines." Raymond pointed at the schematic. "In fact, as you may recall, they were designed with a release mechanism, allowing us to selectively float them to the surface in order to maximize their impact."

Desmond looked up at him. "*Man of War* was a joint venture between us and the Brits. We'd need their approval to activate them."

Statler nodded. "It's a phone call away, sir," he said, glancing at his watch. "And last I checked, the Lubov was about 30 minutes out from the American flotilla – and then all hell is going to break loose."

16

The *International Space Station* had just completed its tenth orbit of the Earth that day.

Hannah Weber, the German member of the European team, and Vivian Dubois, her French counterpart, sat in discussion over their latest findings.

"I want to show you something," said Hannah as she tapped a screen. Her fingers worked the keys, bringing an image up. "On our last pass over the Ross Ice Shelf, we got this."

Vivian leaned closer, touched the screen and expanded the image. Her head cocked to one side as her brow furrowed. "Is that what I think it is?"

Hannah nodded. "It's a fissure, there is no doubt about it. But that's not the most alarming thing," she paused as she tapped the screen once again and brought up a chart. "These are the most recent spectrometer readings from Apex."

Vivian's eyes widened. "The density reading is 50% less than the rest of the ice."

Hannah eyed the chart as she nodded. "Suggesting that there's a massive cavity under that rift, Viv, and when we fly over it again ..." she paused to check their flight itinerary, "at 23:00, we can intensify the spectral scan and get an even better reading."

Vivian leaned back, her face rippling with concern as her eyes flitted from the computer chart to Hannah. "Should we tell ESA or wait until we get more evidential material?"

Hannah shrugged. "We should alert them now. The next flyby is only going to corroborate what we already know."

Vivian exhaled. "My god, the Ross Ice Shelf is actually melting away faster than we knew."

17

In view of the potential for a military confrontation, Captain Harper had ordered the civilians removed from the ship and returned to Ireland.

After two stops to refuel and several hours inside a shaking and rumbling tin can, Kaetlyn was more than happy to set foot on Irish soil.

The pilot had been instructed to drop them at the Bantry airstrip, a small one at that, but nonetheless, it was just ten minutes from home.

Three lone figures dashed across the asphalt to meet them.

Her mum squeezed Kaetlyn so hard that it took the air from her lungs, refusing to let go until Kaetlyn forced the issue so she could breathe again.

Tears rolled down Claire's cheeks. "I missed you, darling."

"And what about me, did ya miss yur ol' man?" huffed Harry with a jovial glint in his eye.

"Aye, ya big lard," she squeezed him.

Kaetlyn turned just in time to receive an embrace from Alana, her best friend. "You little bitch, why didn't you tell me?"

"It all happened so fast. I promise to fill in the bits for ya."

Standing next to Alana was Shamus, a reserved look on his face, clearly unsure of exactly how to negotiate the matter. In his heart he was exhilarated to see Kaetlyn, but he knew that now was not the time to express his feelings. "How are ya, Kaet?" he asked.

18

"We've got minutes left to make a decision here," said Desmond, sitting in a conference room with Raymond Statler, while speaking to the Irish Minister of Defense, and her counterpart in London.

"This sounds very rash," responded the British MOD.

"It is," responded Desmond. "However, given the circumstances, it is the most sensible thing we can do to avert a military confrontation and to get some leverage on this situation."

The Irish MOD spoke. "We are assuming that by setting off one or more of those underwater buoys, that it will somehow activate this … "thing"," she said, her voice clearly conveying her incredulity, "but what it if does something else?"

"You're suggesting that it might affect other vessels in the proximity?" asked Desmond.

"Precisely. What if an America sub is neutralized? Or what if the Russians, or the Americans for that matter, perceive the explosion as provocation on either side."

Desmond tipped his head at Statler, giving him a tacit go ahead to speak.

"Ma'am, my name is Raymond Statler. I am a naval engineer under Colonel Desmond's command…"

"I'm familiar with your name, Statler, you are after all, the one who dug this thing from the cliffside."

"I have studied the schematics for *Man of War*, in quite some detail. The location of the buoys, and the range of the EMP is very specific. We can only activate a buoy if we know that the *Lubov* is within its proximity, otherwise the effect of the blast would be minimal. If there should happen to be another vessel within range of that explosion, the worst-case scenario is that their electronics would be rendered entirely dysfunctional."

"You mean, destroyed?" she retorted.

"Yes ma'am. The EMP was designed to permanently disable an enemy craft, literally frying its electronic circuits. It's not fatal to humans, but of course, there can be collateral damage of which we cannot entirely control."

The British Minister of Defense interceded.

"I am of the mind that we should proceed with this plan, if only to disable the trawler, and if it means getting that thing out of the hands of the Russians. I believe it is worth any collateral damage."

"And how do you propose we explain this to the Yanks and the Ruskies?" inquired the Irish woman.

Desmond tipped his head at the screen. "If it works, and that thing does what we hope it will do, we'll just have to talk our way out of it."

"That's a very slippery slope, Colonel."

"Ma'am, may I speak freely?"

She consented with a nod.

"In less than ten minutes, we'll be past the point where this plan is effectual. At that juncture, it'll be out of our hands anyhow, and a shite-fight will ensue between the Yanks and the Russians. We can either stand by and spectate, or we can take our chances at neutralizing a worse-case scenario."

The Irish Minister of Defense sat in silence, her eyes skidding away from the screen as she weighed all the factors. Normally, she would consult with the PM first, but there were clauses, military contingencies that gave her the power to make snap decisions in the event of such a crisis.

She turned to the screen.

"You have my consent, Desmond. I hope to hell this works, or all of our arses will be in the fire."

19

The Captain of the *Lubov* scanned the seas ahead with a nervous tick in his brow.

He wasn't cut-out for warfare. He was a civilian, a commercial pilot of a fishing trawler, who, admittedly, and secretly, occasionally did special errands on behalf of Moscow. *But this*, he huffed, *was outside his comfort zone.*

His stomach had been twisted up in knots for days, ever since they first arrived over the object, winched it aboard his vessel, and set off back to Russia.

Ahead, the string of American ships hovered, like sharks in wait, and below, to each side of his vessel, he knew that two American subs were ghosting him.

"Sir, it's the Captain of the Nikolay Kuznetsov, he wants to speak to you."

Sergei took the headset.

"Sergei," sounded the authoritative voice of the man heading up the flotilla just some kilometers ahead.

"Yes, Captain."

"Hold your bearing at your current coordinates. Do not deviate your speed. Is that clear?"

"Da."

"Good."

"But, what if the Americans ..."

His question was cut short by a curt reply. "You do not deviate, you do not slow down. I will deal with the Americans, da!?"

"Da."

Sergei drew in a deep breath, feeling the last of his stomach muscles surrendering to the mounting pressure, and a sickly feeling consuming him like murky water seeping through his veins.

Was he committing his crew and his boat to a deep-sea burial, he wondered?

Was this cargo so valuable that two nations would go to war over it?

He pulled the binoculars to his eyes and peered at the massive aircraft carrier close in pursuit, the words, *Gerald R. Ford* imprinted on its bow, close enough to be read.

He sighed, wondering if he'd ever see his wife and kids again as he silently prayed for a miracle.

20

Captain Harper stood like a block of granite, matching the sway of his ship as it plowed through the whitecaps of the North Sea.

Ahead, the *Lubov*, was dancing in rhythm to the rising waves.

"How long before it reaches our ships?" he demanded.

"At its current speed, 13 minutes," answered the navigator.

"Get the Captain of the Enterprise on the horn."

A moment later, the voice of his counterpart spoke. "Hi Jim, how are things shaping up at your end?" asked the Captain of the lead vessel in the flotilla now facing-off with the Russians.

"The Lubov doesn't appear to be slowing down."

"No, it isn't. In fact, they're holding steady on their current course."

"So, if they pass the line of scrimmage – what then?"

"We'll fire a shot over her bow, as ordered," answered the other.

"You think the Russians will idly sit by and do nothing?"

"They might show some muscle, but I don't think Ivan is going to do anything drastic – they know better. How 'bout you, your team ready?"

"I've got two skimmers ready to deploy. My team will board the Lubov in ..." Harper glanced at his watch, "... roughly six minutes."

"Tighter than a nun's ..."

"I know," Harper cut him off. "Ivan isn't going to be happy when we board that trawler."

"Well, if it's any consolation, they drew first blood, Jim, they stole it from us. We're just taking back our property."

"Yeah," sighed Harper. "I'm not so sure that Ivan will see it that way."

21

Despite her mum's best efforts at leveraging her magical wand, with the aroma of freshly-baked scones and coffee, nothing abated her growing sense of dread. All Kaetlyn could think about was the theater some eight hundred kilometers north of her.

On the way home from the airstrip, Shamus had expressed his concerns, that while the video he had posted, revealing the whole story to the world, had garnered over three million views so far, there were veiled, even direct threats in the commentary thread. Some people saw Kaetlyn as a harbinger of disaster, an omen, a satanic figure in disguise – and the threats were very real.

She hadn't paid it much attention then, but now, alone in her room, she wondered about it.

Why were people so afraid of finding out the truth, she thought?

Her fear that the US government would hush it all up and secret the craft to some military installation, never to be seen or heard of, was now aggrandized by another growing trepidation – that people were threatening her life.

Visions of her encounters at school, her deliberate confrontations with the faculty, challenging their statements about God and Divine creation, the Theory of Evolution, the very paradigm of human existence – now played across her mind.

She had never understood why ignorance, selective or taught, was acceptable, and why turning a blind eye to the potential of much greater truths, was so abhorrent to some; but as she scrolled through the commentary thread posted on the video, the statements showed the depth of people's beliefs; their assertions that there are no aliens, no life elsewhere in the Universe, that all of this is sheer heresy against the word of God and his truth, a mad tirade of denial and veiled threats, as if her very existence threatened theirs.

She looked to the window and noticed a lone figure trudging through the rain toward their house. She dashed to the door and opened it.

"Hi Shamus," she said, clearly happy to see him.

He wiped the rain from his face. "Figur'd you might like some company."

Claire O'Sullivan smiled at him as he stepped into the house. "Hi ya, Shamus," she said, as if they had known one another for a long time.

Harry looked up from his paper with his usual poker face in play, but Kaetlyn knew that he was just biding his time, like her, waiting to hear the outcome of events on the North Sea.

She led him to her room, closed the door and pulled a chair out for him.

Shamus shook off the cold as his eyes met hers.

"I feel a bit weird 'bout it all," he said with a cautious smile.

"Oh, you mean the fact that we both share the same experience from a past life," she quipped. "What's so weird about that?" she ended with an impish smile.

"It's just that ..."

Kaetlyn reached out a hand and touched his. "Look, Shamus, this is new to me too."

He sighed as he relaxed a little. "Were we...?" he paused.

She smiled. "Apparently so."

"Shite, that's so mental to even have to reckon with. Anyhow, maybe its best we shelve that part of this whole thing until later, we have more important things to discuss, agreed?"

She nodded.

"Do you think you'll get another shot at talking with the computer?" he asked.

She shrugged. "I hope so. I don't know what to expect."

"Yeah. But, if you do get back inside the ship, what will you do?"

Kaetlyn was silent for a time before answering. She looked up at him. "I'm going to do the right thing."

"Meaning?"

"If it comes down to it, I will lock the computer."

"How?"

She sighed. "I'll just tell LIN to shut up and not talk to anyone except me."

Shamus' head wagged. "That's dangerous, Kaet."

She cast an eye at the growing line of commentary on her computer screen. "Any more dangerous than that?" she nodded.

22

The Captain of the *Lubov* spoke as his eyes remained fixed on the *Enterprise*, the massive carrier now looming directly ahead, literally towering above his own vessel, it's prow capable of crushing his boat in a single run.

"Are they changing course?" he demanded of his First Mate.

"No, Captain."

"Pizdets!" he exclaimed.

"Captain," the voice sounded over the loudspeaker. "Skimmers are approaching from the rear."

Sergei sprang to the port observation deck, and peered through his binoculars at two inflatable US navy skimmers speeding his way.

"Fucking, Christ, the Americans are going to board us," he exclaimed.

He turned to issue orders to speed up, when the shock wave hit.

The tremor shook his ship, like an earthquake.

His eyes worked the sky above, and the line of ships facing him, but nothing was different.

"Captain!" the alarmed voice of his First Mate, sounded.

He turned to see the man staring at the ship's control panel with a ghostly pale face.

The panel was dark, completely dead and nothing the First Mate did was changing it.

Suddenly the bridge lights flickered and died. In fact, every light within view was suddenly gone.

"Go to reserve power," he commanded.

The First Mate pressed his palm to the emergency button– nothing happened.

"Go to back-up power," screamed Sergei.

The First Mate turned to him with a dreaded look. "Every single electronic aspect of the ship is dead, sir, even the radio."

"What the fuck could do that?"

The Captain rushed back out onto the observation deck, looking down at his crew who scurried about in confusion.

In the odd silence that ensued, the brief seconds between something and nothing, another rumbling ensued, one that vibrated throughout the ship.

The Captain raced down the stairwell, following the source of the sound.

Dashing to the aft portion of the ship, he skidded to a stop and watched in abject shock as the anomaly, their precious cargo, slowly rose up from the belly of the holding bay where it had sat since being winched up from the bottom of the sea.

The high-pitched whine grew more sonorous as it rose level to his eyes, a sight so bizarre and so mesmerizing, that he could not move.

A tremulous rumble filled the air, and then it streaked away with an explosive concussion that drove them to the deck.

23

Donovan O'Neil monitored every bit of news concerning the events unfolding on the North Sea.

Naturally, because of the circumstances and the potential for conflict, not to mention that a Russian trawler was carrying an alien spacecraft, something that Shamus Maguire's video had spotlighted to the entire world, the military had issued a no-fly-zone injunction to within 100 kilometers of the area.

Civilian flights over the North Sea had been halted. Commercial and civilian ships had been put to anchor.

In other words, a total lock-down, and it was only by the grace of god, or maybe just his sense of adventure, that Donovan had even managed to fly in and out with the Cessna pilot, just before the lid was clamped tight.

Unfortunately, their military sources were providing no information whatsoever – all of which suggested that there was a lot more credence to Shamus and Kaetlyn's story.

He didn't have to wait long, in fact, he heard the voice cutting the air, calling his name. The editor seemed to have a genetic aversion to using intercom or other means of calling people to his office, preferring simply yelling out their names into a sea of journalists.

As he entered the office, the man's look of repressed shock was as visible as a storm cloud on a sunny day.

"There's been an explosion."

"The Yanks?"

"No. My source tells me that the Yanks did not fire on the Lubov."

"So, what happened?"

"All we know is that the Russian trawler is sitting dead in the water, its entire operating system, its engines, anything electronic, has been rendered dysfunctional."

Donovan twisted his brow upwards. "What could possibly do that?"

The editor shrugged. "That's not the real concern. The issue is that thing, whatever they had on board the Lubov, it took off."

"What?!"

"Yes. No one's been able to track it yet."

"Oh my god."

The editor pressed forward. "Get hold of your source, Donovan. Find out what you can, and fast."

This time Donovan raced from the office, his heart pounding against his chest as he dialed up Shamus.

24

Aengus Cafferty had been fishing these very waters since he was nigh-on five years of age, having plucked his very first catch off these shores, using a small harpoon while his dad, a fisherman by trade, cast him an approving wink. That singular praise had started him on a life-long career.

Now, at 77 years of age, his hands ached, and his skin, though tough and leathery from constant exposure to the touch of the Celtic, no longer weathered the elements so well. He knew his time was coming to an end.

And though the sea still beckoned to him, like a siren afar, it was becoming harder to answer her call.

Soon he'd have to cash in a lifetime calling and join some of his peers in that lonely and forgotten land called *retirement*, a place where people dreamed of how good things used to be, while waiting for the day when some higher power would whisk them away and end their agony.

He rolled in the net as the white caps sloshed against his small boat, pressing a knee against the side to keep his balance, while dumping his latest catch into a metal basin.

With one eye on the sea, the other peered up at the darkening sky, a foreboding one and a precursor to an approaching storm.

With his hunt flopping about in the bin, he started the engine with a crack followed by a plume of gray-white smoke that shot upwards, and then angled its rudder, aiming inland.

Ahead, was the one-eyed monster, as some called *Sheep's Head Lighthouse* – it's singular beam streaming through the mist of an incipient twilight. The lighthouse had stood on that very promontory, never failing in its duty, since he could remember. It had saved his arse many times, the only beacon visible in these often fog-ridden shores.

As his small boat plugged along, tacking into the waves at just the right angle, he caught sight of a flash ahead.

Age may have stolen his vitality, but not his sight. His eyes were as sharp as a gull's, and he knew that the odd flash was not coming from Sheep's Head. This was different as it cut through the twilight like a bullet speeding downward at a steep angle.

In the split second of its existence, the flash vanished not far up the coast.

Never short on courage, and often accused of lacking prudence, he throttled the motor and turned in that direction.

The sky thickened with the haze of a growing crepuscule, and the shore ahead dimmed in the growing murk. Without *Sheep's Head* to guide him, he was on his own.

He turned on the spotlight, casting a white tunnel ahead, and continued to plow through the seas as the waves pressed him dangerously close to the rocky shoreline.

When he arrived at the spot where he figured it must have come to, whatever "it" was, there was no sign of anything.

Maybe it was a meteor, a plane, or maybe even one of them satellites, he thought, but there should have been flotsam, something revealing the crash.

Not easily deterred in his quest, the old man grabbed the spotlight and manually cast its tunneled-beam, following a 360-degree path around his small boat.

Nothing. Just waves and the sound of an impending storm blowing in.

He sighed. *"Aye, could'a been somethin' – could'a been noth'n,"* he mused aloud. *"Time to go home."*

He gripped the throttle of the engine and brought the boat around on a heading back up the coast, and that's when he saw it.

The old man froze as consternation gripped him to his very core.

Slowly, he reached for the spotlight, angled it upwards into the sky, and there, to his utter shock, was something that in all his days he had never witnessed.

25

Raymond Statler had been monitoring the Naval radio frequencies for hours – listening for anything, any sightings, any indication of where the anomaly might have disappeared to.

He hadn't involved himself in the fall-out in the wake of the EMP they had set off below the Lubov; that he left up to others to deal with.

The real concern was where did it go?

And how could it disappear without leaving a trail?

No satellite tracking system, nor radar, not even surface monitoring systems that could track of thousands of airplanes in the air to an accuracy of inches, had revealed its location.

Clearly, the technology aboard that craft exceeded anything they had on Earth – an ability to fly invisible, undetected and literally off the grid.

Taking a sip on his lukewarm coffee, he rubbed his tired eyes, and wondered how it would all end?

Would the object just simply disappear for good, this time buried in the sea or in a mountain side somewhere, or maybe it had escaped the Earth's atmosphere and was now streaking back to its home world?

Everything that had happened in the past two weeks felt oddly surreal to him – as if maybe none of it had really happened at all. And yet, it had.

His eyes turned back to the screen as he scrolled through the coast guard site. Suddenly, something caught his attention; a short memo just recently logged by a coast guard station, and in that brief instant, his fatigue, his despair, his disillusionment vanished like smoke in the wind as he sprinted from the room.

26

Kaetlyn's mobile buzzed.

It was Alana, her best friend.

"Kaet, you best look at the news. Now!" she practically screamed.

Kaetlyn's fingers worked her phone, pulling up the newsfeed. "Fook!" she exclaimed.

Tearing from her room, with Shamus in tow, she found her dad lolling in his armchair, half asleep. "Get up!"

Harry O'Sullivan jerked to a start. "What!?"

"We need to go, now," her voice pitched high as she vibrated with excitement.

Harry pushed himself to his feet. "What's going on, lass?"

"The ship, dad, it's back. It's hovering above the shore, exactly where they found it in that cliff."

27

The rocky shoreline was already crowded with locals.

News had spread like wildfire, and given the remoteness of the region, its sparsely populated villages, the appearance of this many people was itself a phenomenon.

Harry parked the car on the promontory above, overlooking the site, and from there, he and the others descended a steep path, arriving just as several military helicopters swooped in for a landing.

The crowd backed up giving the machines a wide-berth.

Even though she had seen it a dozen times during her sessions aboard the Largs Bay, Kaetlyn was breathless at the sight.

The choppers settled to the rocky ground, spewing up a storm of dirt and particulates that forced people to cover their faces.

A familiar face emerged from one of them, that of Colonel Desmond – followed by Raymond Statler.

From the other choppers came a covey of armed military personnel who rapidly formed a perimeter below the anomaly which hovered some fifteen meters above.

Kaetlyn caught the eye of Desmond who waived her through the military cordon, along with her entourage.

"I must say," began the man, "you have an uncanny ability to be in the right place at the right time, Ms. O'Sullivan." His eyes rose up in the air to the object directly above them.

Desmond nodded to Harry O'Sullivan and turned to the other two. "Shamus Maguire, I assume?"

"Aye, sir."

Desmond pinched his lips. "You created a real shite-storm for us, lad."

"Aye, I did," answered Shamus without an ounce of remorse.

Kaetlyn turned to Alana. "This is my best friend, Alana. She is cousin to Shamus."

Desmond nodded respectfully and then faced-off with Kaetlyn.

"You know that ship better than anyone, why did it come back here?" he asked.

Kaetlyn fixed him a glare. "I could ask you the same thing, Colonel."

Desmond raised a brow, accentuating it with a subtle smile. "We've bought some time, Kaetlyn, that's all. Let's use it wisely. The Yanks are sailing back this way as we speak, and I expect they're going to insist on getting inside that thing."

"And the Russians," asked Harry.

Desmond shrugged. "They're probably drowning their sorrows in vodka right about now." He grinned.

Kaetlyn stared up at the ship. "I need to speak with LIN."

Desmond's head bobbed as he considered the problem. He turned to Statler. "Get your men to move that crane over here," he pointed to one of the large lifts they had used to excavate the anomaly from the cliffside.

Desmond turned back to Kaetlyn. "I will get you inside, but this time, I'm coming with you."

She nodded. "Fair enough, but I want Serena and Shamus in there too."

Watching as the crane rolled across the rocky beach, crushing stones beneath its tonnage, Kaetlyn turned to see Serena pressing herself through the crowd toward her.

"Came as fast as I could," she said through broken breaths as she suddenly stared up at thr craft with renewed awe. Up until now, she'd only seen it sitting on the deck of the Largs Bay. But now, it hovered silently above her, a sight that could hardly be called normal.

"Why is it here?" she asked as her eyes levelled with Katelyn's.

"I don't know, but we're going to find out soon enough."

Book Five

1

The Molly, a fishing vessel out of Cape Town, South Africa, was technically a *catch-and-freeze trawler*, one designed with all the facilities necessary to slice, preserve and package them as market-ready fillets.

67 meters in length, with a crew of 33, *The Molly* was seaworthy for six weeks at a time, returning to Cape Town with a sizeable tonnage of product after each outing.

Captain, Lawrence Biggard, usually referred to as, "Biggie", had been commanding the vessel for twenty years. This would be his 80th and final haul, given that they did the same itinerary every quarter.

At 59 years of age, Biggie was a veteran of the south seas, having navigated much of the Antarctic, particularly the Ross Sea.

It was a brutal and harrowing domain, with tempests that sometimes shook his ship to the bone, threatening to sink it at any moment.

Then of course, there was the cold, a frigidity of which his home town, in South Africa, had never experienced. A place where a casual mistake, touching a metal rail with a bare hand or exposing skin for just minutes, could result in injury.

He had seen his share of dire moments, with waves, trough to crest, the size of a ten-story building, but each time, they had come out of it, returning home with a decent haul.

This would be his final voyage on *The Molly*. When they arrived back to Cape Town, he would pass the torch and assume a rather innocuous position in administration, coasting along in his final years before retirement and then, the ultimate voyage - death.

Standing on the bridge, he eyed the sea ahead.

Despite its ruthless side, the Ross Sea was a thing of extraordinary beauty.

To his right, a wall of ice rose high above the ship, like a towering skyscraper, but one that extended along the edge of the Ross Ice Shelf as far as the eye could see.

Ahead were the caps of ice floes, some large, some small, some which his radar man had to constantly observe, because beneath the surface could be an iceberg that would crush the hull of his ship and send them into the abyss of history.

"Captain," the voice of his First Mate sounded.

Biggie turned to him.

"I'm pick'n up something strange on the sonar."

Biggie sidled over and looked at the screen.

"Those spikes are very unusual," commented the other, his finger lingering over several surges on an otherwise level chart.

Biggie glanced at the calm sea ahead. "Don't make sense, does it? No storm clouds, no seismic activity, why the spikes?"

As Biggie pondered the anomaly while a voice inside his head cautioned him with a warning signal. It was the same voice he had listened to before, when tiny red flags appeared, when something didn't seem right, and when his prerogative as Captain had given him the authority to turn the ship, to speed away, or to take a different course and avoid some unseen, yet imminent danger.

Was this a time to listen to that voice, he wondered.

"What do you think?" he asked the First Mate, a man who had sailed these very seas with him for nearly twenty years.

"Don't know, Cap, never seen anything quite like it."

"Can we get a bearing on where it's comin' from?"

The First Mate tapped the screen. "To our right somewhere," he nodded at the wall of ice that towered above the ship.

Biggie looked out the curved window that encompassed the bridge. "That's the Ross, man, that makes no sense."

As they watched the image on the screen, it suddenly shifted again, the sonar picking up more disturbance, and spiking by nearly two times.

Both men's eyes widened, never having seen such readings before.

A deep and sonorous growl suddenly filled the air around them.

The ship resonated it, like a gong, and Biggie felt his teeth rattling.

They turned to see plumes of white suddenly shooting up above the Ross, like geysers from multiple volcanos.

More plumes speared upward and with them came a cracking sound, as if a piece of the world had just broken off.

Their eyes widened with shock as the air above the Ross Ice Shelf thickened with a shroud of white, and with it, came a sight that stultified them, watching as the edge of the ice shelf, some 40 meters high, splintered, like a fracture in a massive dam.

"Get us the fuck out of here," he screamed to his First Mate.

The man whipped the wheel, hard to port.

The ship lurched forward, its net still dragging through the water behind as the Captain issued orders to cut it loose.

He turned a frantic eye to the icy wall that stood like an ancient fortification, watching in sheer consternation as its face lurched forward, like the side of a building suddenly canting. "Oh my fucking Christ," he exclaimed. "It's coming apart."

"Keep that throttle full-on!" he commanded as he ran from the bridge, sprinted to the aft section of the ship where his men were struggling to disengage the massive net, one already heavy with their first catch of the day.

As the ship surged ahead at full speed, the drag and the pressure exerted on the winches used to draw in the net, had already exceeded their limitations. All three winches locked tight, followed by the sound of metal grinding and clashing, like the scream of anguish.

Biggie grabbed the winch-controls from one of his men.

In his peripheral vision, he could see the wall of ice now separating itself, careening to one side, and then it happened.

They watched as a fatalistic sense of defeat blanketed them; as an entire section of the Ross Ice Shelf, possibly kilometers in length, ruptured and exploded outward with a crack that filled the world, and then toppled into the maws of a waiting sea.

The tidal wave that followed, ripped across the Ross Sea at a speed that exceeded anything that *The Molly* could ever hope to outrun – barely enough time to issue a mayday before it joined the ranks of the Titanic.

2

With her daughter and husband safely back home, Claire O'Sullivan had tried to steal an hour or two of desperately needed sleep since returning from the airport, but that was not to be.

As Kaetlyn, Shamus and Harry rushed out the door she had tried to get their attention, a task quite impossible to accomplish considering the sudden reappearance of the alien craft.

The nervous quaking inside her, the specter of her recent haunting, all of it, had left her with a terrible sense of dread.

She sat at the kitchen table with a cold cup of untouched tea in front of her, wondering whether she should call Harry, or if it was best to lock it inside her, and just hope for the best.

She did not consider herself a religious person, certainly not a God-fearing one, but her upbringing had imbibed her with certain cultural beliefs and one of them was the appearance of the banshee.

With the background noise of the television, and the media spilling out a fountain of news about the strange alien craft hovering just miles from her home, she picked up her mobile and dialed the number.

"Harry!" her voice sounded with repressed emotion.

"Everything's fine, Claire, if that's what you're call'n 'bout," he said before she could utter a word.

"No, Harry, listen to me, I don't think it's fine at all."

Harry O'Sullivan, standing amidst the crowd, watching as his daughter and the others were hoisted into the sky on the platform of a crane, was in no mood for discussions.

"Claire, what the fook are you chatter'n 'bout?"

"I had a vision. T'was a Banshee visited me."

"Ah, shite, woman, you and your fook'n myths, let it go, Claire."

She paused. "Harry, ya know what it means, don'a ya?"

He sighed, his eyes still rivetted on the crane high above. "Claire, please, I don'a want a hear about banshees and dire myths, not now."

She bit her lip. "Just you be careful, and make sure our daughter is okay, promise me that."

"I will, and I'll call ya later," he said.

When the call ended, she remained stone cold as her vision blurred with tears.

Maybe it was just an old myth as Harry claimed, a mere wive's tale, Irish lore and all, but as much as she tried to deny it, the specter of the banshee she had seen during her fitful sleep, now filled her mind, and with it came the dreaded message – that whenever a banshee appeared in a dream, it was a sign of death to come, that someone in the family was about to be taken.

3

Rear Admiral, Norman Patterson, sat staring into a screen at the faces of the Commander of the Navy, located in Virginia, and the Captain of the *Gerald R. Ford,* Jim Harper, thousands of miles away.

"Well, "said Patterson, "we dodged a bullet with the Russians – if that's any consolation.

The Commander of the Navy shook his head. "True, but the President is having a fucking meltdown next door. He's pissed."

Patterson refrained from expressing his thoughts on the matter. In his experience, perfect plans were never perfect, and no matter the contingencies, Murphy's Law ruled – that is, *whatever can go wrong will go wrong.*

"Sir, with all due respect, none of these incidents were under our control."

The Commander crimped his lips. A stern look passing over his face. "I know that Norm, we all do, but politicians live in a different world than you and I. They think their plans are perfect before their time." He paused to draw a breath. "That said, I have to appease the President with something. Listen up, Harper, once the GRF is back at that coastal area you anchor it close enough to show those damn Irish that we're not disappearing and that we have every intention of reclaiming our property, and meanwhile, we'll let Anne Lansing and her team in the State Department, smooth it over with Ministry of Foreign Affairs in Dublin. I want that thing on the GRF today – end of story."

"Understood, sir" acknowledged Captain Harper. "Although, I'm wondering how we're going to do that if that ship is in the control of its computer."

"Better figure out a way to use this young woman to get that computer playing ball."

"And what about the Russians, what are they saying?" asked Patterson.

"Radio silence right now," answered the Commander. "Once that thing left the *Lubov*, the show was over. We called off the Northern Fleet, the Russians hauled the Lubov away, and right about now, I figure they're hacking every computer they can get their hands on. I don't think we have to worry about them right now. They played their best hand and they lost."

Patterson spoke. "Captain, Harper, as you well know, that thing is hovering over the exact spot where it was excavated from, and according to the news reports, Kaetlyn O'Sullivan is about to step foot inside that ship. I suspect that this time, when she comes out, she'll be coming out with pure gold, and we need to be ready to move fast, because that news is going to hit the airwaves. We already know she has her own agenda."

"I am quite aware of this young lady's intentions."

"Okay, you have your orders, Captain," said the Naval Commander as he closed the line to Harper.

"Listen, Norm," he began, "this shit-storm is far from over. Right now, that girl is holding all the aces, and the Irish have control over that craft because it's back in their territory. We don't know what's going to happen, but I'm pretty sure they're going to stall until she opens Pandora's box. We need a continency plan, something to help expedite the matter in our favor."

"I understand, sir. And just where do we draw the line on this contingency?"

The Commander's face soured. "Considering its importance to our national security, anything within reason, maybe even more."

"I'll get my team to work-up a proposal."

"Good, because I'm scheduled to meet with the President in an hour and I need something to appease that man."

4

Standing on the platform, high above the beach, as it gently swayed to the push and tug of a Celtic wind, Kaetlyn cast a cursory glance at the crowd below.

"My god, how many people are down there?" she murmured.

Colonel Desmond glanced at the crowd. "Oh, figure on at least three, maybe four-hundred, but I guarantee you it will be in the thousands soon."

The crane eased toward the portal of the craft, and then gently kissed its side.

Desmond turned an eye to Kaetlyn. "It's your show now, lass."

She stepped forward, placed her hand against the portal as she had done a dozen times before, but this time her heart was racing as adrenaline pumped through her veins, in the knowledge that the world was now watching.

The door silently whooshed open.

Serena and Kaetlyn stepped into the antechamber without delay, while the others, slack-jawed, stood back, hesitant.

"Come on," motioned Kaetlyn, "it doesn't bite."

With the others in tow, Kaetlyn navigated two more doors and took them to the large control room – the bridge of the craft.

Shamus was gripped by an overwhelming awe as he walked the perimeter – his face filled with wonder.

Colonel Desmond was beside himself as he approached the control panel and then ran his hand over its perfectly smooth, yet alien surface.

"Look familiar?" asked Kaetlyn with an eye to Shamus.

"It's mental," he responded.

"Well, feel free to look around, but best if everyone stays quiet for this next part."

Drawing herself onto one of the over-sized chairs, she placed her left hand on the console and tapped in the code.

The holographic image materialized above, with the digital face of LIN, and a soft incredulous voice spoke.

"Hello, Kaetlyn – good to see you again."

5

As time marched on and the air grew colder and the wind growled even meaner, the crowd was becoming surly – people wanted to know what was happening inside the strange ship.

The questions were bandied about, and even the media, with its cameras poised into the air, was asking the same questions.

Raymond Statler tried to allay their concerns as people pressed against the ring of soldiers, demanding answers while tossing questions at him like stones from a mob.

Suddenly, another chopper swooped in from above, and from it emerged more brass. They approached him.

"Where's Colonel Desmond?" asked a senior officer with more braid than Statler had seen on most.

Statler's eyes rose to the crane above. "He's inside, sir?"

"Doing what?"

"I can only assume that Colonel Desmond is doing his job as head of Military Intelligence."

The man turned to the others, engaging in a short discourse and then turned back to Statler. "I want to go up there."

"You can't, sir."

"Why not?"

"Because, the only way into that ship is with the young woman, and they're inside now. Until they come out, no one gets in."

Raymond caught sight of Harry O'Sullivan approaching. "Who are these blokes?" he pointed.

Raymond shook his head. "Don't worry 'bout them, Harry. Just more dicks trying to get a piece of the pie."

Raymond's attitude had clearly shifted in the past days. Two weeks ago, when he had first engaged this mission, he was both skeptical and aloof about what it all meant. But now, it had become personal for him in way he could not even quite fathom. He was championing Kaetlyn, and moreover, like her, he wanted to see the secrets of that craft made available to the entire world.

Watching as Harry O'Sullivan returned to his spot in the crowd, Raymond's gaze drifted upwards to the spectacle that held the world spellbound.

What secrets it possessed could change the course of humanity, he thought, or, in the worst-case scenario, *send it spiraling down another road.*

The world was waiting for an eighteen-year-old woman to tell them which it would be.

6

News of the phenomenon on the southwest coast of Ireland, had, indeed, transfixed the entire world.

Across the globe, people were glued to television sets, mobile phones and hand-held devices as the media, difficult as it was to gain any insights into what was happening, provided live-streaming of the on-goings.

It was estimated that that 17% of the world's population had watched the first man, Neil Armstrong, step on the moon back in 1969. But today, as Kaetlyn was ferried up to the alien craft, that record had been smashed, as a whopping 23% of the global population watched on or listened to news of what appeared to be First Contact with another race of beings.

The internet, particularly social media, the court of public opinion and disinformation, reflected countless tens of thousands of commentary threads.

Some heralded the event as a precursor to the second coming of Christ.

Others vociferously asserted it was the harkening of doomsday.

Most saw it for what it really was; *First Contact* with another sentient species, catalyzing a flood of discussions challenging accepted mediocrity, with its asserted theories about creation, the Universe, the very paradigms of our culture.

Amongst the commentary were the hateful ones, the extremists, the righteous puritans, the religious zealots, who referred to Kaetlyn O'Sullivan as some kind of witch, the spawn of Satan, something evil – a herald of imminent doom and destruction – an ungodly thing.

Their threats were couched in words of suspicion and hatred, some even alluded to violence, while others offered up threats of death – as if her very existence now threatened the world and god himself.

Stan Murphy was one of them, having openly declared himself a card-carrying member of this latter club.

After the altercation in the pub, a week earlier, where he openly and quite deliberately insulted Kaetlyn, calling her a witch to Harry O'Sullivan's face, an act which had earned him a knuckle sandwich, the man had not been dissuaded from his mission.

Murphy's ego was sustained by three pillars.

First, his claim that God was the source of everything and that science answered to the Almighty, none other.

Second, a consummate racist, believing to his core that only pure-blooded Irish deserved to live on Irish soild, and the rest, the darkies, the towel heads, the slope heads, every rendition he used to judge and objectify those who were not white skinned and of Irish descent, belonged elsewhere.

Finally, the last stanchion was his hateful arrogance toward others – of which the man seemed to have no scarcity of.

Stan Murphy saw the world through a veil; as if looking through colored glass his perception of it and those around him was entirely self-serving and self-empowering. If others didn't see things his way, he would take them down a notch. If they were not god-loving and god-fearing folk, he would objectify them as "different", "stupid" or just "not good people". In other words, the man's hypocrisy had no limits as he played the hand of judgement, as if he was the ambassador of God himself.

"*It's the Devil's work*," he brazenly announced at the pub, where several of his drinking mates nodded in silence, as they avidly watched the news on the television screen.

He gulped down yet another glass of ale as he stood and declared, "*I'll not stand by and let this vile girl*," his words seethed from his mouth, "desecrate the good name of our Lord. This little witch, this little cunt from hell, has to go."

When he disappeared from the pub late that morning, no one paid him much mind, figuring as usual that Stan would go home, sleep off his latest rant, and he'd be back the next day to start blustering all over again.

Unfortunately, they were wrong.

7

Everyone inside the ship was transfixed at hearing those words, "Hello Kaetlyn ..." – just spoken by the ship's computer.

"Hi, LIN," she answered.

"I think it would appropriate," said LIN "if you introduced me to your associates." Her holographic image turned to face them.

Shamus, first and foremost, felt a sudden release in the depths of his soul, as if some encysted pool had been unlocked. He smiled.

Kaetlyn nodded. "Yes, of course. You've met Serena already. This is Colonel Desmond, and this is Shamus, my ..." she paused, "... friend."

LIN's eyes lingered on Shamus, as his locked on hers.

"What is your relationship to Kaetlyn," asked LIN.

Shamus felt his throat go dry as sand, as he struggled to answer. "It's complicated."

LIN nodded, but the nuances of her face suggested she understood more than she was saying.

She turned back to Kaetlyn. "Our meetings seem to occur under very strange circumstances," said LIN with a twist of her head, a gesticulation that made her seem so lifelike, and yet, her holographic form towered over them by nearly a meter.

LIN's ebony skin was framed by braids of long silver hair and her slightly protrusive forehead was accentuated by deep-set eyes – emerald in color. She was a mesmerizing sight to all. If she was a reflection of the race of beings who had created her, then they were not only beautiful, but stately too.

"To be honest, it's been quite mental," said Kaetlyn.

"Nonetheless, it seemed appropriate that we meet again."

"Is that why you brought the ship back here?"

LIN nodded. "In truth, I didn't know if I could get the navigational system to work. It appears that I am limited to brief stints for now."

"I'm sorry to hear that."

LIN grinned. "I'm sorry you died. You had an important mission to do and now it seems that may not occur."

"You said in our last talk that our task was to save the planet."

"That is correct. This planet is, or at least was, based on the most recent reconnaissance at the time, considered a Type 5 Classification."

"Please explain what that means for the benefit of everyone here."

"It is a world on the tipping point of a global disaster."

Another holographic image appeared next to her – a 3-dimensional vision of the Earth. LIN pointed a finger into it. "Sometime before your mission was launched, a scout-droid was dispatched to this planet to observe its state. When then information was studied, it was discovered that Earth was headed for a global event."

"What kind of event?" asked Colonel Desmond, no longer able to hold his tongue.

LIN turned to him. "An extinction-event, Colonel Desmond."

"How?" he asked.

"Like other habitable planets, there is a threshold between the proper balance of planetary conditions and coexistence of its dominant species – in this case, you."

"What determines the threshold?" he asked, now feeling more comfortable about speaking to LIN.

"I believe you already know the answer to that question, Colonel Desmond."

"1.5 – is that it?" interceded Kaetlyn.

"Thereabouts, yes," answered LIN, as she reached out with a digital hand and touched the hologram of Earth. It's usual blue-green luster began to fade to a dull dusty gray. "Every habitable world in the known system of stars, has a temperature gauge, if you will, and when the planet, by whatever means, overheats, it is forced to reset itself. That re-set, or recalibration if you will, can be quite dramatic, depending on the circumstances." She turned to face them. "The drone which passed your planet several of your decades ago, revealed to us that your Earth was on a lethal path – with rising temperatures, a scenario that has an inevitable end."

"Meaning?" asked Kaetlyn.

LIN leveled her eyes on her. "Do you not remember anything about your role on this mission?"

Kaetlyn shook her head. "Sadly, no."

Again, without a word, the forward screen came to life with the image of the female crew member. "This is you, some 18 or more of your Earth years ago," said LIN with a tip of her head. "Possibly this will help to jog your memory.

You were the ship's Captain and Science Officer. It was your duty to evaluate the parameters of this planet's declination, and to provide the exact formulation for its recovery through terraforming."

Kaetlyn was momentarily bewitched by the image of her previous self – her remarkably dark skin, not unlike today, with long silver hair and deep green eyes.

Finally, she broke the spell and looked at LIN. "I don't understand. If we were sent to save this planet, as you say, how would that even be possible with a ship this size?"

"You are mis-judging size for effectiveness. The technology in my data-banks, if used properly, could help to terraform your world avert an imminent extinction event. The nature of your mission was a critical one, Kaetlyn," continued the Ai computer. "It was estimated that Earth had less than three or four decades in terms of your years, before the rapid declination would become an irreversible one."

"What exactly does that mean, declination?" asked Shamus, feeling frustrated that he could not remember a damn thing about their mission.

"It means that when a planet's overall global temperature passes a certain point, it will begin a process of reclamation to restore balance to itself. Your polar icecaps, which are already melting, will, to a very large degree, disappear. Coastal areas of all current landmasses will be submerged under water. Climatic changes will be dramatic, swift and brutal, such that it will disrupt food production, farming and the like, and even the oceans will be affected. In short, the billions of people on this planet will be subjected to an event which they cannot control nor stop, and for which they are not adapted to survive."

"So, most will die?"

LIN nodded. "Earth is not the first civilization to have perished by its own hand. Statistical precedents show that when such an event occurs, roughly 90% or more of the inhabitants perish from starvation, disease, insufferable weather and natural catastrophes."

Colonel Desmond stepped closer. LIN turned to face him, her prodigious face hanging before him like a massive Grecian statue. "You referred to terraforming – how was that meant to be done?"

"There are several factors which must be answered before I can provide you with a succinct statement of how exactly the terraforming will accomplish its objective, Colonel."

"What kind of factors?"

LIN turned to face the second hologram, which morphed and revealed detailed imagery of the Earth. "These images were taken by a droid passing by your planet, as I said." She pointed to the polar regions. "As you can see, the ice caps were diminishing, even then, and the recorded temperature rise was significant." She turned to face them. "I do not know the current state of Earth. Our mission was, unfortunately, cut short. But, if the declination, that is, the rise in global temperatures has continued, I can only conclude that your world must be very close to the tipping point," said LIN with a cool unemotional tone. "It is unfortunate."

Kaetlyn turned to her. "Why is it unfortunate?"

LIN raised a brow. "As I said, there is a critical point, once passed, which cannot be reversed, even with our technology, Kaetlyn."

Kaetlyn felt her heart pounding against her chest as her anxiety rose.

"How can we know for sure and how can we stop it?"

LIN's eyes met theirs as she answered. "Provided with sufficient information, I can assess the situation and provide you with a likely formulation on how to go about terraforming your atmosphere to avert the inevitable, assuming of course that time still remains to do such."

8

Harry O'Sullivan waited anxiously amidst a crowd of people that seemed only to grow, pressing in tighter, on a strip of rocky coastline that probably had never seen more than a dozen or two people at any one time in its entire history.

"What's taking them so long," he grumbled.

Someone pushed into him, almost knocking him to the ground.

Harry turned, annoyed, and came face to face with Stan Murphy.

"Oye, Harry-boy," said Stan with a stony glare and a cutting edge in his voice. "Waiting fer your daughter, are ya?"

"Get out of my face, Stan."

The man grinned as his eyes hardened. "You can be sure that I'll be right here, watching and wait'n to see what happens to her."

"Nothin's gonna happen to her, now get away from me unless yer want'n another knuckle sandwich."

Stan backed up. "I wouldn't be so sure of that, Harry. She's in league with Lucifer now. It's unnatural what's going on here," he yelled as the crowd enveloped him.

9

As the platform touched the ground, a sea of people pressed toward them, as people shouted out and media machine-gunned questions at her.

Kaetlyn wasn't quite sure what to make of it.

There was a distinct ambience that seemed to have catalyzed the collective emotion into something that resembled awe, fear and even trepidation.

Clearly, people did not know what was going on, and she knew that soon enough they would start to fill that vacuum with their own ideas, good or bad.

She turned to Colonel Desmond before stepping off the platform. "We have to tell them what is happening," she eyed the crowd.

Desmond nodded. "I know. This bunch is unsettled. I'll have a word with my superiors," he said as he spotted the small group of officials approaching.

He squeezed her arm, "Leave it to me, lass, you just go get some food and coffee in your belly. It's gonna be a long day."

Raymond Statler stepped up to the Colonel.

"I want guards watching over Kaetlyn and Shamus. And, get some food and hot coffee for them."

10

Desmond had been right to call for an armed escort to surround Kaetlyn.

The second she stepped off the platform, the throng surged in, and had it not been for the ring of soldiers who took their cue, she would have found herself sandwiched between hundreds of people clamoring to know what had happened up there.

Now, safely ensconced between several large boulders, and tucked away from the eager eyes of onlookers, with five armed soldiers forming a protective line, she crouched down to avoid the touch of a bitter wind, with her dad, Serena, Shamus and Alana.

Raymond Statler showed up with a large thermos of coffee and bags of sandwiches.

"It's not Starbucks, but it'll warm your innards," he said with a smile. He eyed Kaetlyn. "You doin' okay, lass?"

"I'm fine, thanks for everything," she answered.

Everyone seemed to be processing what had happened up there as they imbibed the coffee and sandwiches in silence, except of course, Harry and Alana, who were both eager to hear about it.

Kaetlyn sighed as she stole another look to Shamus. "Well, how's your memory, now? Any better?"

He shook his head. "I'm still tryin' to make sense of it."

"And what did HAL say," posed her father with a grin.

"Well," began Kaetlyn, "apparently we were sent here to abduct you and take you back to our planet, dad."

"Oye, that's a load of bull crap if I ever heard some. No aliens wanna to see m'ugly mug."

A small chuckle emitted from the others.

Kaetlyn continued. "Our mission here was save the planet from global warming."

"Global warming, that's all this all about?" exclaimed Harry.

"Dad, I know you think it's a lot of hype, but the truth is that we're facing a real catastrophe if we don't act..."

Her words were cut off as Shamus spoke. "Shite, look at this." He handed his phone to Kaetlyn. Her face paled.

"What!? What is it?" asked Harry.

She turned the phone for him to see. "Fook'n Christ in a handbag, is that a joke?"

Soon they had all read the headline news announcing that a massive portion of the Ross Ice Shelf had broken off, and that a tidal wave was headed for the south island of New Zealand.

"It's started already – just like LIN said would happen," said Shamus.

"So, how are you supposed to stop this?" asked her dad, less jovial and certainly more somber in mood.

"I don't know, dad. We haven't gotten that far yet. LIN, I mean, the computer, needs more input so she can tell us what we can do, and if we can stop it."

Alana reached a hand over to Kaetlyn and squeezed it. The look of deep concern in her eyes was evident. "Kaet, what does this mean for you? I mean, can you just walk away from this now and leave it up to others to deal with it, or what?"

Kaetlyn's head wagged as her eyes looked to the crowd beyond their small enclosure. "I can't. If there is any chance that LIN can provide us with an answer, how could I possibly turn away now?"

Harry eyed the crowd beyond. "People are talk'n, lass. They're worried, they don't understand what's happening here and 'bout you and your involvement, and I'm fearing that this could get worse before it gets better."

Kaetlyn turned to her dad. "I'll be okay, don't worry."

Harry clenched his jaw, repressing his concerns.

Kaetlyn felt herself caught in a vortex of a different kind now. Weeks earlier, when she first began to pull on the thread of her past-life experience, with the help of Serena, she was seeking closure to a dream, a nightmare in fact, which had visited itself upon her more times than she could count.

When the Navy had discovered the craft, the gaping hole grew even wider, darker, deeper, once again drawing her down the rabbit hole.

As the weave of her past-life began to develop into a mural, a picture that was clearer, her recent dialogues with LIN had put the icing on the cake, making it manifest to her that all the feelings of anxiety and guilt which had filled her life, and the sense of subtle dread which had clouded her days, were soundly based.

And now, the shocking news about the Ross Ice Shelf having split off, and the tidal wave rushing outward, simply spelled the beginning of the worst-case scenario.

"Can I have a few moments alone with Shamus," she said to the others. The small enclosure emptied.

A deep and tired sigh escaped her lips as she looked into his face – his eyes watching her in silence.

"I guess we should talk about the elephant in the room." She grinned.

"I really wanted to talk to you about this earlier. Now …" he paused to cast an eye at the throng beyond, "it seems pretty silly to me."

Kaetlyn raised a brow, feeling some nervous tension dissipating. "Yeah, feels kind of weird to me too."

"The thing is, most of my recollections about the event, concern you and us, not so much about the rest of it," he said.

"So, you don't remember the crash and the details of our mission?" she asked.

"Small things drift back to memory, here and there, but it's like flotsam in the sea, I can't get the whole picture. The more you tell me, the more you expose, the more I begin to feel like it really happened just as you say it did. But …" he paused, "the one thing I am and have been completely certain of, is how I felt about you back then. That's been the one thing compelling me all this time."

Her hands trembled as she sipped her coffee. A tremulous smile quivered on the edge of her lips. "I do remember the words you said to me just before that missile hit."

His face blushed slightly.

"You said you loved me."

His head bobbed lightly. "I did."

Kaetlyn's eyes fixed on his. "Do you still feel that way?"

"Yeah, I do, in a weird sort of way."

She shook her head, a look of disbelief rippling over her face.

"But, how is that possible, Shamus?"

"What do you mean?"

"Look at me. I'm not the same person you knew and loved back then. We were relative giants back then, a different species entirely." she nodded at herself. "Our features, our skin, so much of us was different."

Shamus raised a brow. "It isn't the shell that matters, it's what's inside that counts."

She sighed, her face becoming somber.

He nudged closer to her. "It's the reason I sought you out after hearing from Alana about your dream. I always knew that my dreams could not be just dreams. The sense of longing, the feelings I felt each time I woke up from that nightmare, all of it lingered with me – like I was walking through a haze of some kind."

Shamus paused, looking her in the eyes. "I don't expect you to necessarily feel the same way about me. It's probably mental of me to expect that from you, but just the fact of knowing that it was real, that we shared something that strong, has given me some sense of closure – even if I don't grasp the entire thing and even if ..." he sighed, "... it ends here."

Kaetlyn pressed her lips together, feeling the uncontrollable trembling in her jaw as tears pooled in her eyes.

Shamus felt a sudden sense of guilt. "I'm sorry if I upset you. You really didn't need to have this shite added to your plate right now."

Tears streaked down her face as she reached a hand across to his. "You didn't upset me, Shamus. You made me very happy."

11

Colonel Desmond sat amidst a sea of brass in the small tent that had been pitched in the clearing directly beneath the alien craft above.

No one seemed concerned that the ship's computer might decide, on its very own, to suddenly land on top of where they sat, but that wasn't what really occupied his mind.

The tenor of the narrative had completely changed for him after witnessing and engaging in the dialogue with LIN – in fact, First Contact with an alien Ai.

Moreover, what seemed bizarre was now becoming reality – as news of the debacle in the Antarctic was unfolding.

Vaguely listening to the banter going back and forth between the military and the politicos who now tried to determine the best way to deal with this matter, he realized that they were entirely out of their league. There was only one thing to do.

He cleared his throat, catching their attention as he did.

"Gentlemen, and ma'am," he nodded to the Minister of Defense. "As head of Military Intelligence, having been inside that craft and spoken to its computer, I must urge you to speak to the Americans and get them to see the bigger picture." He paused. "I am no diplomat, nor do I navigate the

327

same waters as some of you do in the political arenas, but right now, with the American ship once again coming to anchor off our shores, demanding the return of their property, it is of the utmost importance that we get them to agree to stop this tug of war, and to sit down and discuss what this computer and the knowledge it possesses, now means to our world and our future."

The Naval Commander spoke. "Colonel, that's all well and good, but I'm not even so sure that we're on-board with the idea of a computer dictating the terms to us."

Desmond tipped his head at them, feeling ire welling-up inside. "Sir, with all due respect, an estimated 5% of the Ross Ice Shelf just fell into the ocean – what more do you need?" he openly challenged the man.

"Yes, yes, of course, we must deal with what is happening down there, but surely you do not expect us to buy this story that the world is at risk and that we are facing an extinction event if we do not execute this ..." he paused for the right words, "this plan or whatever this girl claims they were sent here to accomplish."

Desmond drew in a tired breath, exhaustion seemed to be on the cusp of taking hold.

The Minister of Defense spoke. "Colonel, what exactly are you proposing we do?"

Desmond leaned in and fixed his eyes on them. "I propose to escort Kaetlyn back inside that ship and ask her to get the computer to give us the details of how, given sufficient information, it's technology can be used to reverse engineer this global warming. Once we have that, I will ask that you and others in your constituency take the matter to the table, not only with the Americans, but any nation that should and must be involved in whatever it is we must do to address the situation for what it is – a global crisis."

"And why you?" asked the Naval Commander.

"Because I am familiar to both Kaetlyn and the ship's computer. Kaetlyn trusts me. I believe it is in our best interests to avoid entering any unnecessary changes or factors which could complicate the matter at this stage, as time is simply not on our side."

"And you think the Americans will just stand by while you interrogate this, LIN?"

"I believe they have no choice, sir. That craft is on our soil. And besides, we must consider the obvious and irrefutable fact that this ship's computer decisively navigated its way back to this precise location, clearly with the intent of continuing its dialogue with Kaetlyn, whom it still considers to be the Captain of that ship. Right now, LIN controls that ship, not us, and certainly not the Americans. So, yes …" he paused, "it would be in our best interests to continue the process that was begun."

Silence reigned as everyone considered his words.

The Minister of Defense spoke. "I agree with your proposal, Colonel. I will contact the Ministry of Foreign Affairs and ask them to get the Americans to stand down. Meanwhile, I will brief the PM and the cabinet."

She paused, fixing a firm gaze on him.

"But, as you say, time is no longer a luxury we can afford to waste. Get us some solid stuff, Desmond, because according to my sources, about 25% of the world's population has its eyes on this very spot, as we speak, and we need answers, fast."

12

Donovan O'Neil raced through the crowd, that is, if shouldering his way through a wall of bodies could be called such, in search of a familiar face.

"Where the hell is he?" he grumbled as someone elbowed him in the ribs.

"Journalist coming through," he announced.

Someone shouted, "Go fook yourself, ya nabbie!"

Finally reaching the front of the line, he saw someone he recognized. "Sir!" he yelled over the din and rumble of voices.

Raymond Statler turned. "Can I help you?"

"My name is Donovan O'Neil, I'm with the *Times*. You're Raymond Statler, right?"

"I am."

"I'm here to see Shamus Maguire."

Statler shrugged. "You'll have to get line with the other journalists," he said, but Donovan cut him off.

"No, you don't understand. I'm the journalist that Shamus first contacted."

Statler tipped his head at the man and approached closer. "Is Shamus expecting you?"

"I didn't set an appointment, but I know he'll see me."

Statler debated it for a moment. His orders were strict, no journalists. But, as he looked at the faces of people standing nearby, he knew that this crowd was a powder-keg just waiting to explode.

He stepped through the military cordon, grabbed Donovan by the arm and led him away.

"You've got about thirty minutes, at best, before the brass back there start making their own demands," he said to the man over the din of the crowd.

They stopped just short of the small enclave where Kaetlyn and Shamus were now sitting alone.

"I'll probably get my arse in a shite-load of trouble for letting you in there, so you best do a good job of it."

Donovan nodded as Statler waved him through the wall of solders.

Donovan came face-to-face with Kaetlyn, feeling slightly humbled, even slack-jawed, at finally meeting her.

"Kaet, this is Donovan O'Neil, the journalist I told you about," said Shamus.

She reached out a hand and shook his. "Thanks for all your help, so far."

Donovan lowered himself to the rock next to her. "I haven't done shite, to be honest. Shamus is the one who started the whole ruckus with his damn video," he said with affected anger.

He turned back to Kaetlyn.

"Why are you here," she asked.

"When Shamus first contacted me about your story, I thought he was just another exhibitionist looking for the spotlight, maybe even a little mental." He exhaled. "You have certainly made me a believer, Kaet. I was never one to dismiss the idea of alien intelligence, but, by the nature of my work, I never encouraged any stories which people offered me on the subject either. Not until yours came along."

"Why? Why was mine so different?" she asked.

Donovan shrugged. "I think, in part, it was because of Shamus – he seemed so sincere, so believably passionate about it, and of course, when I discovered that he was right, than an American battle ship was parked off our coast, that certainly helped to pique my interest." He paused to catch up with his mind. "I would like to tell your story, Kaet. Not the story that everyone is bandying about right now, not the hearsay and the talk on the street, but your story."

"Why?" she asked in a hushed voice.

"I believe that this event is somehow going to be a turning point for our world. I don't even know what happened inside that ship today, but I'm pretty sure that the size of this crowd, the amount of media I see on this beach, the American ship hovering on the horizon out there, and a global interest in what is happening here unlike anything I have ever seen before, that your story is a critical one to tell."

Kaetlyn was silent for a time, her eyes growing waxy as her thoughts faded back in time.

Shamus reached out and touched her hand, bringing her back from the past.

"Kaet, you don't have to do this. You're already doing so much as it is."

She smiled at him, squeezed his hand and turned to Donovan. "We best do it now. I suspect that people will want me back in that ship very soon."

Donovan pulled out his phone and started recording.

13

The Prime Minister of New Zealand stood watching the wall screen, with several members of her cabinet next to her as the Minister of Defense spoke to them from another location.

"That chunk of ice has started a tidal wave heading our way, ma'am," he said.

"How big will it be when it reaches the south island?" asked the PM with a clenched jaw.

"There is no way of telling exactly, but the first wave just passed our seismic buoys off the coast of Campbell Island."

"And?"

"If the readings are right, we've got a mega-tsunami, anywhere from 50 to 75 meters high."

Consternation filled her. "What is its trajectory?"

"Satellite footage shows it will strike the south island, posibly reaching as far as the Chatham Islands – before dissipating."

"And Campbell Island?" she asked.

"It's roughly 400 kilometers south of us, ma'am," answered the man. "But ..." he hesitated.

"But what?" asked the PM.

"Ma'am, Campbell Island is gone. Satellite footage shows that the tsunami washed over it like it never existed."

"There are no people living there that I am aware of," said one of the cabinet Ministers.

"No, there aren't," said the Minister of Defense, "but there were two research teams there studying local fauna."

"How many people?" asked the PM as her stomach began to turn.

"We're getting the figures confirmed, but it appears to be around 48 people." His face was filled with dread. "No one could possibly have survived that wave."

"How long do we have before it reaches the south island?"

Another dour look ensued. "Dunedin will be the first to get hit, and probably the worst of it too. We estimate two hours at best."

"Oh god," the expletive escaped her lips as her body filled with a sense of trepidation.

She turned to the other heads of her government. "Initiate emergency evacuation of all coastal areas south of Christchurch, including the Chatham Islands."

14

Colonel Desmond showed up in the enclave where he found Kaetlyn and Shamus speaking to the journalist.

Of course, he could have been angry that someone, and he suspected who, had permitted the journalist to get in, but then again, he had come to realize that both Kaetlyn and Shamus were not about to be stopped. And what was the point anyhow – if anyone should tell the story of what was happening, it should be these two.

Kaetlyn raised a smile to meet his somewhat dour look.

"Calm down, Colonel, I didn't tell him any national secrets, not yet at least," she flicked a brow.

Desmond stepped closer and sat near to them – hovering close enough to make Donovan realize that his interview had coming to a sudden end.

"I think I have enough to go with," said Donovan as he stood. "And I hope that as the story develops, you will think of me for the next installment."

He nodded to the Colonel and left.

"So," began Desmond with an affected grin. "Are you ready for the next talk with ..."

"LIN," said Kaetlyn.

"Yes, her, it ... whatever." He flicked a dismissive hand to the air.

Shamus fixed a firm look at him, "May I ask you a question, Colonel?"

Desmond nodded.

"What are your intentions?"

"My intentions are of little concern, Mr. Maguire," answered Desmond. "I am not a politician, I'm a military intelligence officer. My only interest in this entire affair has been with regards to its security implications to our nation. Beyond that, this is entirely outside my league." He offered a tenuous smile. "However, that said, and off the books, I find myself championing another player." He fixed his eyes on Kaetlyn with a nod.

"And what about those other people out there?" asked Kaetlyn. "The suits and military brass?"

Desmond shrugged. "I can't account for them, Kaetlyn. They have their agendas and they answer to their own masters. I can only say that I did manage to convince them that myself, along with Shamus and Serena, would escort you back into that ship one more time and continue our dialogue, but, on one condition."

"Which is?" asked Kaetlyn, her suspicion suddenly piqued.

"That you establish with the computer, I mean, LIN, that following this next dialogue, that a team of scientists of our choosing, can question her and that she will respond."

Kaetlyn's head wagged. "That'll be up to LIN, I reckon, depending on her security protocols, but of course, the more the merrier." She paused.

"I sense there is something you're not saying," he tipped his head at her.

Kaetlyn looked to Shamus and back to Desmond. "I just want you to know that I'm not trying to be the sole proprietor of that ship or its contents. But, if anyone plans to abscond that ship and all it contains, I will shut it down."

"Meaning?"

She shrugged. "I'll tell LIN to clam up."

He pressed his lips together as a grin crept across his face. "Oh, I see. You had your own ace to play, didn't you?"

Kaetlyn sighed. "It's not what I want, Colonel, and I think you know that. What I want is that the information we learn from LIN becomes public knowledge, and I do mean that in a literal sense. I will not let that ship, my ship, disappear into some dark hole where scientists can dissect it. We're going to find out how to save this planet, and that information, every bit of it is going to be made available to every living soul on this planet. That's my ultimatum."

"You truly believe that LIN would shut us out if you told her to do so?"

Kaetlyn looked up to the ship hovering over the shore. "LIN navigated that ship back here to be in touch with me. She knows who I am. She knows my implicit connection to the mission. If I shut it down, I am quite positive that no one will get in that ship, and most certainly, LIN herself."

"I must tell you, Kaetlyn, you're putting yourself in a very precarious spot by making these demands. You are up against a tremendous amount of vested interest." He paused to look at Shamus and then back to her. "I know you want to do the right thing, and frankly, I'm cheering for you all the way, but do not under estimate the lengths that these powers will go to in order to claim that ship as their own. The Yanks and the Ruskies nearly started a military conflict over it."

"Which you stopped," she interjected.

"That was Raymond Statler's idea, a brilliant one I must admit. We all dodged a bullet on that incident, but as you know, the American carrier is out there again, and from what I know, they are pressing us to deliver the craft, now."

Kaetlyn chuckled. "They're blustering, as usual, because as we all know, LIN is calling the shots now. No one can move that ship unless she does it."

"Nonetheless, the drama has not ended. I just want you two," he glanced at Shamus, "to choose your battles and to be smart about it, for your own safety."

"We appreciate the advice, sir," said Shamus.

Desmond stood and turned to leave, but then he hesitated and looked back to her. "One question has plagued me since the first time you entered the ship."

She turned an eye his way.

"The code you use to enter it and to access LIN, it appears to be nothing more than a series of taps. Why is that others have not been able to replicate it?"

Kaetlyn smiled. "Oh, I forgot to mention that little detail," she grinned impishly. "I asked LIN that exact question."

"And?"

"It's not just the act of putting in a code, Colonel. LIN and the ship, are calibrated to register an entirely different code."

Desmond turned to her, his face confused. "I don't understand."

She shrugged. "I'm not so sure I understand it either, not yet, at least. Apparently, every person has their own innate signature, so, when we use the physical code, LIN confirms it with our individual signature."

"You're losing me here, what does she mean by a *signature?*"

"Take your mobile phone for example. There are billions of electronic devices out there today, countless billions of electromagnetic signals all around us at all times of the day, literally, an ocean of frequencies, and yet, your phone's signature can be detected amidst that ocean in a nanosecond. If I understand LIN correctly, a person's signature is like an energy emanation, something unique to each individual which can be detected with the right equipment."

"Amazing," he said with a shake of his head. "I guess we have more to learn from her," he said as he walked away.

A soldier stepped into the enclave. "Ma'am, we will escort you to the lift now."

Shamus took her hand in his and squeezed it. "We'll talk more."

She smiled at him and then leaned over and placed a kiss on his cheek. As they stepped out into the crowd, soldiers surrounded them and formed a vanguard, pressing their way through the congestion.

Harry O'Sullivan stepped into the group and poked his daughter in the arm. "Everything okay, lass?" he said, giving her hand a firm squeeze.

338

"Don't worry, dad. We'll talk when I come down from that ship."

Harry rolled his eyes. "Been worry'n 'bout you since you were a chubby little fook. Why would I stop now?" he smiled.

She kissed him on the cheek and then continued forward with the vanguard.

A chorus of voices shouted out at them.

Kaetlyn heard her name called over and over. Everyone seemed to know who she was, thanks to Shamus' video, the media, and of course, social media.

A sea of mobile phones floated above the crowd, snapping off shots and videoing the procession.

A young girl stepped into their path, her finger pointing up at the craft above. "Are you going to save us from them?"

Kaetlyn knelt and looked her in the face. "You don't need to worry about them, they've come to save us."

The young girl smiled and stepped back into her mother's arms.

They finally reached the crane without incident, stepped onto the platform and waited until the cage was secured in place.

Slowly it began to rise into the air, and with it came a sight that caused Kaetlyn to catch her breath.

The sheer magnitude of the crowd exploded into view, now stretching back along the rocky coast as far as the cliffs which overlooked this very spot. In the past hour alone it seemed to have doubled or tripled in size.

She clasped Shamus' hand. "My god, I hope we don't disappoint the world," she said, her face awash with concern.

Shamus smiled. "You won't ...." but his words were cut short by the concussion that cut the air.

Kaetlyn's body suddenly propelled backwards, smashing into the cage, as a moan of pain emitted from her lips and blood spilled from a hole in the side of her head.

A cry erupted from the crowd below.

It was the last thing she heard before her world went black.

15

Several weeks had passed since the shooting.

During that time, teams of military and civilian engineers, manned by both American and Irish personnel, had tried, quite unsuccessfully, to get through the portal of the ship, including countless attempts to cut through pilot's glass, and even drilling into the hull. Nothing worked. Nothing penetrated it. Nothing.

The ship remained as it was, like a mountain hovering in the air.

The crowds had disappeared, and what remained was a military and scientific contingent, dozens of both, engaged in either protecting the site, or trying to figure out a way to penetrate the craft.

It was, as Kaetlyn had told Colonel, Desmond, the fact that the ship's computer recognized her primary signature, and hers alone, and was not about to permit access to anyone else.

Some meager attempts had been made to see if Shamus could try to replicate Kaetlyn's entry code, but it didn't work. And for that matter, Shamus insisted on staying by her bedside.

The world stood by, waiting to hear news about the young woman, the only person, it seemed, who could access the strange alien craft which remained hovering above the Irish coast.

The media expounded the events, and of course, the biggest subject of debate was whether the eighteen-year-old would survive her head injury and wake up from her coma?

That notwithstanding, there was also the other shockwave which now pressed itself upon the world, the one unfolding in the Antarctic, which had sent a wave of sheer trepidation around the globe in its aftermath.

Scientists were poring over the evidential material provided by Dr. Beckett's research time, the ISS and its scientists orbiting the Earth, as well as the recent debacle in New Zealand.

Global warming was no longer a subject of discussion, it was THE discussion.

Mother Nature was fighting back for her relevance, and mankind stood on the precipice of disaster – certainly proof that a woman scorned was no light matter.

16

Donovan O'Neil sat at his cubicle, staring at the computer, his eyes listlessly reading over the article he had finished the day before.

He had taken the transcript of his interview with Kaetlyn, the one he had prosecuted just minutes before she was shot – and from it, he had constructed her story.

He had tried to make it as heartfelt and deep as the girl herself.

He had tried to capture the narrative of someone who had lived with a nightmare for years, who then delved into the depths of that haunting specter and who had emerged with answers to unlocking the secrets of an alien spacecraft.

And on the cusp of providing, what seemed, the answers to the very dilemma now facing the world, she had been shot and nearly killed.

The shooter, a local resident of Bantry, named Stan Murphy, an avowed hater of not only Kaetlyn O'Sullivan whom he proclaimed to be the spawn of Satan, but a man who despised just about anything and anyone who was different than himself, was facing charges for attempted murder.

Nobody paid much attention to him. His circumstances would simply fade and disappear in a black hole from which he would never emerge – and the world would be better for it.

Donovan rubbed his tired eyes.

Ever since that day, while looking up at the gantry as the crane lifted them toward the ship, wondering what great mysteries they would soon unlock, only to witness the assassination attempt, he had lost some zeal, some spring in his step.

Caught in the miasma of his mental maundering, he failed to hear the calling – the voice.

"Oye, mate," someone poked him in the shoulder.

Donovan blinked and turned to look up at the man. "Boss is call'n ya, bloke."

The editor looked up at him as Donovan entered his office.

"Ya know, Donnie, over these past 40 years I've seen a lot of things," he began, as he took his glasses off and rubbed his eyes.

He leaned back against the desk and looked Donovan in the face.

"My father sat in this very chair. He covered the Korean War, Vietnam, the lunar landing, Nixon's impeachment, even fucking ABBA. Me, everything since then." He paused, his eyes drifting to one side. "I've tried to reconcile everything that has happened recently, and being the Devil's advocate, part of my job, I have to ask myself if all of this hasn't been contrived."

"Unlikely," responded Donovan with less zeal than normally displayed.

The editor shrugged. "I know, but it's how I process things. Just like when the planes struck the Twin Towers and George Bush announced to the world that a handful of terrorists in the Afghan desert had executed a flawless attack." He smiled. "We both know, even then, as did many others, that those buildings fell with perfect demolition precision and that it wasn't the planes that took them down. So, why not this? Why not a hoax?"

"That's what the Americans would want the world to believe."

The editor threw a hand to the air. "Just mess'n with your head, Don. I've been wrong a few times in my career. Don't like to admit it, but right now, I figure you're right. In fact," he waved a piece of paper in the air, "any doubts I had have just been vanquished by this," he handed off the paper.

Donovan read it. "Where did this come from?"

"I called in a favor."

"But this ..."

The editor turned to face him. "Aye, bizarre, ain't it?"

"What do we do with it?"

"I can't publish it without some official confirmation, and you can't mention it either, but I happen to know that you've been caressing that fook'n article about Kaetlyn O'Sullivan for the last two weeks, one that I expected to have in my hands already, and yet, has not appeared on my desk."

He paused to smile at Donovan. "You're the only journalist in the world who has heard her story first-hand. You're the only person who can tell it for her." He nodded to the paper in Donovan's hand. "I'm not sure what that thing portends for us, but I think now would be the right time to tell her story, to remind the world that the narrative has not come to an end. In fact," he hesitated a moment, "to let them know that Kaetlyn O'Sullivan's story might even have more chapters yet to come."

Donovan returned to his desk and read the memo provided by military intelligence.

"At 23:19 hours, on December the 1st, an unidentified object was spotted by a British military satellite, descending through the Earth's atmosphere and slowing over Wales, on a direct trajectory toward the southwest coast of Ireland."

17

It was early in the morning, 1:59 am according to the wall clock he had just passed at the nurse's station.

The corridor was empty – filled only by the sound of silence.

He entered the room and lowered himself to a chair next to her bed.

Her gentle breathing, barely tangible to the ear, the subtle rise and fall of her chest, and a rhythmic beep emanating from a heart monitor nearby – were the only signs that Kaetlyn O'Sullivan was still alive, buried deep inside the coma where she now resided.

It was hard to let go of the trauma, seeing her falling, blood spilling from her head and the look of both shock and anguish in her eyes, that picture would not erase itself from his mind.

It was the last cognizant moment they had shared, the last time she had looked him in the eyes.

Ever since that moment, he had not left her side except for a brief interlude when he was asked to attempt accessing the ship, which of course, was futile.

Kaetlyn was battling for her life – and maybe, deep inside the caverns of obliviousness, she was doing battle with other demons – who could know.

He desperately missed her.

He had never been able to say the words, the words he felt and thought every minute since that fateful moment, the chance to tell Kaetlyn that he loved her.

He reached a hand to hers. Her skin felt oddly lifeless, as if she was indeed hovering somewhere on the threshold of death itself.

"I hope you can hear me," he whispered.

"I hope you can understand when I say that I loved you then, in another life, and that I love you now, and that I will always love you, wherever you go."

His lips quivered as tears pooled in his eyes.

"I miss you Kaetlyn. I know you're in there, and I know that your fight'n to come back."

He wiped his eyes and leaned closer, his lips next to hear ear. "I need you back, the world needs you back, Kaetlyn."

He placed a gentle kiss to her cheek.

18

The Joint Emergency Council, comprised of military personnel from 153 nations and headed by the Commander of the Icelandic Forces, met in Reykjavik, at the *Naval Air Station Keflavik*, next to the *Keflavík International Airport*, Iceland.

The meeting had been called to discuss a new development, one that now involved all countries and one that could not be denied by any.

Commander Gunnar Helgason began as the room quieted.

"Gentlemen and ladies," he nodded, "the purpose of this meeting, as you all know, is to discuss the new incident – that is, the second anomaly on our doorstep."

He clicked the remote in his hand, causing a large wall screen to come to life and then pointed a small laser pen at it.

"What we know so far is that the object followed this trajectory, entering the atmosphere here, where it was first detected by a British telecom satellite, and then disappeared here," he pointed, "just over the southeast coast of Ireland. From there, we lost track of it."

He waited a second or two before continuing. "It is safe to assume that this is either a sister ship to the one currently hovering in that region, or possibly associated with it in some other way."

"Or, it could be something else altogether," voiced his German counterpart.

Helgason nodded. "Yes, of course, we cannot dismiss any possibilities at this point. However, there is one rather significant factor which supports the current theory, more than any. Ever since the original craft returned to that coastal region of Ireland, the Irish Navy has had it under 24/7 surveillance, filming it from different angles. The video I am about to show you is quite revelatory," he finished with a press of the remote.

They watched the short segment, possibly two minutes in length.

"The lights on that ship stopped blinking," said someone aloud.

"Precisely, the forward and aft lights which had been blinking on that craft for the past many weeks, suddenly stopped. However, that isn't the most relevant factor here." He pointed a laser to the time stamp in the bottom right corner of the video. "At precisely the same time as the second anomaly appeared on the outer edge of our atmosphere, and then disappeared over Ireland, is precisely when the lights on the first anomaly disappeared."

He turned to face them. "In short, while other factors cannot be dismissed, this would seem to corroborate our theory that the two objects are somehow connected, if not even, communicating to one another."

"I assume search teams have scoured the Irish countryside and coastal areas for evidence of this second anomaly?" asked a Canadian military official.

The Irish Commander of the Military spoke up. "We have dedicated every resource available to tracking it. Heat and spectral sensors, sonar, radar, you name it. Even satellite footage has not revealed a single thing."

Commander Helgason tipped his head to the screen, pressing the remote and bringing up an image of the first anomaly.

"It would seem, ladies and gentlemen, that we have visitors, not of our world. What their purpose is, we do not yet know. We can only hope, as originally signaled by the first ship's computer, that their reasons are altruistic – but nothing can be certain at this time."

He turned to face them all.

"One thing is very clear; now, more than ever, we must come together as a global alliance, to either protect our world from something intrusive, or to prepare our world for a cooperative endeavor with another race of beings – as bizarre and outlandish as that may seem. We no longer have the luxury of hiding our heads in the sand, protecting our own small turfs and pretending that we are alone in this Universe. And ..." he paused, "we are also now faced with

a global crisis which these visitors seem to have the answer
to, or possibly even, a global intervention, of which type we
cannot yet say."

19

It was a place, or maybe it wasn't at all.
Maybe it was just a feeling.
Maybe nothing at all.
Maybe it was a delusion.
Was it cold she felt? She couldn't tell.
Should it be cold? She couldn't say.
A misty veil of black embraced her.
A depthless black, without dimension, somehow
intangible and yet pervasive.
Was this death, she wondered?
*Was this how it felt, without warmth, sense or sight,
just nothing, a vaporous domain of endless dark, without
borders or edges – just...*
Feeling herself being drawn into its boney clutches,
she sensed something else clawing at her soul, something
desperate, something alive, something wanting her to stop
and turn around.
Somewhere beyond the depth of oblivion that
surrounded her, a voice gently echoed, a voice she knew.
*Could she remember anything if she was now in
death's domain?*
*Could she even reach past the shroud of oblivion that
thickened around her?*
A small spark ignited inside.

Like a pinpoint of light in a tunnel of endless black she reached to it, willing herself to touch it, to feel it, to be it.

The voice of the abyss echoed back to her, coaxing her onward to its waiting arms, but the light lured her with a sense of animation, its aperture growing larger, wider and brighter.

She focused on the echo, the sound of the voice gently filtering through the thick layers of unconscious.

The more she focused, the more she began to sense something else.

Pain!

Something hurt, and that pain, like a beacon in a storm-ridden sea, drew her to it, because it meant she was still alive.

Pain was life – death was nothing.

Feeling the darkness receding behind her, like old skin shedding away, she suddenly felt as if she were standing on the edge of a cliff. Beyond, on the other side, she could see the veil of light washing through a blanket of gray, like the aurora borealis rippling through the night sky.

The darkness clawed at her from behind, its tendrils invoking her to come back to it, but ahead, the light teased and played with her, like pixies invoking their magic spell, and the sound of a voice still beckoned her.

She threw herself over the abyss, a leap of faith – floating, flying, as if movement was as simple as willing it and nothing more.

Suddenly, she gasped, her lungs burning as if she had just taken her first breath after being submerged in cold dark water for a very long time.

She lurched upward, her arms flailing about, weakened and atrophied from weeks of disuse.

Breathing, as if she had never breathed before, she sat there, her chest heaving and her eyes nervously darting about the room as sweat poured off her.

Pain throbbed from her skull.

She touched the tender spot, aggrandizing it more.

The night nurse, sitting at her station down the corridor, heard the monitors ping. She rushed to the room, opened the door and stared at the sight of Kaetlyn O'Sullivan, sitting upright, her face awash with confusion, pain and bordering on sheer consternation.

She approached her in her calming way.

"What happened to me, why am I here?"

"It's okay, Kaetlyn, you've had a very traumatizing experience."

The nurse eased her back down into her bed with a soothing smile.

"You were shot – you have a serious head wound."

Kaetlyn's eyes grew wide as those words suddenly breached the veil of occlusion which had taken hold of her world; and like a dam, everything poured in on her, every memory, every moment, down to the last nanosecond before the bullet had pierced her skull.

She looked up at the nurse.

"Shamus, Shamus Maguire – where is he?"

"I'm here, Kaet," his voice broke the air as he stepped into the room with a smile on his face, one so wide that it threatened to crack his cheeks.

He approached as she reached out and took his hand.

Tears suddenly pooled and drifted down her pallid cheeks.

"I missed you?" she said.

"And I you."

The nurse turned to Shamus. "Just a few minutes, Mr. Maguire, she needs her rest."

He nodded and waited until she left the room.

"I saw everything ..." she began.

Shamus squeezed her hand. "What do you mean?"

Her face rippled with incredulity. "While I was out, I relived it, every moment it seemed, from the time we boarded the ship to the second we died." She smiled. "We have to get back inside that ship," her voice quivered near to panic as her breathing escalated.

"It's okay, there's time."

"No," her head shook as she grimaced with pain, "... there isn't. I think I know how to reverse the global warming, but we don't have much time left."

20

Sitting atop the cliff, with his back against a struggling pine tree, he faced off with Ol'man Celtic.

Just several feet away was the edge of the precipice, a drop several hundred feet to the rocky coast below.

The wind bellowed and shook his frail frame.

Undaunted, and certainly not to be dissuaded from seeing his long-sought-after secret, old-man O'Brien remained, steadfast and unmoving, despite the cold creeping along his extremities.

When the Irish Navy had first approached him and his grandson, insisting on their secrecy regarding the discovery, he had given it little thought. But now, sitting here and staring down at the alien craft still hovering over the coast, he felt his calling, a duty to see it, to experience it and find closure in a lifetime spent climbing these rocky slopes in search of his pot of gold, the very one his father had sparked him on a journey to find over 80 years before.

As twilight escaped the approaching grip of night, the strange object below was an eerie sight.

Spotlights lit it up like a candle in the night.

Military personnel could be seen surrounding it.

Media hovered on the perimeter providing a constant view to the world.

But old man O'Brien, he had the best seat in the house.

From his perch, a small indenture in the cliff, and the pine behind him, he could sit for hours and enjoy a view that few would ever see.

Further along this very ridge, some three or four-hundred meters, was the enclave his father had first taken him to – his secret place that he had called his own.

O'Brien turned an eye back to the craft.

He shuddered as another blast of cold winter air slapped him in the face. It wasn't personal, he knew it. He'd been offended and abused by the coastal weather his whole life. If anything, it had toughened him – giving him more steel, making him appreciate the eternal and immutable touch of Mother Nature.

As the cold continued its assault on what little body warmth he had left, slowly replacing it with a numbing sense of nothing, he realized that now was a perfect time to end his journey.

He had left his one and only friend, Trouble, behind, in the hands of his grandson. The dog had been with him on every outing, but not this one.

He didn't fear death, he was too old to care about that anymore.

But dying, that was a process he hated.

Growing old, becoming feeble, losing vitality, afflicted by creaky bones and constant pains, those were the vanguards of approaching death, and he resented them.

Night's mantle had now cloaked the sea ahead, and below, the site of the alien craft was all that illuminated the otherwise starkly black coastline.

O'Brien drew the collar of his coat to over his neck, reminding himself that this very jacket had been a gift from his departed wife.

He missed her.

He missed their life together.

He missed their past.

As he sat there, caught in the maunderings of the life he had led, a glow caught his eye.

It approached from the far left, like the spotlight of a ship breaching a fog-ridden sea.

As he watched, it moved fast, canting to the right, and then suddenly, it burst into view, a light so bright and white that it stung his eyes.

O'Brien raised his hand to shade his eyes from its intensity, watching as it suddenly stopped midair and then slowly, yet decisively, descended until it was hovering next to the other alien craft.

Was it a helicopter, he wondered?

But there was no sound to be heard – just that of the waves lapping the shore far below and the endless blow of a winter wind.

Seconds passed before the intense light vanished.

O'Brien sidled closer to the edge of the cliff to get a better view.

As his eyes acclimated to the darkness, he caught his breath.

Hanging in the air was another ship, twice the size of the other.

"Well, I'll be damned," he chuckled.

Eighty years I climbed these rocks, bruised m'fook'n shins and cut my hands, while shiver'n m'arse off. And now you show up.

Father would be proud, he thought.

21

The next morning the world woke up to the startling news.

A second alien ship had arrived during the night and was hovering next to the smaller one over the coast of Ireland.

Moreover, teams of scientists announced yet another imminent debacle as the southern face of Greenland's ice-capped coast, now rumbled, a sign that the same fate that had already touched the Antarctic, was now playing its hand in the northern hemisphere.

As news swept across the globe, a military detail combed the cliffs high above the two anomalies, and came across the lifeless body of an elderly man, tucked into a stony indenture, wrapped in his Henry White forest-green tweed, with a smile on his face.

(to be continued…)

Find out what happens next in L.I.N.
The sequel to The Other